The Love of God
Revealed through Jesus,
The Only Begotten Son

The Love of God Revealed through Jesus, The Only Begotten Son

PAUL C. JONG

Hephzibah Publishing House

A Ministry of THE NEW LIFE MISSION
SEOUL, KOREA

Sermons on the Gospel of John (I)
The Love of God Revealed through Jesus,
The Only Begotten Son

ISBN 89-8314-595-1
Cover Art by Min-soo Kim
Illustration by Young-ae Kim
Printed in Korea

Hephzibah Publishing House
A Ministry of THE NEW LIFE MISSION
48 Bon-dong, Dongjack-gu
Seoul, Korea 156-060

♠ Website: http://www.nlmission.com
        http://www.bjnewlife.org
♠ E-mail: newlife@bjnewlife.org
♠ Phone: 82(Korea)-11-1788-2954
♠ Fax: 82-33-637-4440

Table of Contents

CHAPTER 2

CHAPTER 3

Preface

The disciples of Jesus said, "Oh, what does He mean? It is very difficult. Who can understand His sayings?" It is because the Lord said that He Himself as the bread of life, saying, *"The bread that I shall give is My flesh, which I shall give for the life of the world" (John 6:51).* Again, He said, *"Unless you eat the flesh of the Son of Man and drink His blood, you have no life in you. Whoever eats My flesh and drinks My blood has eternal life, and I will raise him up at the last day. For My flesh is food indeed, and My blood is drink indeed" (John 6:53-55).* He concluded, *"He who eats My flesh and drinks My blood abides in Me, and I in him" (John 6:56).*

We see here that we can eat the flesh of the Lord and drink His blood with the faith of believing in the gospel of the water and the Spirit. We become to know that we are sinless when we eat the flesh of the Lord. If you eat the flesh of the Lord with the faith, you become sinless. My fellow believers, if you eat the flesh of the Lord by the faith of believing in the fact that Jesus who received the baptism from John the Baptist in the Jordan River has taken all our sins, we are then able receive the grace of the remission of sins. We become sinless if by faith we eat the work that the Lord has done with His flesh. However, what about those people who do not eat the flesh of Jesus by faith? They remain sinners no matter how fanatically they believe in Him. Those who eat the flesh of the Lord with spiritual faith become sinless people.

Let us say that there are delicious foods prepared where we are invited. No matter how the sumptuous feasts are, if I do not eat them, I can never be full. Likewise, we receive true remission of sins only when we eat by believing with our mind that our Lord made us sinless, taking the sins of the world, by receiving the baptism on His body. Put differently, our sins will be blotted out only when we eat the flesh of the Lord with the faith of believing in that 'Jesus has blotted out our sins by receiving the baptism.'

We have to eat the flesh of the Lord often with the faith of believing in the gospel of the water and the Spirit. Only then will our spiritual stomach become full. And we receive the peace of mind when we drink the blood of the Lord by believing in its spiritual meaning. There is a possibility for people to misunderstand these sayings, but all of these metaphors are referring to spiritual faith. We can eat the flesh of the Lord and drink His blood only when we believe in the gospel of the water and the Spirit that the Lord has given us. I mean to say that by believing in this gospel we can eat the Truth that says that the Lord gave us His life to fulfill the gospel of the water and the Spirit.

I speak to you once again wondering if there are some unbelievers among you who only know the gospel of the water and the Spirit but do not eat it. If you are in this category, I admonish you to eat the gospel of the water and the Spirit with faith when it is prepared, without any hesitation. I wish for you to drink His blood as you would enjoy a cool beverage and eat the flesh of Jesus as spiritual food. I wish for you to enjoy the eternal life eating and drinking, by knowing that the Lord has blotted our sins out by taking them onto His body through the baptism and paying them off with His blood on the Cross. And I wish for you to have the assurance that we are chosen to eat the flesh of the Lord and drink His blood by believing in the gospel of the water and the Spirit.

Jesus told His disciples to eat His flesh and to drink His

blood. People considered it so hard when Jesus told them to eat His flesh as the bread of life. They were so troubled with these words saying, "Who can understand these words?" Likewise, almost all Christians nowadays are also troubled with this part of the Scriptures because of their spiritual ignorance.

So, our Lord said, *"What then if you should see the Son of Man ascend where He was before? It is the Spirit who gives life; the flesh profits nothing. The words that I speak to you are spirit, and they are life" (John 6:62-63).* This passage means, "You have to listen to My Word spiritually. I have taken all your sins in the Jordan River to save your souls from the sins of the world. I, the Son of Man, have taken all your sins through the baptism I had received from John the Baptist. And I am dying in place of you; I will give my life for you. And what will you say if I will go back to My throne where I was before in 3 days after I have died?" However, there were many among the disciples of Jesus who did not believe that Jesus is the Son of the Lord or that He is the Lord. Blessed are the people who eat the flesh of Jesus by faith.

Are you eating the flesh of the Lord and drinking His blood by believing in the gospel of the water and the Spirit at this moment? Eat and drink his blessings everyday. As you have to eat the food for the flesh everyday, eat the spiritual food by faith as well. If you eat the spiritual food only once, you will become more spiritually hungry in three days. Then, you should eat them again. My fellow believers, you have to eat the spiritual food as often as you can.

Those Who Eat the Flesh of Jesus Come to Receive the Life-sustaining Food

Those who have eaten the flesh of Jesus have become sinless people. My fellow believers, do you know that you became sinless people when you believed in the gospel of the water and the Spirit? We have become sinless people by eating the flesh and the blood of Jesus by faith. The Lord granted us salvation by giving us the gospel of the water and the Spirit that says we can become sinless people by eating the flesh of the Lord and drinking His blood. So, we are born again as truly sinless people because we eat and drink the flesh and the blood of our Lord Jesus.

How full of grace is our Lord that gave us His body? What would we do if the Lord did not give us His flesh? How clean does it feel our conscience that we are sinless because we eat His given flesh as our daily food? My fellow believers, it is so impressive and delightful that we have become sinless people.

How do we dare say that we are the sinless people? Can we be sinless by paying money for it? Can we be sinless by performing good deeds? Or, can we be sinless by living nicely? We cannot be sinless by our deeds or abilities. We cannot be sinless people if not for the flesh of Jesus. We became sinless people by eating the flesh of Jesus because Jesus has given His flesh to us. Do you have sins? –No, I do not have sins. Let us say with our voices, "I do not have sins." Yes, we do not have sin any more, for we have eaten the flesh of Jesus. If people see us, they might say, "Oh, there are such strange people." But, you are the sinless people in whom God is well pleased.

My fellow believers, we do not have any sins because we have eaten the flesh of the Lord. Jesus gave us His flesh. He also gave His blood to us. He took all our sins with that flesh through His baptism, and paid for them by shedding His blood on the Cross. So, we became sinless people by having faith in this gospel of the water and the Spirit.

The Lord said, *"It is the Spirit who gives life; the flesh profits nothing" (John 6:63).* We can be born again when we believe in our minds what the Lord has done for us. We became the people without sins in our mind on this account. As well, we became sinless people in our spirits. Do you agree, or not? I am sure you do. So, the Lord said, *"It is the Spirit who gives life; the flesh profits nothing."* If we think physically, can we actually eat the flesh and drink the blood of someone? We cannot do that. And if we eat the flesh of other people physically, are we saying that we are a cannibalistic tribe? If we obey these words literally, the Bible would be commanding that we do barbarous acts. That is why He said to us not to think physically.

The Lord saved our souls from sin and gave us new life. He has taken our sins once and for all by receiving the baptism on His body from John. Thus, He made us sinless people. We became sinless people by eating the flesh of the Lord. It is so marvelous. The fact that we became sinless people by eating the flesh of the Lord is marvelous. It is so amazing that we came to receive true salvation. How powerful the flesh of the Lord is! Those who eat the flesh of Jesus are sinless.

How can you eat and drink the flesh and the blood of Jesus? We do so by believing in the baptism of Jesus and His shedding of the blood. We eat the flesh of Jesus by believing that Jesus took all our sins through His baptism in the Jordan River. Therefore, we have to eat the flesh of Jesus everyday by faith. We have to eat whenever we feel hungry spiritually. We have to eat the flesh of Jesus whenever we feel like we have sins or feel spiritually weak. We have to eat His flesh as often as we can by believing in the fact that the Lord took our sins through His baptism. This is how to become a man or woman of spiritual faith.

Even among the disciples of Jesus, there were many who did not believe that Jesus was the Son of God, or that Jesus had taken all the sins of the world. Even now, there are many people who do not believe that Jesus has taken the sins with His flesh. It is evident that Jesus has taken the sins of the world by receiving the baptism, but, even among Christians, there are so many people who do not believe in this Truth. That is why Jesus keeps on talking about it.

There was a disciple named Judah among the twelve disciples of Jesus. Jesus knew that Judah belonged to Satan the Devil. The Lord also knew that some of the disciples of Jesus did not fully believe in Him, and that some among the crowds who followed Him did not believe in Him. Then, who were they? The Lord said, "Those who were not led by God the Father are the people who do not believe in Him." He said, *"No one can come to Me unless it has been granted to him by My Father" (John 6:65).*

Many people have left Jesus even while saying, *"No one can come to Me unless it has been granted to him by My Father."* Many people left Him who did have the faith to eat and drink the flesh and the blood of Jesus. My fellow believers, you cannot be led by God the Father if your minds are deceived. God knows all our situations. Therefore, we must not have deceived minds. We have to confess the real situation of our hearts as they are before Him: We have to say, "Oh, my Lord, I have sins in my heart, and I deserve to be condemned because of these sins. Please, have mercy on me!" Then, the Lord will meet such an honest soul with the gospel of the water and the

Spirit without fail.

Jesus said to His twelve disciples, *"Do you also want to go away?"* Simon Peter answered Him, *"Lord, to whom shall we go? You have the words of eternal life. Also we have come to believe and know that You are the Christ, the Son of the living God" (John 6:68-69).*

There must be the same confession of faith to us. Can we live leaving the Lord? Can we go else where leaving the Lord? The Lord had received the baptism on His body and gave His blood to us. And He told us the gospel of the water and the Spirit that is God's Word of Truth, which enables us to receive eternal life.

Now, we have become His sinless people. Whoever believes in the gospel of the water and the Spirit can receive the eternal remission of sins and earn eternal life. Halleluiah! ⊠

CHAPTER 1

Jesus Christ, Our Life

< John 1:1-4 >
"In the beginning was the Word, and the Word was with God, and the Word was God. He was in the beginning with God. All things were made through Him, and without Him nothing was made that was made. In Him was life, and the life was the light of men."

How Great Is Jesus Who Loves Us So Much That He Has Delivered Us from All Our Sins!

John chapter 1 describes Jesus as the Creator of the entire universe. If we were to compare ourselves to the boundless universe that God created, we would realize what small and dismal creatures we are. This is why we cannot thank God enough for being able to meet such great God. It was the greatest of all miracles. Even now, I think that it is the greatest of all miracles that I have met with God, who came by the gospel of the water and the Spirit.

Jesus was the Creator, who created this vast universe that spreads millions upon millions of light years wide. God has also prepared the eternal Truth and the true salvation, which are invisible to our eyes. God is truly an amazing God. God's utmost work was creating humans, out of all other God's creations, as His own children.

Yet, how could we not give thanks to God, when we were able to encounter such a great and marvelous God? God has accomplished such great works that are impossible for us to comprehend with our intelligence. The world that God has created is full of mysteries which are incomprehensible to the human mind. We cannot but help praise God, since we were able to meet with such a great God on our own discretion. We cannot help but praise God, when we look at the universe that is filled with many galaxies that are beyond our imaginations. The universe, which God has created, is magnificent. We are such small beings who are incomparable to God's created world. Each person is no larger than a flake of dust in the eyes of God. Still, how could we not give thanks to God, when such small beings as we were able to meet with God, the Creator of this magnificent universe? With a heart full of gratefulness, I give my thanks to God once again.

However, it is a shame that there are so many people who are trying to meet with the great and holy God without having the gospel Truth of the water and the Spirit. It is absolutely impossible for us to meet with Jesus without first having faith in this true gospel. Also, it is impossible for us to receive the remission of sin without the gospel of the water and the Spirit.

Then, how is Jesus Christ able to meet with us humans? There is no other way through which God is able to meet with us except through Jesus, who became a human just like you and me. Jesus received the baptism from John the Baptist to take all our sins onto Himself at once, and He wholly blotted out all our sins once and for all by being crucified on the Cross. Through His baptism and crucifixion, Jesus made it possible for God to adopt us as His own children. In other words, there is no other means of salvation except the coming of God as our Savior, who has delivered us from all our sins once and for all. However, if God were to meet with us in His fundamental character, no sinner would have been able to escape the judgments accorded to their sins, for He is the most holy and solemn Judge. Because we were fundamentally sinners, we would have died if we were to stand before God's holy light. Thus, for God to meet with us, He had to come to us in the flesh of man, just like us.

Our Lord Himself has thus come in the flesh of man so that He could meet with us and deliver us, who are weak and insufficient, from all our sins. In order to take the flesh and blood of a man, just like the bodies we possess, Jesus was born into this world through the Virgin Mary. Just as it is written, *"Behold, the virgin shall conceive and bear a Son, and shall call His name Immanuel" (Isaiah 7:14),* God has come to us in flesh and blood like ours to be with us. This promise was prophesized by the Prophet Isaiah over 700 years prior to Jesus' birth. If our Lord had not lowered Himself to our humble level and approached us, you and I would have never been able to meet with the Lord. Our Lord had come to this world in the flesh of man, just like ours, to meet with us.

God Who Has Become Immanuel to Us

"Immanuel" means "God with us," and the name "Jesus" means "He who will save His people from their sins" (Matthew 1:21, 23). John 3:16 says about Immanuel Jesus the following: *"For God so loved the world that He gave His only begotten Son, that whoever believes in Him should not perish but have everlasting life."* Because God so loved us, He took the flesh of man and came into this world to meet with us.

Jesus Christ came to this world in the flesh of man and made us sinless by the gospel of the water and the Spirit. Thus, He has made us into His own people. Our Lord has given us the gospel of great blessings. He has come into this world by the gospel of the water and the Spirit. When we listen to and believe in our hearts the gospel Truth of the water and the Spirit, we can meet with the most Holy God and become a part of His own people. We are able to meet with God because we have been delivered from all our sins by the gospel of the water and the Spirit. We are also able to have true fellowship with God because we have become His own people. Because of this, we must realize that we cannot meet with God on our own without first believing in the gospel of the water and the Spirit. Therefore, we can meet with Him only through faith. Although our Lord is fundamentally God, He has visited this world by the gospel Truth of the water and the Spirit to meet with us who are fundamentally sinners.

We believe in the gospel of the water and the Spirit, and we believe that our Lord is the King of kings, the Creator God, and the true Savior. We are thankful that Jesus Christ has come to this world in the flesh of man. We are able to meet with Him when we believe in His spoken gospel Word of the water and the Spirit. Whoever wants to meet with Jesus Christ must realize that this is possible only by believing in Him who came to this world to deliver us from all our sins. We are not able to meet with Him merely because we desire to do so. Because we believe in the gospel of the water and the Spirit, we are now able to meet freely with God. By believing in the Lord-given gospel Truth of the water and the Spirit, we have become God's own people. Dear fellow believers, do these words make sense to you?

Every person grew up in a distinct environment, and one's belief system is molded mainly by this environment. You might be a Christian because of the environment that you have been raised in. Among believers in Jesus, there are also those who have come across the gospel for the first time later in life.

Although the gospel Word of the water and the Spirit may sound a little odd when hearing it for the first time, we know that it is still right. It is natural for us to initially be confused when we enter into the power of the gospel of the water and the Spirit. Everyone goes through the same experience at first. However, your confusion will surely be overcome when you place your faith in the gospel of the water and the Spirit.

There are many Christians who praise God out of their affection for God despite not knowing the gospel of the water and the Spirit. Is He really pleased with this mistaken praise of sinners? Those who have become righteous by their faith are praising God with a joyful heart. If you go to a church of God, you can find other people who are praising only the righteousness of God.

Whoever comes to the church of God will eventually hear the gospel Word of the water and the Spirit. This gospel of the water and the Spirit is the gospel Truth that cannot be heard anywhere else in the world. Those who hear and believe in the gospel Truth of the water and the Spirit gather at God's Church to lead their spiritual lives. Also, since there cannot be a single spot of sin in their hearts, they come to praise God with completely sinless hearts. They can praise God from deep within in their hearts because they have met with the Lord in the Truth and therefore have conviction of their salvation. In God's Church, the grace of the remission of sin, which our Lord has given us, is overflowing at all times.

How was it possible for us to meet with our Lord? Actually, this is impossible through mere human means. It's nonsense for us to try to meet with God with solely our own effort. We are unable to meet with God with faith that is based on human thoughts. It is only by believing in the gospel Truth of the water and the Spirit that we are delivered from all our sins and are also able to meet with God the Creator of all Heavens. For us to meet with God, we are in absolute need of the gospel of the water and the Spirit. There is no defect in our remission of sin which is gained through the faith in that gospel. Now, whoever believes in the gospel of the water and the Spirit can meet with God and become God's own people through their faith.

Our true Mediator is Jesus Christ (1 Timothy 2:5). And the Lord-given gospel of the water and the Spirit is true salvation. No one can meet with Jesus except through the gospel Truth of the water and the Spirit. None of us can be exempted from eternal condemnation unless we know the gospel Truth of the water and the Spirit. We are able to meet with Jesus Christ, our Lord and Savior, only by believing in the real Truth of salvation which came by the water and the Spirit. Thus, I tell you now that you, whoever believes in the gospel of the water and the Spirit will be the most blessed.

However, those Christian ministers who have not come across the gospel of the water and the Spirit cannot preach true sermons because they have not yet met with God. Thus, they are able only to preach sermons of untruth. They may preach the Word of God in their own way, but they are unable to share the Truth that enables people to solve the problem of sin in their spirit. It is absolutely impossible for them to speak of the realm of the gospel Truth of the water and the Spirit, for they have no idea about this gospel Truth. Many preachers give sermons to their congregants, but their words are nothing but theoretical thoughts out of their own flesh.

What Is the Love of God Truly Like?

What is the love of God like? In this world, there are many kinds of love. There exists the love of people, of friends, of a lover, of one's parents, and the love of God. Then, which kind of love is the most precious? Since never changing and unconditional love is the most precious, God's love beats out all others without a second thought. We all desire to possess the love of God in our hearts. How are we able to possess the love of God in our hearts then? When we believe in Jesus Christ, who came by the gospel Word of the water and the Spirit, to be our Savior, we are able to possess the love of God.

Until the last generation, people used to think that they could gain worldly knowledge by going to church. However, nowadays, people don't even think of such an advantage. These days, because there are so many places to learn in the world and because people have already learned so much, people are dissatisfied unless the gospel of the water and the Spirit is preached.

The gospel of the water and the Spirit is preached only in the church of God. People come to church these days not to learn worldly knowledge but to learn about God and to hear the voice of God through the gospel of the water and the Spirit. Yet, how can a minister, who is ignorant of the gospel of the water and the Spirit, lead the souls of others to the Word of God? Those who are still ignorant of the gospel of the water and the Spirit have neither received the remission of their sins nor met with God because they do not know this gospel Truth. How then could they possibly discuss the gospel of the water and the Spirit, which is the Gospel of God? Furthermore, how could they possibly talk about your spiritual condition? They are unable to discuss the remission of sin and the true salvation.

They only confuse the hearts of spiritually blind Christians with their doctrines. Everyone must be washed completely from all their sins by their faith in the gospel of the water and the Spirit. Otherwise, it is impossible to share this true gospel clearly manifested in the Bible.

Yet, we who believe in the gospel of the water and the Spirit were able to meet with Jesus through this gospel Truth. Since Jesus came to this world by water and blood (1 John 5:6), we are made born again as well as God's own people by our faith in that gospel.

In today's Scripture passage of John 1, it is written that Jesus Christ is God: *"In the beginning was the Word, and the Word was with God, and the Word was God. He was in the beginning with God. All things were made through Him, and without Him nothing was made that was made. In Him was life, and the life was the light of men. And the light shines in the darkness, and the darkness did not comprehend it" (John 1:1-5).*

In the beginning, there was the Word. This Word was in fact the Word of God. This world was made through the Word of God, and there was nothing in this world that was not made through the Word of God. In the Word of God, came life for all things. That life also gave life to men.

God the Creator of the entire universe is the very Triune God; the Father, the Son, and the Holy Spirit. God made the universe into a reality by His Word, "Let there be something." When God spoke, it became thus. What I am saying is this Omnipotent God has come to us as our Savior. With our Lord, who came to this world, came the authority to cleanse us from all our sins. Yet, so many people do not know the Lord and die as sinners. *"And the light shines in the darkness, and the darkness did not comprehend it" (John 1:5).*

However, you and I who believe in the gospel of the water and the Spirit have received much love from God. God our Savior came to this world in the man's flesh just like ours. By receiving the baptism from John the Baptist and dying on the Cross, He took all our sins onto Himself and expunged all of them. By resurrecting from the dead, He has given us, who believe in the gospel of the water and the Spirit, the grace to call God the Father as "Abba Father." By knowing and believing in the gospel of the water and the Spirit, we have been delivered from all our sins and adopted as God's own children. Thus, through the gospel of the water and the Spirit, we have met with our Savior, Jesus Christ. Since we have met God by this gospel Truth, what great love have we received from God?

We, who have been born again by believing in Jesus as our Savior through the gospel of the water and the Spirit, have received the great grace of salvation. Yet, many people remain sinners in the darkness, although the light of the gospel of the water and the Spirit has shone upon them. What great shame is it that so many people are still wondering in the darkness, when Jesus Christ has already delivered everyone from all their sins by coming through the gospel of the water and the Spirit? We have certainly received abundant grace, since we have met Jesus through our faith in the gospel of the water and the Spirit.

If we take a moment to reflect on ourselves for a moment, we have not met our Lord because of our intelligence. If we were able to meet the Lord by our fleshly abilities, we would not have been able to meet our Lord. How could such insignificant people such as us meet with such awesome God?

If we look at each individual person in comparison to the universe, we are like dust. No, not even dust. If such beings tried to meet with the Lord, it is only reasonable to think that it won't be possible. That's why He came to us and met with us. We have not met with God through our excellence in the flesh, but we were able to meet with God because our Lord has delivered us by the gospel Word of the water and the Spirit. Those who have believed this and met with the Lord have received His true love. As I am wearing a formal suit right now, those who have believed in the gospel of the water and the Spirit are wearing the clothes of God's righteousness. We who have put on the love of God are wearing His great love indeed. It is a great privilege to receive blessings, grace, salvation, and love from the Almighty God, who is the Creator and the Savior.

We have not loved God, but God loved us first and unconditionally by the gospel Truth of the water and the Spirit, meeting with us and covering us with His love (1 John 4:19). Thus, we have become God's own people, been adopted as His children, and gained the right to enter into the eternal world. There is nothing we have done on our part in completing this amazing Truth of God. God did it all from His side.

For us to go after that love of God is as hopeless as traveling all around the world looking for one's unknown mother, as a fairy tale tells. We will not be able to find the Savior, even if we were to search in ever corner of this universe. We are able to meet God only because He Himself came to meet with us. We can meet with the Lord and are delivered from all our sins only by believing in the Lord-given gospel of the water and the Spirit. No one can receive the remission of sin by ones own deeds or abilities.

Thus, we have to abandon our human thoughts that stand against the will of God. All salvation comes out of our Lord. To think that we will do something with our own worldly knowledge is a delusion. It is forgetting one's place, acting like a puppy that's not afraid of a tiger. If we really want to meet the Lord of Truth, we must pay attention to the Word of God with our eyes and ears. The problem is that people are deceived by false teachings and, therefore, fail to realize the gospel Truth of the water and the Spirit.

Those who are ignorant of the Truth of the water and the Spirit will not meet the Lord even when they are given a second chance. Those who have not been washed completely of all of their sins by their faith in the gospel of the water and the Spirit cannot comprehend even a line of the Bible correctly. They can only say that the Word of God is composed of the white part which is the paper and the black letters. They may come to know the scholastic knowledge of this world, but the written Word of the Bible is indescribably complicated to them. If Jesus said the Word in the beginning to create the heavens and the earth, that Word is the Word of God. And this universe was solely created by His Word. But religionist Christians try to interpret His Word only through their own limited logical understanding. Therefore, it is impossible for those, who do not know the gospel of the water and the Spirit, to comprehend how God came to this world in the flesh of man.

I met the Lord through the gospel Word of the water and the Spirit 10 years after I started believing in Jesus as my Savior. While studying theology I have realized that even at the graduate level, it was utterly impossible to know the essence of Jesus Christ through such theology. "Ah! It's utterly impossible to know Jesus. The more I learn about the Bible, it only gets harder to comprehend. I can understand every variation of Christian doctrines. I can memorize every detail of soteriology, systematic theology, and pneumatology. But the Bible is different. One day I think I have a firm grasp on it, the very next day I am uncertain. The more I study the Bible, the more confused I get." So I rather gave up. I eventually thought to myself, "I am quite ignorant of the Bible."

When I first believed in Jesus, I thought that I knew the Bible fairly well. Although I claimed to have believed in Jesus as my Savior, everything I thought I knew came into doubt after 10 years. Fortunately, I realized the gospel Truth of the water and the Spirit while reading the Scripture. Through it, the sins of my heart were completely blotted out. I received God's blessing of being born again by knowing and then believing in the gospel of the water and the Spirit through the written Word of God. That gospel of the water and the Spirit states, "Jesus terminated all the sins of the world by receiving the baptism from John the Baptist and by dying on the Cross." Only after I had known the gospel Truth of the water and the Spirit, I was able to truly meet with Jesus my Savior. In short, when I knew the gospel of the water and the Spirit, I was truly able to meet Jesus.

Since then, I have been able to preach the gospel Word of the water and the Spirit. When I shared the gospel Word of the water and the Spirit, those who heard the message were able to meet the Lord properly just as I have met the Lord my God.

In retrospect, I had an incomplete belief in God before I knew the gospel of the water and the Spirit. However, my faith is quite different now. I am quite busy with work, but when I take some time off to pray and read the Bible, a thought occurs to me; "How did I meet with God?" This was a question that I couldn't answer precisely before.

"Lord Jesus, You have come to me with the gospel Word of the water and the Spirit. You have visited me by coming into this world in the flesh of man. You took all my sins onto Your body by receiving the baptism, and died on the Cross in my stead. On the third day, You rose from the dead, and ascended into the Heavens. The Word You had spoken was recorded so that I may know myself and God through it. When I know in my heart and believe that God has delivered me from all my sins, I receive my salvation. This was utterly due to Your grace and love. How could I meet with God any way otherwise?" I cannot help but confess like this. What I am saying is that it was not through the efforts on my side by which I met with the Lord. The Lord has delivered me from all my sins by His grace, He has loved me by His grace, and He met with you and me by His grace. I give thanks to God, as I reflect on these.

I am a mere creature, weak and deficient, having nothing to boast about. Not only before God but even before people I have nothing to boast about, but He met with me out of His love. "He became a human being for my sake and brought salvation to humanity by coming down to us by the water and the Spirit. That's why the Lord desires to meet not only with me but also with the rest of the humanity. The Lord always is near to the people. Yet, most of them have not met with Him, although we have." My heart is gladdened whenever these thoughts occur to me. As I see the congregants and servants of God's Church, I am glad because I feel that "They are people who truly have met God."

Dear fellow believers, how many people are there in this world who have believed in Jesus and met with the God of Truth? Are there many? Dear fellow believers, there are not that many Christians who have met God by the gospel of the water and the Spirit.

This is why we are serving the gospel Word of the water and the Spirit. The reason we hold revival meetings at God's Church is so that those who have not met God yet may indeed meet with God. Although the Bible is a pretty thick book, it can be summarized into a few words: They are the gospel of the water and the Spirit. If after hearing the Word you understand it and check it and discover yourself through it, the Lord will come to you. If you know and believe that Jesus bore all your sins and expunged all your sins by the baptism and the Cross, then you can come to meet the Lord.

You may inquire, "How it is possible for mere creatures to meet with God?" If we meet the Lord through our faith in the gospel of the water and the Spirit, we comprehend the gospel of the water and the Spirit at that moment with an exclamation of "That's it." However, those who lack a humble heart are difficult to receive this special love of God. Numerous babies are being born every moment. Yet, is there any one who has met God, the Creator of the entire universe, through his own method? No, no one can meet Him for himself.

Then, how can I receive the love of God and the blessing from Him? The correct answer is that "The Lord has met with me." In order to meet with me, the Lord came to this world in the flesh of man like mine: He took all of our sins onto Himself by receiving the baptism from John the Baptist. When He died on the Cross, He received the judgments for all our sins in our stead. And on the third day, He was resurrected from the dead. Through these righteous acts, the Lord has met you and me. Thus, we have received our salvation from all our sins.

I am standing before you as a pastor who believes in the gospel of the water and the Spirit. Though I am insufficient in many areas, it is my sincerest desire to lead all people who have not met the Lord to the Him and to introduce to them about the God and Jesus whom I have met. I am not a VIP. I am comparable to a tour guide. Like a guide at a tourist attraction, those who have met the Lord through their faith in the gospel of the water and the Spirit are gospel preachers, leading others to Jesus. If we are to be good spiritual guides, we need to believe in the gospel of the water and the Spirit and receive proper spiritual training. Regardless of how articulate a person is, unless he knows about the tourist attraction and about the role of a guide, he cannot be a good guide. Therefore, we, first of all, have to know about the Gospel of the water and the Spirit.

I was able to approach God because I first met with the gospel of the water and the Spirit. And only because the Lord chose to meet with me by the gospel of the water and the Spirit, I was able to meet with the Lord. I have worn the love of the Lord because the Lord has truly loved me first. Because I have worn the love of God, I am trying to spread that love all over the world. Also, because I have met Him, I am trying to introduce Him to you and lead you to Him. Because I am thankful of the fact that the Lord has met with me, I am so happy that the Lord has also met with you. Through these sermons, I hope you all experience how honored and grateful we should be that the Lord has met with us. Still, I am confident that we are of one heart, since we have all been born again of the gospel of the water and the Spirit.

The gospel Truth of the water and the Spirit is the cornerstone of salvation for all sinners. If we lack the faith in this Truth, we are unable to meet the Lord. If any of you does not believe in the gospel of the water and the Spirit, you will be deceived by the false ministers and deprived of your souls as well as your money.

Is there still any one among you who has sin in your heart? How can you say that you have accepted Jesus as your Savior in your heart, when the sins in your heart are still intact because you do not know the gospel of the water and the Spirit? What other Truth is there besides the gospel of the water and the Spirit by which you can encounter Jesus and receive salvation? Your foolish claim that you have been born again without believing correctly in the gospel of the water and the Spirit is leading you to hell. That's why we must continuously blow the trumpet of salvation so that everyone of the world may hear the gospel Truth and be saved from sin. If people fail to meet the Lord and receive eternal salvation again because they choose not to hear to the gospel of the water and the Spirit when we are faithfully preaching it, the blame is on them.

We should love, thank, believe, and glorify God during the days of our lives. We should share what we have received. And as God met with us, we should also share the gospel of the water and the Spirit and introduce God to those who are ignorant of Him so that they also will meet with Him. That is what we the righteous should do.

The Lord has delivered us from all our sins. We should live our lives praising the Lord and giving thanks to Him. ✉

We Must Be Born of God

< John 1:12-18 >

"But as many as received Him, to them He gave the right to become children of God, to those who believe in His name: who were born, not of blood, nor of the will of the flesh, nor of the will of man, but of God. And the Word became flesh and dwelt among us, and we beheld His glory, the glory as of the only begotten of the Father, full of grace and truth. John bore witness of Him and cried out, saying, 'This was He of whom I said, 'He who comes after me is preferred before me, for He was before me.'' And of His fullness we have all received, and grace for grace. For the law was given through Moses, but grace and truth came through Jesus Christ. No one has seen God at any time. The only begotten Son, who is in the bosom of the Father, He has declared Him."

We have to believe in Jesus Christ our Savior, who came by the gospel Truth of the water and the Spirit, in order to receive salvation from all our sins. John 1:10 says, *"He was in the world, and the world was made through Him, and the world did not know Him."* Here, the phrase "He was in the world" implies that Jesus Christ has actually existed in this world. The Lord is the Creator of this world. Thus, the Creator of this world came to the creatures He had created and lived together with among them. However, everyone in this world, not even the Jews, recognized Him as the Savior.

Jesus was the God who spoke to us of the gospel Word of

the water and the Spirit. Jesus Christ was in this world, which was created by Him. Yet, we did not recognize Him as the Lord and Savior. Even now, Jesus Christ has come by the gospel of the water and the Spirit to the world He Himself has created, but there are more people who reject Jesus than accept as their Savior. Many people of this world did neither know nor acknowledge that Jesus is God the Creator of the universe and the Savior, who has expunged all their sins. They must realize how they are indifferent and ignorant of Jesus so far, and must return to Him by believing in God's own gospel Truth of the water and the Spirit.

Why Did Jesus Christ Come to This World in the Flesh of Man?

Jesus Christ came to this world to deliver sinners from all their sins by totally receiving the judgments for all the sins of humanity through His baptism. Put differently, He became a human being to deliver all of humanity from all their sins. Then, was it really possible for Jesus Christ to become a mortal creature? It was possible because Jesus Christ the true God came as a human being. Thus, Jesus Christ was the God of Mercy as well as the Son of God. Because He much loved us His own created humans so much, He came to this world as the Savior according to His Father's will. Jesus Christ came to expunge all sins of humanity which has separated us from God the Father. Jesus Christ necessarily had to become a human being in order to deliver sinners from all their sins. He came to all humanity as a human being through the body of the Virgin Mary just like He had promised.

Yet, so many people these days say words of disbeliefs.

People doubt how a virgin could possibly give birth to a baby. Still, God had come to this world as a human being just like it was promised through the prophet Isaiah some 2700 years ago from now. Quoting from Isaiah 7:14, Matthew 1:23 says, *"'Behold, the virgin shall be with child, and bear a Son, and they shall call His name Immanuel,' which is translated, 'God with us.'"* Jesus Christ came to this world through the body of a virgin just like it was promised.

Scientifically speaking, the question is how a virgin can give birth to a baby without going through the natural process. If you asked me if it is possible, I would answer, "No." However, it is possible because Jesus is fundamentally God. He had such absolute power and authority. Why should He do so? It was necessary because man has been deceived by Satan the Devil, and we all have fallen deep into sin. Specifically to deliver us from all the sins of the world, the Lord had to come in the flesh of man just like ours through the body of a virgin.

Do you understand the message I am trying to convey to you? If we think from our fleshly perspective, what I am saying does not make any sense. However, God is speaking through the Word of the Bible that "He was in the world" and that "the people did not accept Him when He came to this world." Thus, only by believing in the gospel of the water and the Spirit is such understanding possible.

How Does God Reveal Himself to Us?

How does God reveal Himself to us? He reveals Himself through His Word. God exists in the Holy Trinity of God the Father, the Son, and the Holy Spirit. We are able to meet God only when we believe in our hearts His Word, the gospel Truth of the water and the Spirit.

God repeatedly tells us that the Word recorded in the Bible is the very Word of God. Then, what does it mean by "God is Spirit"? (John 4:24) To say God is Spirit entails that God is not a material being. And the Bible also says, *"Let all the earth keep silence before Him" (Habakkuk 2:20).* We have to listen to Him in silence when He says to us, for He always speaks the truth. Although it is difficult for us to believe that God is Spirit, it is not difficult to know who God is once we know and believe in Jesus Christ who came by the gospel of the water and the Spirit. Just as our hearts turn toward God through the Word of God, all our problems of sin are solved by our faith in the Word of Truth.

God has appeared to all people through His Word. The entire 66 Books of the Holy Bible are the very Word of God. Thus, if we believe in the love of God by believing first in the gospel of the water and the Spirit, we come to meet with God. Hence, this Word of the Bible is the very Word of God. The most mysterious and wonderful fact is that all our sins can be blotted out and we can become God's people when we believe with our hearts in the gospel Word of the water and the Spirit. We are truly led to God when we believe in the gospel Word of the water and the Spirit, which is the very Word of God. Truly, having faith in the Holy Word of God means living with the faith in the gospel Word of the water and the Spirit, which is the Truth of God.

When We Believe in Our Hearts the Gospel of the Water and the Spirit, Which Is Recorded in the Word of God, We Are Made God's Own People at That Very Moment

We have to accept the Word of God into our hearts. John 1:11-13 from today's Scripture passage says, *"He came to His own, and His own did not receive Him. But as many as received Him, to them He gave the right to become children of God, to those who believe in His name: who were born, not of blood, nor of the will of the flesh, nor of the will of man, but of God."*

We have to believe in Jesus as our Savior: We have to believe that Jesus Christ came to this world through the virgin birth to deliver us from all our sins; that He took all our sins by receiving the baptism at the Jordan River at the age of thirty; that He bore our sins onto the Cross where He was crucified and left to die; and that He rose from the dead and ascended into Heaven and now sits on the right hand of God the Father's throne. God has given those, who accept in their hearts that Jesus received the baptism and shed His blood so that we sinners may be delivered from all our sins, the power and authority to become God's children.

God desires to speak to us all the Word through the gospel Word of the water and the Spirit. We who are merely creatures can be born again as God's children when we accept the gospel of the water and the Spirit, by which all our sins were blotted out. God's love towards us is comprised in the Word of God. Thus, we simultaneously accept the written Word of God with the gospel of the water and the Spirit. By believing in the Word of God, we can truly experience the remission of sin as well as eternal life.

The entire Bible is not easily understood by those who believe in Christ as one's Savior. Yet, through the Word of God we can understand who we are as human beings, where we come from and where we will go eventually. We must know the love of God though the gospel of the water and the Spirit, for the love of God is revealed in this gospel Truth. If it is written that God created us humans with dust, we must know so and believe so. According to the written Word of God, the LORD God formed man of the dust of the ground, and breathed into his nostrils the breath of life; and man became a living being (Genesis 2:7). Also, the written Word of God says that, when we die, we shall return to dust. It is also written in the Bible that humans are sinners born with innate sins. It also says that our God will resurrect all of us on the last days.

Though we are made of dust and will return to dust, it is entirely by God's grace that we are able to become God's children and have our names entered in His family book. All this is possible because we have met God, and all our sins have been washed away by our faith in the gospel Word of the water and the Spirit, which the Son of God gave us. Dear fellow believers, do you believe and are you thankful that Jesus came to this world to expunge my sins as well as yours? Do you believe that Jesus took not only all of our sins but the sins of the all humanity when He received the baptism at the Jordan River? Do you believe that Jesus bore the sins onto the Cross and vicariously received all the judgments corresponding to them? By believing as such in the gospel of the water and the Spirit, our names are added to God's family book. When you and I believe in the Creator God who came to this world as the Savior of all sinners who shed water and blood to deliver us from all our sins, we are able to accept Jesus as our personal Savior. Thus, we receive the power and authority to be transformed into God's children from mere creatures. Now, God has given the right to become God's children only to those who have received the remission of sin and become righteous.

Dear fellow believers, have you received the remission of sin? Have you become God's children by being washed away of all your sins? Those who have become God's children in actuality have no sin in their hearts. If a person accepts Jesus Christ as one's personal Savior and accepts the Word of God as recorded, he comes to experience all his sins being purged away. Thus, because we have become the righteous and holy, our names have been added to the family book of God.

Is Believing in Jesus as One's Savior the Same as Believing in the Truth? Or Is It Believing in a Worldly Religion?

What we believe is the gospel Truth of the water and the Spirit and not some worldly religion. Because Jesus is the Savior who delivered us from all the sins of the world, we wear the love of God by believing in Him with all our hearts. The God-spoken gospel of the water and the Spirit, which brings the remission of sin, is the definite Truth of salvation. It is also the just and pure gospel of God that makes our hearts as white as snow.

Jesus has truly saved us by coming to us through the water and the Holy Spirit. To believe in Jesus is equivalent to believing in God the Father. Believing in Jesus as one's true Savior is only possible when one believes in the gospel of the water and the Spirit, which is the Truth that delivers us from all our sins. Believing in Jesus is the way to the remission of sin and to eternal life. The history of Christianity is not made by men, but is made by God. Christianity is the fruit of God's love. Out of His love and providence, God Himself planned and executed the salvation of the entire humanity. Christians are people who believe and follow Jesus. When we say we believe in Jesus, we are confessing Jesus as the true God and eternal life (1 John 5:20). By our confession of faith in Jesus, we attain our eternal life, that is, we are transferred from death to a new life. To say that we believe in the Son of God is to believe Jesus as our Savior, who came by the gospel of the water and the Spirit.

The difference between faith and religion before God is as follows. Faith professes that God has blotted out all our sins, while Religion lies in the heart of people who made their own god out of their thoughts and believe in it. This is the difference between a man of faith and a religionist.

A person is able to receive salvation from all his sins and gain the right to become God's child by believing in God's living Word, the gospel of the water and the Spirit. True faith of salvation does not come out of one's own thoughts but out of the faith in the gospel of the water and the Spirit, to which the Word of God testifies. Every Word in the Scriptures is the written Word of God. Believing in the gospel of the water and the Spirit is the only way of gaining true life.

A person becomes God's child not through flesh or blood or even human will but only through faith in the gospel of the water and the Spirit, which is the Word of God. Believers in the gospel of the water and the Spirit receive the right and blessing to become the children of God. We become God's children not through our biological heritage but through the faith in the written Word of God. Again, it is not through the human emotion that we become the children of God but only through the Word of God. Hence, those who are born of God are the ones who are born of the gospel of the water and the Spirit, which is the Word of God. Just as the heavens and the earth were created through the Word of God, we are created again through our faith in the gospel Word of the water and the Spirit, which is the Word of God. By believing in the gospel of the water and the Spirit, we are regenerated into the children of God.

If people were only to inherit through their biological heritage, naturally only the sons of kings would become kings. If we were to determine such things through bloodlines, this makes perfect sense. This may work in the earthly world, but becoming a child of God is a completely different matter. Anyone who believes in the God-spoken gospel Word of the water and the Spirit can become a child of God. There is no way to become a child of God and be acknowledged of one's faith without first believing in the gospel of the water and the Spirit.

We Cannot Become God's Children by Means of Pedigree, nor by the Will of the Flesh

A family line is merely of the flesh and cannot become Godly heritage. Thus, it is impossible to become God's child through one's pedigree. It does not matter whether a person belongs a good family line that consists of men of faith. If he still has sin in his heart despite believing in Jesus as his Savior, that person cannot be said to believe in the gospel of the water and the Spirit. How can a person profess to be sinless when that person clearly has sin in his heart? If a person claims to be sinless despite the sins of one's heart, that person would be lying in front of God. Regardless of whether a person professes to believe in Jesus, those who have sins are still sinners. And the wage of sin is death. A sinner cannot go to Heaven to be with the Lord because of his sins.

You and I have become the children of God through our faith in the gospel of the water and the Spirit, and not through any specific family line. We receive the remission of sin by the faith in the gospel of the water and the Spirit, for this gospel Truth is the very Truth of salvation. The gospel of the water and the Spirit is truly an amazing Truth which blots out all the sins of all people.

Some people profess to have received their salvation because they feel sure of their salvation emotionally. But, this is not the case. Nor are we made God's children because some people acknowledge our faith. We have received the remission of sin neither through the fullness of emotions nor through our human will but only through our faith in the gospel of the water and the Spirit. We do not become the children of God by becoming good theologians. We are not made the people of God by believing in the signs and miracles of God. All these are false forms of faith that are created by spiritually blind people.

The worldly religionists create their own salvation. They are trying to make their own offspring into Christian ministers without first receiving the remission of sin by the gospel of the water and the Spirit. They think that they should make their sons into pastors. Thus, there are many who send their sinful sons to seminary to train them as pastors. We cannot make servants of God solely through sheer human will. Why, then, are they sending their unqualified children, who are unaware of the gospel of the water and the Spirit, to seminaries? Still, parents are proud when their sons go through seminaries against their own will and somehow become pastors. Parents say proudly, "My son is a pastor." However, that is not something to be proud of.

A person does not become a child of God or a servant of God out of the human will but only through the faith in the gospel of the water and the Spirit. But the reality is far different from this truth. This is why there are so many false pastors in this world. Thus, everyone has to know and believe in their hearts the gospel Word of the water and the Spirit, which is God's Word of Truth, and receive the remission of sin to become God's own people. By doing so, they must receive Jesus Christ as their true personal Savior, who came by the gospel of the water and the Spirit. Only then can they become children of God and His workers.

Are We Made the Righteous Only by Believing in the Truth of the Water, the Blood, and the Holy Spirit?

Only those who believe in Jesus as their Savior and accept the gospel of the water and the Spirit in their hearts can directly become the children of God and be washed away of all their sins completely. Is it possible for a person to accept Jesus as one's Savior without first knowing the gospel Truth of the water and the Spirit? It is absolutely impossible. How could we believe in Jesus as our personal Savior if we did not know the correct gospel Truth of the water and the Spirit?

Which kind of faith enables us to accept Jesus as the Savior? It is only possible when we believe in our hearts the gospel Truth, the Word of God. We are able to accept the Savior truthfully and know that the gospel of the water and the Spirit is Truth by our faith in the Word of God. Why is it so? It is because the Word of God is Truth itself.

Every human being is a sinner from his or her birth: Coming into this world, they are born with the 12 sins (Mark 7:20-23). Unfortunately thus, people cannot help but sin against God throughout their entire lives. We are sinners with sin as black as a crow. Still, our Lord has taken all the sins of this world—including those we have already committed and will commit throughout our entire lives, the sins of our hearts and deeds—onto Himself once for all by receiving the baptism from John the Baptist at the Jordan River. He bore those sins onto the Cross, vicariously receiving the judgments accorded to our sins. He thus blotted out all our sins at once, has taken the judgments for our sins himself, and has given us the remission of sin instead.

Our faith in the gospel Word of the water and the Spirit gives us the very remission of all our sins. Also, by this faith, we receive a new life from the eternal and living God. That is, we become born of God. By knowing and believing in our hearts the gospel of the water and the Spirit, which is the Word of God, we have become born of God.

In this world, the expression "being born again" is easily found in everyone's mouth. Even our congressmen say saying, "I am born again," "I am trying everything to be born again." However, being truly born again is nothing like this. It is a spiritual concept implying that a sinner becomes a righteous one by receiving the remission of sin.

In today's Christianity, there are many who claim that they have been born again from all their sins through their own actions or ability. However, the problem is that there are many among them who believe that one has to experience signs and miracles to be born again. Some others still think that one has to do a lot of charitable works. This is truly foolish, for God clearly says that we are born, not of blood, nor of the will of the flesh, nor of the will of man, but of God (John 1:13).

God has created the universe and everything in it. God has created us so that we are to die once spiritually and be born again by our faith in the gospel of the water and the Spirit. And He will recreate everything once again in His Day (Revelation 21:5). The real Truth of being born again is that God has made a way to transform imperfect sinners into the perfect righteous.

When God first created us humans, He created us imperfect so that we may be deceived by Satan the Devil. Hence, we the humanity had fallen into sin. The hearts of humanity was soaked with sin. Thus, humans had become sinners who cannot but help sin throughout their entire lives.

Yet, God the Father so loved us and sent His Son as the propitiation out of His love. When Jesus Christ came to this world, He received the baptism from John the Baptist at the Jordan River to take all the sins of the world. He delivered us from all our sins, death, and condemnation by dying vicariously on the Cross. We have been born again by believing that Jesus Christ, who has done such righteous acts, is our personal Lord and Savior.

God describes throughout the entire Bible how we are born again by our faith in the gospel Word of the water and the Spirit. *"And the Word became flesh and dwelt among us, and we beheld His glory, the glory as of the only begotten of the Father, full of grace and truth" (John 1:14).*

When it says that "the Word became flesh," who is this Word? It says that it was Jesus, who was also God. What did God become? He wore the flesh of man. God became a creature. Why did God do such a thing? It is because of God's fundamental love for humanity. "For God so loved the world" (John 3:16), God has come in the flesh of man to deliver us from all the sins of the world.

"And the Word became flesh and dwelt among us, and we beheld His glory, the glory as of the only begotten of the Father, full of grace and truth."

We have seen the glory of God in Jesus Christ. We have seen and experienced the love of God through Jesus Christ who came by the gospel of the water and the Spirit. God is so holy and He hates sin so much that He was willing to send His Son into this world to expunge all our sins. Thus, God sent His Son, our Lord, to this world, who received the baptism from John the Baptist by which all the sins of humanity were transferred onto Himself. Also, God had His Son receive all the judgments accorded to all our sins by being crucified to His death on the Cross. That was the gift of salvation, which is the love of God.

Jesus, the only glorious Son of God, came to this world and took all our sins by receiving the baptism from John the Baptist at the Jordan River to expunge all the sins of His creatures. The gospel Word of the water and the Spirit is the real Truth of salvation. Believing in this Truth, which is the Word of God, was equivalent to believing in God as our personal Lord. The word "grace" in the phrase "full of grace and Truth" means the gift from God. God has given us the gift of salvation abundantly so that we can become His children without fail. Since God has delivered us from all our sins by His acts of salvation out of His abundant love, we must receive the remission of sin by believing in His righteous acts with our hearts.

Our faith in the written Word of God enables us to know the true salvation. Truthful faith in the gospel of the water and the Spirit places its foundation in the Word of Jesus Christ. We have become the righteous by believing in Jesus Christ as our personal Lord and Savior. We were truly wicked sinners before we believed in Jesus Christ, who came by the gospel of the water and the Spirit. Yet, the Son of God is the very Word that became flesh and dwelt among us, and whose glory is of the glory of the only begotten Son of God, full of grace and Truth. He has sufficiently made us into the righteous. Furthermore, God has given us who believe in the gospel of the water and the Spirit abundant gifts: He has given us the gift to become His children.

God is speaking to us now. God has given us the grace to become the children of God by coming into this world wearing the flesh of man. Thus, it is not only by word but also by His actual gospel of the water and the Spirit, that God has made us His rightful children so that we may live with Him happily for eternity.

What Is the God-Given Grace of Salvation to Us?

God tells us the Truth of salvation. *"John bore witness of Him and cried out, saying, 'This was He of whom I said, 'He who comes after me is preferred before me, for He was before me.'' And of His fullness we have all received, and grace for grace" (John 1:15-16).*

How can everyone in this world know the fact that Jesus Christ took all the sins of the world by receiving the baptism from John the Baptist? Every person is able to know this by the testimony of John the Baptist that all our sins were transferred onto Jesus Christ through the baptism and that all our sins expunged once for all by the bloodshed on the Cross. Today's Scripture passage says, *"And of His fullness we have all received, and grace for grace."*

Those who believe in the gospel of the water and the

Spirit have been emancipated from all their sins and have become righteous at once. This came as the gift of salvation on top of the Lord-given grace and Truth. The Lord of grace over grace not only delivered us from all our sins but also blessed us in body and spirit so that we may lead a blessed life. As we call God the Father "Abba Father," we the believers in the gospel of the water and the Spirit have become the children of God. Therefore, we also call the Father of Jesus "God our Father." Then, what do the believers in the gospel of the water and the Spirit gain in front of God? They receive the full rights of sons, just like Jesus. This is the very grace of God, the grace over grace. The book of Romans records Jesus Christ as the First Son of God.

Even from the moment when God created the universe and everything in it, God's intention of creating humans was to adopt them as His children. This was God's purpose for creating humans. It says in Genesis that God created humans in His own image. Genesis 1:27-28 says, *"So God created man in His own image; in the image of God He created him; male and female He created them. Then God blessed them, and God said to them, 'Be fruitful and multiply; fill the earth and subdue it; have dominion over the fish of the sea, over the birds of the air, and over every living thing that moves on the earth."*

Also, if we look at Genesis 1:26, it says, *"Let us make man in Our image, according to Our likeness."* The Lord uses the word "Our" when creating humans. Therefore, God is God of the Holy Trinity. That is, God the Father, the Son, and the Holy Spirit, these three are one and the same God to us. The Triune God made humans in "Our" image, in "Our" likeness. In this word "Our" is included God the Father, the Son, and the Holy Spirit. This Triune God is God to all of us. God has created the universe and everything in it in 5 days, and on the sixth day God created humans.

Back then in the beginning, the entire universe was dark. In a world full of darkness, God created and let light come to this world. The first work of God was to let the light shine in the darkness. This was in order to give every human being the new life in Jesus Christ. On the first day, the light was created when God said, "Let there be light."

What did God do on the second day? He made the firmament, and divided the waters that were under the firmament from the waters that were above the firmament. What did God do on the third day? He said, *"Let the earth bring forth grass, the herb that yields seed, and the fruit tree that yields fruit according to its kind, whose seed is in itself, on the earth."* And it was so. On the fourth day, God created two great lights; the greater light to rule the day, and the lesser light. On the fifth day, God created the birds in the air and the fish under the water. On the sixth day, God created us humans.

God made the universe and everything in it for the first five days and on the sixth day said, "Let Us make man in Our image, according to Our likeness; let them have dominion over the fish of the sea, over the birds of the air, and over the cattle, over all the earth and over every creeping thing that creeps on the earth." Thus, God created humans in His image, both male and female.

Why did God create humans? The reason is as follows. God intended humans to live with God. And He wanted to share love with humans and to be praised by them. This is God's purpose for creating humans in His own image. God created humans so that they could eventually become the children of God by being delivered from all their sins through the gospel of the water and the Spirit. Apart from other creatures, God created humans uniquely in His image for this purpose. God has the intention to adopt humans as His own children, and for this reason He has us born in this world through our parents. We realize that God has created us in His image to adopt us as His children, because if we were to live our lives without any meaning, we would lead worse lives than animals.

Thus, every human being is born into this world crying. Every human being loves eternal life, which belongs only to God. God has given every human being the yearning for eternal life (Ecclesiastes 3:11). And God has given His eternal Kingdom to those who have received the remission of sin. Because God has given those whom He loves the eternal Kingdom of God, we also yearn for His Kingdom. Why is that? It is because we have received the eternal Kingdom. God has fundamentally made us as such beings. Thus, although we live in this world for 60 or 70 years, every human being has the yearning for the eternal Kingdom in their hearts. Thus, everyone longs for the eternal Kingdom of God. Everyone instinctively longs for their eternal homeland throughout their lives.

As God lives for eternity, we are also beings that exist for eternity. Hence, when a person dies, his spirit goes upward to God to be judged by Him (Ecclesiastes 3:21). That is why we only need to believe in the gospel of the water and the Spirit while we are living in this world. God was determined to send His Son into this world to blot out all the sins of the entire humanity once for all by having Jesus receive the baptism. To those who believe in this Truth, God has sealed them as His children.

Therefore, we can fulfill God's will when we believe in the gospel of the water and the Spirit. For that reason, God has created us in His image and given us the gospel of the water and the Spirit, after we had fallen into sin. Therefore, God admonishes us to believe in His purpose for creating us. We are told to believe that God is our Creator and that God is dwelling within us, delivering us from all our sins by the gospel of the water and the Spirit. And Jesus Christ is the true God who delivers us from all our sins.

We Can Become God's Children Only by Believing in the Word of God

Through the written Word of God, He speaks the gospel Word of the water and the Spirit and gives the gift of salvation to the believers. All sinners come to know that they are sinners through the Word of God. Through the Word, they also recognize their need for Jesus and are delivered from all their sins by their faith in the Lord-given gospel of the water and the Spirit.

What we have to know first of all is the function of the Law of God. Through whom was the Law of God first delivered to us? It was done through Moses. Through whom was the God-given salvation to humanity accomplished? It was done through Jesus. We are allowed to know the gospel of the water and the Spirit through the written Word of God. And by believing in that gospel Truth, we receive the remission of sin and eternal life. We receive our salvation through the Word of our Lord.

The Scripture passage in John 1:17-18 says, *"For the law was given through Moses, but grace and truth came through Jesus Christ. No one has seen God at any time. The only begotten Son, who is in the bosom of the Father, He has declared Him."*

God says, "The Law was given through Moses." God through His grace has given people the salvation to become His own children. That salvation came through the Son of God, Jesus Christ. Jesus has blotted out all our sins by giving us the gospel of the water and the Spirit. Whoever believes in the gospel of the water and the Spirit was made sinless – without even a single sin – and also made a child of God.

However, God first told His Law to Moses. Put differently, the Law was delivered in this world through Moses. Through that Word of the Law, we were convicted of our sins and realized them. When we admitted that we were such grave sinners, God allowed us to meet the gospel Truth: We received the blessing of salvation from all our sins by believing in the baptism Jesus received and the blood Jesus shed. Now we can become children of God when we receive the remission of sin by believing in the gospel of the water and the Spirit, which Jesus has given us. Through this gospel Truth, God has adopted us His children. Thus, it is written that the Law was given to us through Moses, while God's grace and Truth came through Jesus Christ.

What we have to know is that anyone who has seen Jesus, the only begotten Son of God, has also seen God. Also, whoever believes in the Lord-given gospel of the water and the Spirit has already received the gift of salvation from the Lord.

God continues to say as follows. *"No one has seen God at any time. The only begotten Son, who is in the bosom of the Father, He has declared Him" (John 1:18).* We are able to see God when we receive the remission of sin by believing in the gospel of the water and the Spirit. Although it says that no one has seen God, the Son of God Jesus who rests in the bosom of God the Father has revealed what kind of Person God is. The gospel of the water and the Spirit reveals who Jesus is. God has declared that Jesus has blotted out all our sins by the gospel of the water and the Spirit and that He is the Son of God. By coming in the flesh of man, God has shown us the remission of sin through His baptism and bloodshed.

Therefore, we the believers in the gospel of the water and the Spirit can declare who God is as follows: God is Savior, Creator, Love, God of Justice, Holy, and Truth. God is also our Savior who has granted us the remission of sin. God is our blessings. God is the Lord who has granted us the gift of salvation. God is God in Trinity to us. He is the God who came to us by the flesh of man, water and the blood.

God has revealed Himself to us that He is the God of love and that He is the One who has granted us the remission of sin and the eternal life. God has revealed to us that He hates sin. Thus, He has blotted out all the sins of this world once for all with the gospel of the water and the Spirit.

Fundamentally, people who were born to this world were not born as children of God. However, He has given us the gift of salvation for us to become His children through the gospel of the water and the Spirit. Although there was no one who had seen God, we have actually become children of God, able to call out the most holy God "Abba Father," by our faith in the gospel of the water and the Spirit. It is through Jesus the Son of God and God the Father as well as through the gospel of the water and the Spirit that we are able to receive the remission of sin. We have met the gospel of the water and the Spirit through Jesus. And through the Word of God, we have come to know what kind of Person God is. Through the gospel of the water and the Spirit, which is the Word of God, we have met God and heard His voice, and have been able to become the children of God by receiving the remission of our sins.

God has told us that those who believe in the gospel of the

water and the Spirit will receive abundant grace and Truth. The Scripture says that God has loved us so much that He has delivered us from all the sins of the world. God has certainly come to everyone once by the gospel of the water and the Spirit. All the sins and iniquities we commit with our bodies and hearts were transferred onto Jesus when He received the baptism from John the Baptist at the Jordan River, and later all these sins were blotted out completely. Every Word of God is the Word of Truth. Therefore, believers in the gospel Truth of the water and the Spirit receive the remission of all their sins once for all through their faith and are adopted as children of God to live happily for eternity in His eternal Kingdom.

My beloved saints, through God's Church, instead of worldly knowledge you have to learn and believe the Truth of God to receive the eternal life. Only then are all the problems of our lives and those of our sins completely taken care of. The realities of all our lives are like a puzzle or a ball of tangled strings. The only one who can untangle the complicated problems of sins in our lives is Jesus Himself. We must acquire the faith in the gospel of the water and the Spirit, which is the Truth of salvation for every one of us. The Truth of God is the Word of the water and the Spirit.

We do not know where we come from nor whereto we are going. Still, by realizing the gospel of the water and the Spirit, which is the Word of God, we know that the Lord has blotted out all our sins and that He has delivered us from all our sins. By believing these truths in our hearts, we enter into the blessings God has granted us. By this faith in the true gospel, we have come to know the purpose for why we were born in this world and why we are living in this world now.

My beloved fellow believers, we must hear the Word of God spoken to us by God every time we have a meeting at the church of God. By doing so, we have truly entered the full grace of God, and we also have received the Lord-given gift of salvation as well as the gospel of the water and the Spirit. Through the gospel of the water and the Spirit, all of our entangled problems are solved. That is why we must receive the grace of the Truth of God by the gospel of the water and the Spirit. And then we will go to the Kingdom of God after we finish living in this world.

God is inviting us into the gospel of the water and the Spirit, saying, "Come into the Truth of the water and the Spirit." Jesus Christ is the Lord of the Truth who came by the gospel of the water and the Spirit. And the Lord has given abundant grace of salvation as well as the grace of the gospel of the water and the Spirit.

I give thanks to the Lord for delivering us from all the sins of the world and for His love. All of us must become born again from God by our faith in the gospel of the water and the Spirit. ✉

The Love of God Revealed through Jesus, The Only Begotten Son

< John 1:15-18 >

"John bore witness of Him and cried out, saying, 'This was He of whom I said, 'He who comes after me is preferred before me, for He was before me.'' And of His fullness we have all received, and grace for grace. For the law was given through Moses, but grace and truth came through Jesus Christ. No one has seen God at any time. The only begotten Son, who is in the bosom of the Father, He has declared Him."

In today's Scripture passage, we can see that John the Baptist, who had baptized Jesus, and the Apostle John the gospel writer are witnessing to us about Jesus, who has become our Lord and Savior: *"John bore witness of Him and cried out, saying, 'This was He of whom I said, 'He who comes after me is preferred before me, for He was before me'''* (John 1:15). John the Baptist witnessed about Jesus Christ by saying, "When He comes, He will judge with the fire and deliver with the water." The Apostle John witnessed about Jesus, saying, *"And of His fullness we have all received, and grace for grace. For the law was given through Moses, but the grace and truth came through Jesus Christ"* (John 1:16-17). Furthermore, it continues on, saying, *"No one has seen God at any time. The only begotten Son, who is in the bosom of the Father, He has declared Him" (John 1:18).* There is no one among us who has seen God through the naked eye. However, we are able to see Him through the one and only begotten Son of God who was at the bosom of the Father. This means that only Jesus Christ, who was in the bosom of the Father, had revealed to us what God is like.

Really, we have never seen God with our own eyes. We cannot say that we have met with God through any other senses either. Then, how was it possible for us to meet with that God and believe in Him? Through the baptism Jesus had received and His bloodshed on the Cross, we were able to know that Jesus Christ the Son of God was the true Savior.

Have You Ever Received the Love of God?

Every December we await Christmas. On that day, we remember the coming of the only Son of God into this world. Both the Apostle John and John the Baptist knew that the only Son of God, Jesus, was the true Savior of the entire humanity and revealed that to us. They tried to let us know who Jesus was to us. We know that God is the God of love. What kind of person was Jesus Christ who had appeared to all of us? We know that He is the Son of God who delivered us from all our sins, and that He is the true God who loves us. He is the true Savior to us, the One who delivered us from all our sins.

God truly loved us all, and not only by words. God showed us His love Himself by actually delivering us from all of our sins. Since He is the God of love and justice, He revealed to us that He has delivered us from all of our sins by

His own love and sacrifice, even though all sins must be judged and accounted for. This love of God was the absolute love toward us. This love of God was revealed to us through the only Son of God Jesus Christ.

The essential Truth of the Scriptural Word is that God so loved the world that He gave His only Son to deliver us all from all of our sins. If we are to look at how God revealed His love toward us, it is as follows. "Because God so loved us, God gave His Son Jesus to deliver us from all the sins of the world at once through Jesus' baptism and bloodshed and then made believers into His own children." Thus, God revealed what He is like through His only Son Jesus Christ. Jesus Christ gave His life completely away for us so that we may have the salvation of Truth and be delivered from condemnation. Through all of this, God revealed His love for us.

Truly, God teaches us that this love of God is incomparable to anything else in this world. Now, we can feel the love of God through the gospel of the water and the Spirit. Parents sometimes give away their lives for their own children, patriots for their countries, and friends for their friends. If a person gives up his life for the sake of his own country, he has done it for a great cause.

However, it is not comparable to what God has done for us in order to deliver us from all of our sins and give us eternal life. Even if a person gives up his life for his friend, it is only because of a friendship toward a single friend, it does not reach the level of the love of God. Sometimes, people give away their lives for their lovers. Although they sacrifice themselves and choose death because their emotions are hard to bear and uncontrollable, it still cannot be compared to the love of God. All these people are at most revealing only a tiny fraction of the love of God.

Yet, the love of Jesus Christ is special. The only Son of God revealed God nature to us and we cannot fathom His love because of the sacrifice of His own life for us. In order to give a new life to us sinners, Jesus was predestined to give up His own life for us. The love of our Lord was to give away His own life so that we may be revived and have the true life. How could we discuss the love of God through with ideals of love between people?

Every nation has its patriots who sacrificed their own lives for their own countries. Then, why did Jesus sacrifice Himself? It was in order to deliver all humanity from all sin and inequity. Because we, the human beings, were collapsing and dying due to our sins, He sacrificed Himself to give new life to us. Because He loved us, He gave us the gospel of the water and the Spirit so that we may have new life. Jesus Christ clothed us with the glory and honor of becoming God's children and gave us the power and authority to reign over all things. Furthermore, He enabled us to live happily for eternity. In order to do so, He revealed His love towards us. The reason Jesus Christ became a sacrifice after coming to this world was as a presentation of God's love.

All living creatures in this world exist for themselves. Yet, the only Son of God came to this world to give true life to His creatures. His birth and reason of being were different from our own. The only Son of God, Jesus, was born and existed in this world to show us what kind of being God was. Jesus carried out the righteous works of the baptism and the bloodshed to fulfill His reason of existing in this world. Our Lord demonstrated His own love toward us, and we now know and believe in that love.

It says in the Bible that God the Father loved us so much that He gave His only Son to us. During the 33 years of His life in this world, Jesus saw that many people had a hard life because of their illness and death and that His people were suffering from the loss of their land. Because of their sins these people could not help but face their destruction and condemnation and lose the only life they had. Before Jesus Christ came to this world, every person could not avoid the eternal fire of hell, where they would become servants of Satan the Devil and suffer for eternity, because they could not receive the remission of sin.

However, Jesus had compassion for everyone. Thus, He received the baptism on His own body, by which all the sins of humanity were transferred onto Him, and shed His own blood on the Cross so that we may have new life. To allow us to live for eternity through the salvation from all our sins, our Lord sacrificed Himself, enduring all the sufferings and pains. This was the love of God given to us to deliver us from all the sins of the world, from death, and from condemnation. The Lord-given gospel of the water and the Spirit is the love of God, which allows us to live for eternity by receiving new life. The Truth was a gift to us from the love of God. Now when we are asked who God is, we can answer in our faith that He is the One who sacrificed Himself so that we may have new life.

Is There Any One among You Who Has Seen God Directly?

Still, there were those people who had seen the sacrifice of Jesus. They had witnessed that to deliver us from all our sins, Jesus bore all the sins of the whole of humanity through His baptism, gave up His body to the Cross where He bled to death, and resurrected from the dead. We can realize and believe how much God has loved you and me through their accounts.

Because I too believe in the gospel of the water and the Spirit, it is not easy to articulate the love of God through words. God's love is too big to be understood. Yet, I am able to experience the love of God through the gospel of the water and the Spirit. Of course, I am grateful for the love of God that came by the water and the Holy Spirit. I believe that Jesus has wiped away all of our sins and that He has given us the gift of eternal life, glory, and honor. I also believe that He has given us His own life. It is true that we are still not capable in deeply knowing and feeling the love of our Lord, even though we believe in it. It is because we have not loved someone to the point of death. We have never given up our lives to someone else so that the person could have a new life and live for eternity. Hence, I myself lack the knowledge of and ability to feel the entire depth of the love of God. I also believe that the love of God is indescribably big. Still, I firmly believe one thing in my heart. It is true for myself, all of you, and everyone in this world that we have all received the love of salvation. The only Son of God clearly demonstrated who God is toward us. Hence, we were delivered from all our sins. I surely believe in that. I am sure you believe in that as well.

We naturally compact ourselves when the weather becomes cold. But, this does not mean that our hearts have to shrink as well. Although we are not perfect in our actions, out of compassion we want to deliver the love of God to the wandering souls. Although we cannot love humanity perfectly like Jesus, we still want to become instruments that deliver the love of God. Although we may compact our bodies in the winter cold, the thought of the magnitude of God's love for us makes our hearts warm. Truly, when we think of God who gave us new life by sacrificing Himself, we are thankful in our hearts. Although we may crouch in our bodies, we have rest in our hearts and our hearts become warm as if we have a little campfire in them. It is good that we can share His love for we have received it first, despite our weaknesses.

If we look at the saving works of Jesus in this world, we can easily know that God is like that. Thus, we must believe. Looking at Jesus Christ, we come to confess, "God was truly like that. Jesus was truly omnipotent, but He did not abuse His power. Jesus truly humbled Himself to give new life to all humanity and wash all our sins away. Jesus sacrificed Himself, and delivered us from all of our sins by the perfect love of sacrifice, not a false love." And we know that Jesus has clothed us with the glory of becoming the children of God. We must truly give thanks, honor, and glory to God in our faith for this Truth. This winter as well as in all the winters to come, we must think deeply about God's love whenever we crouch in coldness. Also, we must serve the Lord and do the works of God with that kind of faith.

If we have a legalistic faith instead of ruminating over the love of God, we will become nothing. If we believe in the gospel of the water and the Spirit, which is the love of God, we must be clothed with the true love of Truth by standing firm on the Lord-given Truth. Because we were given and clothed with the love of God, we are witnessing that love to everyone in this world. We are serving the gospel of the water and the Spirit, even though we feel very weary due to the works of God we have to do everyday. Whenever we feel weary serving our Lord, we should be reminded of the love of God, just as the Shulamite woman who was working hard as the keeper of the vineyard by wearing the love of King Solomon. We must go forward holding the hands of our Lord tightly despite of all the hardships for the gospel of the water and the Spirit, as it is

written:
"My beloved spoke, and said to me:
'Rise up, my love, my fair one,
And come away.
For lo, the winter is past,
The rain is over and gone.
The flowers appear on the earth;
The time of singing has come,
And the voice of the turtledove
Is heard in our land'" (Song of Solomon 2:10-12).

Every time you and I pray, I hope that God listens to our prayers. The Lord is responding to us with the Word above, *"Rise up, my love, my fair one, and come away."* You can know the love of God by these answers from God.

Sometimes we grow exhausted from hard work. Also, there are times good things happen to us as well as unfortunate things. I wish that things would get better as time goes by, but worries about God's works grow in my heart as time goes by. The gospel of the water and the Spirit, which is the Truth of God, should be spread until the end of the world. This is possible only if we continue to believe and live for our Lord. Although we the servants of God and His people are weak and deficient in many ways, we must be faithful to our calling in our knowledge and faith in the love of God. I worry that we may give up on our tasks and live for our own sake. I worry that we may give up these precious tasks because we love ourselves too much, instead of spreading the gospel, which proclaims the love of God that delivers the sinners from all their sins out of love for them.

Whoever that does not think of the love of God is living selfishly for one's own sake. Whoever lives only for himself does not know the love of God. Because it is clear that God loved us, although everyone may pursue his or her lusts of flesh, we the believers in the love of God cannot live for ourselves alone but must keep spreading the gospel of the water and the Spirit. Because we have received the love of God, now it is in our hearts. Hence, we can love others and sacrifice ourselves for the sake of others. We also can have such faith and can practice God's love according to our faith.

At one time we did not know or receive the love of God, and instead of living for others we lived only for ourselves. However, now we have changed. The more we know about our Lord, and as our new spiritual lives grow, the Lord allows us to share the love we have received despite our weaknesses and deficiencies. We come to recognize that it is right for us to share what belongs to God, although it is only a small part, until the day we will meet the Lord.

We believe for certain that the sacrificial love of God has blotted out all the sins of this world. Jesus Christ really has come to this world for us in the flesh of man and received the baptism so that all our sins may be transferred onto Him. Moreover, He died crucified on the Cross. Although God is the Almighty One who created the universe and everything in it, He has become the propitiation for all of us to fulfill the gospel of the water and the Spirit.

The disciples of Jesus did not believe in Jesus as the God of salvation when He walked on water. Hence, Jesus while in this world had to make known to His disciples clearly who He was so that they can believe in Him as God and be forgiven from all their sins. Because of that, Jesus showed His power to His disciples by walking on water. And most of the time, He acted just like an ordinary person. Jesus lowered Himself to a very weak appearance and came as our Savior. Our Lord has become the sacrificial Lamb of God, lowering Himself to complete His work of salvation: He took all our sins onto Himself by receiving the baptism from John the Baptist at the Jordan River. And in order to receive the tremendous and just judgments for all our sins, He offered His own body to be crucified on the Cross. He has delivered us believers from sin wholly by vicariously receiving contempt and insults. By the love of our Lord, we have become possessors of new life. To recover all of mankind to the status of people created in the image of God, He has taught the gospel of the water and the Spirit to everybody. Because of that, we came to believe.

However, there are still many people who do not believe or know this. This is why the Lord admonishes us to share His love to them. Hence, we have shared the Word of God, are still sharing by our faith, and will continue to share in the future. People have received the same salvation as us, have been clothed with the love of God, and have received the eternal life because they came to know and believe God, who was revealed to them by His only Son Jesus through the gospel of the water and the Spirit we shared.

Thus, I only give thanks to God. There is nothing else other than thanks that we could say to Him. Because the only Son of God has revealed to us who God was, we are able to know His love, to meet with Him, and to receive the salvation from all our sins by believing in Him. We were able to meet with Jesus because of the love of God. We have become His own people by wearing the love of God. We give thanks to God by our faith in the gospel of the water and the Spirit.

God Has Revealed His Love to Us through His Only Begotten Son

Although no one has seen God, people have come to know, see, and believe in God through Jesus. This is true. Those religious people who are highly regarded as men of intelligence, have added nothing to the redemption of the sins of humanity. Sakyamuni died under a bo tree while meditating about the joy and sorrow of life. He only worried to solve the problem of life's joy and sorrow. Put differently, he started thinking to solve his own problem and reached a conclusion somehow, but such conclusion had nothing to do with solving the problem of everyone's sin. Did he actually wash away the sins of each one of us? What did he do to blot out our sins, to receive vicariously the judgments for our sins, to help us avoid God's wrath upon us, or to help us receive blessings?

No matter how eagerly the religious people want to do so, they just lack the ability to do those things for us in the first place. All the sages of this world are all like this. None of them could take all our sins on his body to wash away the sins of each individual person. Only the only Son of God Jesus Christ, who was our Savior, could take all the sins of each one of us by receiving the baptism and sacrifice Himself for our happiness, and eternal life.

If we were to use the water in all the oceans as our ink and the blue sky as the parchment, we would still not be able to write all about the love of God for us. The love of God is that wide. The grace of salvation by which we are made known that God is truly the God of love is in the gospel of the water and the Spirit. Who has comforted you, delivered your souls from all your sins, and given you the eternal life? He is Jesus Christ, who is our Savior. We have not received our true salvation from any worldly authority but from Jesus Christ. Jesus Christ is the true God, the true Savior, and the King of love. He is incomparable to any other person in this world. Jesus was fundamentally God the King of kings, who rules over the angels up in Heaven, the visible world, and the invisible world.

Although there is no one who has seen the glory of God, the only Son of God Jesus Christ has revealed the Father, the Son, and the Holy Spirit by coming to this world. Jesus has revealed the love and justice of our God through the sacrifices of His baptism and bloodshed after He had come into this world in the flesh of man. Alongside the gospel of the water and the Spirit, He has given us the remission of sin. In this way God has shown us His love. Do you believe so?

Dear fellow believers, when your hearts are depressed and you are exhausted, think about how the only begotten Son of God Jesus Christ has revealed His love to us. And by bearing in your hearts the love of God for you and by recognizing and keeping that love, you will then be made grateful and happy. Nothing else in this world can be your true love, happiness, or blessing. Because Jesus Christ is actually our true God and Savior, only He can give us the true love, happiness, and blessing.

When I witness people receiving the remission of sin through our books, I truly realize the power of God's gospel. Many pastors from every corner of the world are saying that they have not even heard of the gospel of the water and the Spirit before. And they are further testifying that by this gospel they have received the true love of God, grace of salvation, blessing of eternal life, and the abundant peace of heart.

Truly, there is no one who has seen God or felt God. Still, we have met with God, received His love, and believed in His love. Hence, we are spreading the love of God through our faith. People throughout the world are meeting with God through our service to the Lord. Truly, they would not be able to meet with God, if it were not for the gospel of salvation we are witnessing to them. It is because of the testimonies of John the Baptist, the Apostle John and the other Apostles that we were able to meet with Jesus Christ. They all testified the gospel of the water and the Spirit. If they had kept this true gospel only in their hearts and refrained from spreading it, we would not have met with God.

There were many men of faith who were called as the Bible writers of the New Testament: The four Gospels were written by Matthew, Mark, Luke, and John in turn; the Acts was written by Luke; the Apostle Paul wrote the Pauline Epistles; the Apostle Peter, the Apostle John, and James and Jude, the brother of Jesus, also wrote their epistles; lastly, Revelation was wrote by John the Apostle.

They were inspired by the Holy Spirit and wrote about what they had seen and heard while they accompanied Jesus. But they still faced many difficulties to follow the will of God. Despite these difficulties, they have recorded and left behind the gospel of the water and the Spirit, which is the Word of God. Of course, God inspired them with special power so that they could not help but write these down. Still, it was possible to do the works of God through them because they were obedient toward God. If they had rejected the will of God, God would have done this through some other means. However, because they obeyed the Will of God, we are able to know and believe the love of God even till this moment.

John the Baptist was despised and cursed by many people of his age. Although we respect the 12 disciples of Jesus, while they were still in this world, they were despised and ignored by the people of their times, being treated below human standards.

Still, the disciples had fellowship with God in their faith in the gospel of the water and the Spirit and imparted this Truth to us. Because the disciples of Jesus lived by their faith, you and I are able to know the love of God and who God is. Following in their steps, we have to serve the Lord and His gospel so that others can also come to meet with God.

Even now, there is no one who has seen God, but whoever believes in the gospel of the water and the Spirit can know what kind of Person God is. Those who have heard the gospel of the water and the Spirit through us confess as follows: "The love of God is too great. Although I have been a pastor, I have neither known the gospel Truth nor met with God until now." I am encouraged when I see people returning to the Truth and meeting with God by the gospel of the water and the Spirit.

Dear fellow believers, it feels like that our weaknesses, deficiencies, and the fleshly thoughts rise to the top since the weather has gotten colder. However, I ask that you remember this verse from the Bible. *"No one has seen God at any time. The only begotten Son, who is in the bosom of the Father, He has declared Him" (John 1:18)*. We should live our lives, remembering this Word, keeping it by faith, and meditating on it always. We should accept in our hearts the love by which the only Son of God has delivered us from all our sins and meditate and propagate this thought by faith. Whatever you may do, I hope you live such a life. Let's meditate on the love of God, share the gospel, and then go up to His Kingdom and live there forever when the Lord returns.

When the weather gets really cold, we think of the warmth of a seat next to the fireplace. We do not realize it when the weather is warm, but we miss the warmth as soon as it turns cold. We are in a cold winter season where we miss warm food and warm hearts. How do our souls feel if our bodies feel that way?

Truly, the only Son of God Jesus Christ has revealed to us who God is and what God's love is. He also revealed to us that God has delivered us from all our sins by that love. Our souls receive the warmth, comfort, blessings and hope by meditating and believing in that love. I think that we should have such faith. We should not think about the works of our flesh but instead think about God's love. There is something we should never forget in our hearts. It is the love of God, with which He has delivered us from all our sins. We should live our lives keeping that love of God in our hearts, not forgetting it, but meditating on it. We should live in anticipation of all the blessings and glory that the Lord has promised us. Dear fellow believers, do you believe this?

Truly, the Law has come through Moses, and the gift of grace, Truth, salvation and the life-giving gospel has come through Jesus Christ. We do not receive our salvation by abiding by the Law, but by knowing Jesus Christ and believing in our hearts the gospel Word of God that Jesus given us. God comes to our hearts as the Holy Spirit and designates that we have become His children. We must give thanks before God through the faith provided by the Holy Spirit and live by that very faith.

Those who have received the love of God cannot lead their lives without loving others, so they live loving everyone in this world. Can you live your lives without loving everyone in this world? Dear fellow believers, the answer to the question "What does a person live by?" is very simple once you know it. The correct answer is that people live by love. Then, what do Christians live by? They also live by love, but their love is different from the selfish love of the secular people. Because the born-again Christians have received the love of God first, they live by loving God and others.

Some people say, "Now that I have received the remission of sin. I just want to live for myself." But they say this because they do not know that there is no enjoyment in such a life. Life is worth living if you live for others and sacrifice yourself out of love for others. Don't you feel this way yourself when you are serving the Lord voluntarily? We truly do feel that way.

If someone told me to give up spreading the gospel and tried everything to prevent me from spreading the gospel, I would try to find other means to do so because I would feel that my life has become worthless without sharing God's love with other people. What fulfillment do we have in our lives if we cannot live doing the works of God? Before we were born again, we used to live for the sake of drinking, eating, and enjoying ourselves with our favorite amusement. However, do we still have satisfaction living like that even now? People who have just recently received the remission of sin might worry about their future saying, "What shall we eat?" or "What shall we drink?" or "What shall we wear?" However, our selfish way of living and our purpose in life changes the moment we realize what Jesus Christ has revealed to us about who God is.

We feel alive when we are spreading the gospel of the water and the Spirit. Hence, we are sharing the gospel of the water and the Spirit throughout the world now and loving everyone in the entire world. In the past, we thought that even loving our own neighbors was a truly great task. But how have we changed now? We have become people who love everyone in this world. God has made this possible. Am I wrong? If it were not for God, how could we have changed?

We would have been satisfied in the past if we could build a nice house with great heating system, and eat delicious food inside of it. However, we can no longer live like that. Even if we have to live in a small single room, we must live for others, just as we would have to if we lived in a large mansion. Whether we eat or drink or do anything else, we should do these things for the sake of others. We must live for the sake of those who have not yet received the remission of sin and protect others who have already received the remission of sin. Isn't this true for you as well?

"The Bible says, *"No one has seen God at any time. The only begotten Son, who is in the bosom of the Father, He has declared Him" (John 1:18).* How perfectly did Jesus reveal the love of God to us! How perfectly did Jesus deliver us! What perfect Truth of salvation is the gospel of the water and the Spirit! We have never regretted receiving our salvation through our faith in Jesus, who came by the gospel of the water and the Spirit. We are not ashamed in believing in Him. Rather, we are thankful to God for the most perfect salvation and perfect love. Don't you feel grateful towards God? Of course, you do.

I hope that all of you believe in Jesus Christ who has revealed the love of God, keep the faith in His love in your hearts, and live daily for the sake of spreading that love. In time, we will meet our Lord and enjoy the glory of God. Before that, I hope that you will acquire the blessing of the remission of sin by meeting with God through the gospel of the water and the Spirit. ⊠

The Truth That John the Baptist Testified

< John 1:19-28 >
"Now this is the testimony of John, when the Jews sent priests and Levites from Jerusalem to ask him, 'Who are you?' He confessed, and did not deny, but confessed, 'I am not the Christ.' And they asked him, 'What then? Are you Elijah?' He said, 'I am not.' 'Are you the Prophet?' And he answered, 'No.' Then they said to him, 'Who are you, that we may give an answer to those who sent us? What do you say about yourself?' He said: 'I am
'The voice of one crying in the wilderness:
Make straight the way of the LORD,'
as the prophet Isaiah said.'
Now those who were sent were from the Pharisees. And they asked him, saying, 'Why then do you baptize if you are not the Christ, nor Elijah, nor the Prophet?' John answered them, saying, 'I baptize with water, but there stands One among you whom you do not know. It is He who, coming after me, is preferred before me, whose sandal strap I am not worthy to loose.' These things were done in Bethabara beyond the Jordan, where John was baptizing."

John 1:6-7 says, *"There was a man sent from God, whose name was John. This man came for a witness, to bear witness of the Light, that all through him might believe."* Here in this passage, 'John' is not the author of the Gospel of John, the

Apostle, but John the Baptist who was God's promised Elijah to come. As it is prophesied in Malachi 4:5, we can understand how the Gospel Truth is being witnessed by John the Baptist.

As we can see from John the Baptist's witness in today's text and in the following witness of Jesus, *"Behold! The Lamb of God who takes away the sin of the world" (John 1:29),* John testified that Jesus was the Lamb of God and the Savior of all sinners, who bore all the sins of the world on Himself.

By being baptized by John the Baptist, Jesus took all the sins of the world onto Himself and brought all those sins onto the Cross. Jesus did not testify about Himself, saying, "I am the Son of God. I bear all the sins of the world." Rather, John the Baptist witnessed to us that Jesus took all the sins of the world through the baptism He received. Thus, Jesus became our Savior by bearing all those sins of the world onto the Cross.

Just as John the Baptist did not testify about himself, Jesus did not testify about Himself either. Rather, He let His disciples witness about Him. We cannot help but believe in Jesus in our hearts because of the witness of John the Baptist. Our Lord has told us that we receive the remission of sin not because we have experienced special miracles and wonders but because we are be born again by the faith in the gospel of the water and the Spirit that we acquired through the witness of John the Baptist. We become God's children by believing in our hearts that God has cleansed all our sins through the gospel of the water and the Spirit.

What Is the Light of Truth?

John chapter 1 is testifying about the Light of Truth. Here the Light is the Truth signifies that Jesus has saved all the sinners from their sins by taking those sins through His baptism received from John the Baptist and then by shedding His blood on the Cross. John the Baptist witnessed that Jesus is the Son of God, the King of kings, the Creator, the Master of all of humanity, and the perfect Savior of all sinners. He witnessed that Jesus our Savior took all the sins of this world by being baptized at the Jordan River and that He bore those sins onto the Cross where He vicariously received all the judgments for those sins in our place. By means of His baptism and His bloodshed, Jesus delivered us all from all our sins. And whoever believes in Jesus as the Savior through John's testimony is delivered from all of his or her sins and becomes one of God's children.

The greatest blessing for humanity is the gift of salvation by believing in the gospel of the water and the Spirit given by Jesus. Because John the Baptist testified that Jesus was the true Savior, we are able to receive the full remission of sin by believing in our hearts that Jesus is our Savior who came by the gospel of the water and the Spirit. As such, the witness of John the Baptist has played a crucial part in the salvation of all sinners from their sins. There may be some people who are opposed to this idea; however, God predetermined John to be a witness to Jesus.

John the Baptist witnessed for Jesus as the Lamb of God prophesized in the Old Testament. *"Behold! The Lamb of God who takes away the sin of the world!" (John 1:29)* This testimony was given the day after John baptized Jesus by laying his hands on him. You may know that Aaron the High Priest had to lay both his hands on the head of a live goat to offer all the sins of Israelites to God on the Day of Atonement (Leviticus 16:20-21).

As a matter of fact, John the Baptist could testify like this because he witnessed the Holy Spirit descending like a dove and alighting upon Jesus when He came out of the water and he heard what God the Father witnessed of Him from heaven, *"This is My beloved Son, in whom I am well pleased"* *(Matthew 3:16-17).* We know this because John the Baptist testifies about it later in the following words. *"I did not know Him; but that He should be revealed to Israel, therefore I came baptizing with water" (John 1:31).* The reason John the Baptist baptized Jesus was to witness that Jesus was the Savior of all sinners, the Son of God, and the Lamb of God who took all our sins onto Himself. To reveal to the world that Jesus is the Savior, he had to baptize by laying his hands on the head of Jesus in the water of the Jordan River.

John the Baptist Had to Give the Baptism to Jesus

The reason John the Baptist baptized Jesus was to transfer all the sins of all sinners to Jesus. In other words, the reason Jesus was baptized was to take all the sins of every person who has lived and will live in this world.

The Scripture passage from Matthew 3:13 to 3:15 says, *"Then Jesus came from Galilee to John at the Jordan to be baptized by him. And John tried to prevent Him, saying, 'I need to be baptized by You, and are You coming to me?' But Jesus answered and said to Him, 'Permit it to be so now, for thus it is fitting for us to fulfill all righteousness.' Then he allowed Him."*

While John the Baptist was baptizing other people, Jesus unexpectedly came to the Jordan River to be baptized by him. Seeing Him, John the Baptist was startled and said, "I should receive the baptism from You. How, then, do You come to me to be baptized?" However, Jesus replied, "I must take all the sins of all people by receiving the baptism by you. Thus, you must baptize Me." Then, Jesus was baptized at the Jordan River by John the Baptist, who testified about Him.

Here comes one of the most important passages for our salvation: *"Permit it to be so now for thus it is fitting for us to fulfill all righteousness" (Matthew 3:15).* By being baptized this way, Jesus took all the sins of the world onto Himself and fulfilled all the righteousness of God. Just when Jesus received the baptism from John the Baptist, all the sins of this world were transferred onto Jesus. Now, everyone in this world may not keep any sin in their hearts anymore because Jesus fulfilled all of God's righteousness by being baptized by John the Baptist and taking all the sins of the world onto Himself.

The baptism Jesus received from John the Baptist was God's planned method of transferring all the sins of all sinners onto Jesus. In order for Jesus to take all the sins of this world onto Himself, Jesus had to be baptized by John the Baptist. The baptism Jesus received from John the Baptist was an indispensable process for the salvation of all sinners from all their sins. After He was baptized, Jesus bore all the sins of this world during his three years of public ministry, until He received the judgments for all those sins on the Cross, died and was resurrected from the dead. In this way, Jesus became the true Savior who took care of all the sins of all sinners.

Is John the Baptist a Descendant of Aaron?

John the Baptist was born in this world six months earlier than Jesus, and was born to the house of Aaron, the first High Priests of the Old Testament times. He was born to a priest named Zacharias, of the division of Abijah among the descendants of Aaron the High Priest.

Then, why did God send John the Baptist into this world? It was to appoint him the task of transferring all the sins of this world onto Jesus. God send John the Baptist into this world for that purpose. And God is testifying that John the Baptist was the very one who transferred all the sins of this world onto Jesus.

Therefore, God planned that people would receive their salvation from all of their sins by believing in the witness of John the Baptist. Thus, the reason that God sent John the Baptist to this world six months prior to Jesus was to appoint him as the High Priest of all of humanity—just like there were High Priests before him in the Old Testament times—who would transfer all the sins of this world onto Jesus. That is, the two missions of John the Baptist were to transfer all the sins of the world onto Jesus and to witness the Truth of salvation to all sinners that Jesus bore all of their sins.

The reason God has left those of us who have received the remission of sin in this world is for us to witness this gospel Truth just like John the Baptist did. Thus, God has entrusted John the Baptist with the ministry to witness as is written in Isaiah:

"The voice of one crying in the wilderness:
'Prepare the way of the LORD;
Make His paths straight.
Every valley shall be filled
And every mountain and hill brought low;
The crooked places shall be made straight
And the rough ways smooth;
And all flesh shall see the salvation of God'" (Luke 3:4-6).
This means that everyone can receive the remission of sin by

believing in their hearts in Jesus Christ, who came by the gospel of the water and the Spirit.

John the Baptist is continuously testifying that Jesus is the Lord and Savior: *"He who sent me to baptize with water said to me, 'Upon whom you see the Spirit descending, and remaining on Him, this is He who baptizes with the Holy Spirit.' And I have seen and testified that this is the Son of God" (John 1:33-34).* The Holy Spirit had already taught him this beforehand. So when Jesus asked John to baptize Him, John recognized who He was and transferred all the sins of the world unto Jesus. To transfer all the sins of the world was the purpose of Jesus' baptism received from John the Baptist.

The Two Kinds of Baptism That John the Baptist Gave: To Jesus and To the Israelites

The first objective of John the Baptist in baptizing people was to have the Israelites repent and turn away from worshipping foreign idols and return to God. But, the purpose of the baptism he gave to Jesus is different. It was to cleanse all the sins of the world by transferring them to Jesus. Through the baptism Jesus received from John, God transferred all the sins of the world onto Jesus by a proper process, and through His righteousness completed the remission of sin for all sinners when Jesus received the judgments of those sins in our place on the Cross.

When we the righteous receive the baptism after receiving our salvation, we are confessing the faith that "I have been delivered from all my sins because Jesus received the baptism from John the Baptist." We are born again by believing that Jesus is the Lamb of God who takes away all the sins of the world and that Jesus completely eliminated all the sins of all sinners by taking them with the baptism He received.

Jesus is the Lamb of God who has taken all the sins of the world. Jesus came to this world about 2000 years ago, took all the sins of the world, and died on the Cross to expunge all those sins. When we mention the sins of this world, what are the limits of these sins? All the sins of the world refer to all the sins from the beginning of humanity to the last days of humanity. It has been over 2000 years since Jesus came onto this world, and all the sins having been committed so far are also included. By the world, we mean everything from the very beginning to the very end, and all the sins that take place in between are all the sins of the world.

Dear fellow believers, we must understand the words "the sins of the world" carefully. John the Baptist proclaimed, *"Behold! The Lamb of God who takes away the sin of the world!" (John 1:29)* He is saying, "Look, people! That Lamb of God, Jesus Christ, the Son of God who bears all the sins of this world, is the Savior of all sinners. That Person has borne all the sins of the world by being baptized from me. By bearing all the sins of all sinners, Jesus has completely eliminated your sins. All the sins of every sinner in the world were completely blotted out by Him." By this witness of John the Baptist, whoever believes in Jesus Christ as his or her Savior becomes able to receive the remission of sin.

Because Jesus took all the sins of the world by being baptized from John and Hr shed His blood on the Cross to atone for them, now He admonishes us to receive the remission of sin by believing in this Truth. Dear fellow believers, do you still have sin? We are not sinless because we have not committed any sin or because we are completely innocent. Rather, it is because Jesus took all the sins of the world through

His baptism. Since Jesus took all the sins of the world by being baptized by John the Baptist, the believers in this Truth receive the remission of all their sins. We are sinless because we believe in the Truth of salvation that we were made sinless. Thus, a sinner receives his salvation by believing in his heart the gospel of the water and the Spirit.

We have received the remission of sin by believing in the gospel witnessed by John the Baptist. Still, we cannot receive our salvation if we do not believe in the God-spoken Word of Truth, the salvation through Jesus' baptism. God appears Himself to sinners through the Word these days. There is not a single person who has seen God. Still, we come to believe in God by believing in His Word. Furthermore, we receive the remission of all our sins through His Word.

John the Baptist continues to witness. It is written in John 1:35-39, *"Again, the next day, John stood with two of his disciples. And looking at Jesus as He walked, he said, 'Behold the Lamb of God!' The two disciples heard him speak, and they followed Jesus. Then Jesus turned, and seeing them following, said to them, 'What do you seek?' They said to Him, 'Rabbi' (which is to say, when translated, Teacher), 'where are You staying?' He said to them, 'Come and see.' They came and saw where He was staying, and remained with Him that day (now it was about the tenth hour)."*

If we look at above Scripture passage, we find that the number of Jesus' disciples increased because of the testimony of John the Baptist. Among the disciples of Jesus, there were many who had been the followers of John the Baptist. However, John the Baptist did not tell them to follow himself. Rather, he witnessed to them about how Jesus bore all the sins of the world after He was baptized *"Behold! The Lamb of God who takes away the sin of the world!" (John 1:29)* "Look! There goes the Lamb of God. That Person is the very Son of God, our Lord and Savior." Because of that witness, two of his disciples left him to follow Jesus. From that moment on, they began their lives anew as the disciples of Jesus.

We who believe in the gospel of the water and the Spirit are also the disciples of Jesus Christ. Everyone who has become a disciple of Jesus Christ has become so through their faith in the gospel of the water and the Spirit, which is what John the Baptist witnessed about. Of course, Jesus Himself also sometimes personally called people to follow Him, and they became His disciples, as was the case with Philip. In the case of Simon Peter and Andrew his brother, Jesus said, *"Follow Me, and I will make you become fishers of men" (Mark 1:17).* Still, John the Baptist convinced his disciples that Jesus is the Lamb of God and the only One to be followed. John the Baptist has made his disciples believers in Jesus as their Savior.

John the Baptist played the role that enables people to follow just Jesus correctly. Even now, if all sinners were to be delivered completely from all their sins and become righteous by believing in Jesus as their Savior who came by the gospel of the water and the Spirit, it would be because of the baptism John the Baptist gave Jesus and the witness that is given by the disciples of Jesus.

Then, all of those who believe in the Word of the Old Testament must also believe in Jesus, who is the Messiah. Who is the Savior and Master of all humanity? That would be Jesus. Who is the servant who accurately witnessed about Jesus? That would be John the Baptist. After hearing the witness of their master, "Behold the Lamb of God! He is the Savior," the disciples of John the Baptist including Andrew followed Jesus and became His disciples, and followed Him. *"Then Jesus turned, and seeing them following, said to them, 'What do you* seek?' They said to Him, 'Rabbi (which is to say, when translated, Teacher), where are You staying?' He said to them, 'Come and see.' They came and saw where He was staying, and remained with Him that day (now it was about the tenth hour)" (John 1:38-39).

Dear fellow believers, we must believe with certainty that Jesus is the Son of God, our Savior. Also, we must believe that Jesus granted us remission from all our sins by His baptism and bloodshed. Jesus had asked, "Why are you following Me?" and John's disciples replied by asking, "Rabbi, where are You staying?" "Come and see." Hence, Jesus took them and showed them where He stayed.

Dear fellow believers, what would Jesus' home have been like? Would it have been like some palaces? Jesus did not have His own house while living in this world. Traveling through the desert for His mission, Jesus sometimes went up to the mountains to pray and even slept there. As the Scripture says, *"Foxes have holes and birds of the air have nests, but the Son of Man has nowhere to lay His head" (Luke 9:58; also Matthew 8:20),* Jesus did not settle down in any one place. That means that Jesus did not live in splendor while He was in this world.

Neither Jesus nor His disciples possessed much of anything. Simply because of the witness of their previous teacher, John the Baptist, that Jesus is the Lamb of God, they became the disciples of Jesus by believing that Jesus was the Son of God, the Savior and Lord. Today, if you and I are to become disciples of the Lord Jesus, we should do likewise. Andrew and another anonymous person became disciples of Jesus by believing in Him and following Him.

Although Jesus did not live in splendor and glory while He was in this world, He was fundamentally the true God and equal with God the Father; He is the Son of God, the Creator of the universe and everything in it, and our Savior. We can become disciples of Jesus and witness about Him only when we believe that He is the Messiah who came in the flesh of man by the incarnation of the Word. If we also want to become disciples of Jesus Christ, we must know and believe that Jesus' baptism was for the transfer all the sins of the world onto Him and that the bloodshed on the Cross was for Jesus to receive the judgments for all sins in our place. Dear fellow believers, do you understand?

"He said to them, 'Come and see.' They came and saw where He was staying, and remained with Him that day (now it was about the tenth hour)" (John 1:39). Here, it clearly tells us how a disciple of Jesus is made. Truly, these people needed the Messiah and not a wealthy landowner or famous politician. The disciples of John the Baptist were waiting for the Messiah and not some earthly glory. They really wanted to receive the remission of sin and enter into the Kingdom of Heaven by believing in the Messiah.

Let's look at John 1:40-42 together. *"One of the two who heard John speak, and followed Him, was Andrew, Simon Peter's brother. He first found his own brother Simon, and said to him, 'We have found the Messiah' (which is translated, the Christ). And he brought him to Jesus. Now when Jesus looked at him, He said, 'You are Simon the son of Jonah. You shall be called Cephas' (which is translated, a Stone)."*

Through the witness of Andrew, his brother Peter was able to meet with Jesus. And he became a disciple of Jesus Christ. Peter became a believer in Jesus and lived a righteous life following Jesus. Andrew witnessed to Peter that he had met the Messiah (which is translated, the Christ), that the Son of God is the very One prophesized by the Old Testament prophets, and that He is the Messiah our Savior who came to this world as an offspring of a woman to deliver us from all our sins. When Andrew witnessed to Peter what he had believed, Peter was led to Jesus and met Him and became a disciple of Jesus.

Here in today's Scripture passage, we can know whom John the Baptist had witnessed about. It also teaches us how important the role of John the Baptist is to those who believe in Jesus as their Savior. If it had not been for the witness of John the Baptist, Andrew and Peter would not have become the disciples of Jesus. And you and I could not have become His disciples. Without the witness of John the Baptist, how could we have become the disciples of Jesus? How could we believe in Jesus as our Savior? The Apostle John, the Gospel writer, emphasizes the importance of the role of John the Baptist and his witness. It is clear that all of us can wholly become God's children because of the witness of John the Baptist.

John the Baptist played an important and indispensable role for the propagation of the gospel. We must understand that our role is the same as John the Baptist's. Just as John the Baptist was the voice openly declaring how Jesus took all of our sins onto Himself by coming to this world, we are also such voices. We the righteous are not saviors and they are not gods. Rather, we the righteous are the servants and disciples of God, and a voice in the wilderness that clearly witnesses about Jesus Christ. This voice led people to meet with the true Life. The Bible records that those who accept the voice (the gospel) of the righteous receive salvation and become disciples of Jesus as well as the children of God. We shall live the lives of disciples who witness the gospel of the water and the Spirit after having met this true gospel, which Jesus the Messiah gave us. That is the role of the righteous.

The role of the righteous is very important today in this age. Just as the light of a lighthouse is the light of safety that leads ships through safe paths in the darkness, the righteous become lights of salvation in this dark world. How important is this role? If it were not for us, there would be no one to witness the gospel of the water and the Spirit. We must live our lives like that of John the Baptist and the disciples of Jesus.

My beloved fellow believers, God is clearly telling us what our role as the righteous is and what the role of John the Baptist was. God is also telling us that Jesus has become the Savior for all of humanity. Just as John the Baptist testified about Jesus, we the righteous should also try to clearly witness about Jesus instead of distinguishing ourselves in this world. People will believe and become children of God after hearing the voices of the righteous, but only when the righteous actively witness who Jesus was, that He is our Savior, that He is the Lamb of God, and that He bore the sins of the world. That is the role of the righteous. We as the righteous should not make ourselves distinguished in the world but witness about Jesus.

The servants and believers of God should not single out their own achievement for praise. We are merely the voice of the one who proclaims in the wilderness. We who have become the righteous should not chase after our own fame and status but instead devote ourselves to witnessing the gospel of the water and the Spirit throughout the entire world. In order to witness about Jesus and propagate the gospel of the water and the Spirit, there cannot be any ego. If we pursue our selfishness, we will be unable to share the righteousness of God. The righteous should play the role of the witness of the gospel. Everything was given to us as a blessing from God. We have been told to be responsible to our duties as the witnesses of the gospel and to live the rest of our lives as the disciples of Jesus.

John the Baptist witnessed that Jesus is the true Savior until he went to Heaven, after he transferred all the sins of the world to Jesus by baptizing Him. After he had led many people to Jesus, he clearly witnessed that Jesus is our Savior, and after he had rebuked the immoral, he was martyred. Because of Jesus Christ, he was temporarily a light that had shone the light of salvation. John the Baptist was a servant of God, living in the wilderness, eating locusts and wild honey and not seeking the wealth and fame of this world. This was the kind of life John the Baptist led in this world. After he had been martyred, he entered the heavenly Kingdom of God, and is now a great servant of God in His Kingdom.

The righteous in this world should likewise play the same role of John the Baptist. By recognizing our transformed status, we should not live our lives according to our own desires, but should devote ourselves to the work of spreading the gospel of the water and the Spirit, which we were commissioned to do. That is the last task God has entrusted us with, and the purpose and meaning of our lives. God is the Lord who let us live such lives. I give thanks to our Lord who sent John the Baptist and Jesus into this world. ✉

The Biblical Evidence That Jesus Bore All the Sins of The World

< John 1:29-39 >

"The next day John saw Jesus coming toward him, and said, 'Behold! The Lamb of God who takes away the sin of the world! This is He of whom I said, 'After me comes a Man who is preferred before me, for He was before me.' I did not know Him; but that He should be revealed to Israel, therefore I came baptizing with water.' And John bore witness, saying, 'I saw the Spirit descending from heaven like a dove, and He remained upon Him. I did not know Him, but He who sent me to baptize with water said to me, 'Upon whom you see the Spirit descending, and remaining on Him, this is He who baptizes with the Holy Spirit.' And I have seen and testified that this is the Son of God.' Again, the next day, John stood with two of his disciples. And looking at Jesus as He walked, he said, 'Behold the Lamb of God!' The two disciples heard him speak, and they followed Jesus. Then Jesus turned, and seeing them following, said to them, 'What do you seek?' They said to Him, 'Rabbi' (which is to say, when translated, Teacher), 'where are You staying?' He said to them, 'Come and see.' They came and saw where He was staying, and remained with Him that day (now it was about the tenth hour)."

Let Us Think about How Weak We Are

How weak is a human being? As we begin to think about this question, we should not place our hearts in high places. A person should know his fundamental nature and humble his heart.

What is a human being? I am asking what a human being is at its fundamental level. When we examine ourselves as human beings, do we really live by lofty ideals, excellent abilities, power, and perspectives? In actuality, we fall short of these qualities. We may have lofty ideals in our heads but people cannot live up to their ideals by themselves. We are such weak beings.

Once we see the reality of ourselves as human beings, we find that there is no way by which we can attain such lofty ideals. That is our current reality. But, often we overvalue ourselves out of our misunderstanding about our fundamental nature. Hence, people struggle because they do not know themselves. That is because people have such great faith in themselves initially, only to disappoint themselves when they find their own weaknesses.

Truly, people have been trying to attain a high level of virtuous living ethically, religiously, and in their deeds. However, what is the reality? Although they have set their goals pretty high, can they live up to those standards? People disappoint themselves once they face reality, because they do not know or acknowledge themselves as they truly are. The reason people disappoint themselves and are disappointed by others is because they set their expectations so high. Hence, we should not think so highly of ourselves and consider ourselves as too noble.

Today, I would like to share the message from John 1:29-

39 with you. Verse 29 of today's Scripture passage says, *"The next day John saw Jesus coming toward him, and said, 'Behold! The Lamb of God who takes away the sin of the world!'"*

Which sins among all the sins of the world did our Lord take away? Did He take only the original sin away? And does God wash away all our personal sins each time we offer the prayers of repentance? Does Jesus take all the sins that we had committed before we started to believe in Jesus as our Lord and Savior? Or did Jesus take all the sins of the world once and for all as today's Scripture passage tells us? The Bible records and tells us that our Lord has taken all the sins of the world onto Himself once and for all.

We commit sins as much as "a thick cloud" while we live in this world (Isaiah 44:22). Yet, our Lord says that He has taken all the sins of the world through the baptism. More accurately, what I am saying is that our Lord has taken all the sins we commit by His baptism. Jesus knows very well that you cannot help but commit sins while you are awake or sleeping. We repeat our lives of eating and sleeping, and also repeatedly committing sins like a hamster in a treadmill. However, the Bible tells us that Jesus has taken all the sins of the world we commit until the day we breathe our last breath once and for all through His baptism received from John the Baptist.

We must pay attention to the Word that states that our Lord has taken all the sins of the world by being baptized. What are we like? It is written in Psalms 51:5, *"Behold, I was brought forth in iniquity, and in sin my mother conceived me."* As such, we were born with sin and still continue to commit sins in this world. My dear fellow believers! Don't we continually commit sins while we are alive? Am I not right?

Just as people end up being stained with coal if they go through a coal mine or end up drinking if they go to a bar, like so, everyone ends up committing so many sins while they are living in this world.

Dear fellow believers! Are you not committing much sin in this world? Are you committing any sin at all? If you say that you are not committing sins at all, you are lying. We know that people will continue to commit sins while they are living in this world. Whether it is this sin or that sin, we will commit sins in this world. Thus, in order to deliver us from all the sins of the world, our Lord has taken all those sins onto Himself once and for all by being baptized. Then, by bearing all the sins of the world onto the Cross, where He received the judgments for all our sins by shedding His precious blood, He has delivered us from all the sins of the world. Thus, to the believers, there is no sin of this world in them. Although we are weak and deficient in many areas, believers have no sin in them because our Lord has taken all their sins onto Himself.

It is obvious that you and I would not have been delivered from all the sins of the world, if Jesus had not been baptized by John the Baptist, through which Jesus took all the sins of the world.

The Biblical Evidence That Jesus Bore All the Sins of This World

Let's look at the Word in Matthew 3:15-17. *"But Jesus answered and said to him, 'Permit it to be so now, for thus it is fitting for us to fulfill all righteousness.' Then he allowed Him. When He had been baptized, Jesus came up immediately from the water and behold, the heavens were opened to Him, and He saw the Spirit of God descending like a dove and alighting upon Him. And suddenly a voice came from heaven, saying, 'This is My beloved Son, in whom I am well pleased.'"*

When our Lord tried to receive the baptism from John the Baptist at the Jordan River, He commanded John the Baptist, "Permit it to be so now. It is right for us to fulfill all righteousness by doing thus." Then, John the Baptist obeyed and baptized Jesus.

When Jesus received the baptism, He ordered to John the Baptist, *"Permit it to be so now, for thus it is fitting for us to fulfill all righteousness" (Matthew 3:15).* Our Lord took all the sins of the world by receiving the baptism and blotted out all those sins by bearing them onto the Cross. Our Lord fulfilled all righteousness by receiving the baptism from John the Baptist. To declare that Jesus fulfilled all righteousness when He received the baptism means that Jesus bore all the sins of the world through His baptism.

If we were to declare this incident from our perspectives, His baptism means that all of our worldly sins were transferred onto Jesus once and for all. Our faith was made perfect, because Jesus Christ took all the sins of the world onto His own body once and for all through His baptism.

Dear fellow believers, we have faith that Jesus took all the sins of the world, but it is also true that we commit many sins until we die. Do we commit all kinds of sin while living in this world or not? From the day of our birth until the day we die, we are constantly commit sin. Whether they are sins in our thoughts or in our actual deeds, every sin we commit is a sin of this world. Did our Lord take all those sins of the world or not? It is written in the Bible that He has taken all of the sins of the world. When John laid his hands on Jesus, all the sins of the world were transferred onto the head of Jesus Christ, and Jesus has taken every sin in this world. It was fulfilled according to the exactly same manner of the sin offering in the Old Testament (Leviticus 1:4, 4:27-30, 16:21). Thus, all the sin we commit in this world does not exist anymore. Jesus has taken all the sins of the world, and so we are delivered from all the sins of the world by our faith.

By receiving the baptism from John, Jesus took all the sins we commit in this world. Therefore, we must believe as the Bible says. Without any exception, Jesus has taken every sin that is committed in this world through His baptism. We receive the remission of sin by believing in this. Because Jesus received the baptism from John the Baptist, Jesus was able to take all the sins of the world and bear those sins onto the Cross, where He was crucified unto His death to pay for the wages of those sins. This is the gospel Truth of the water and the Spirit, by which we can receive the remission of sin.

Some theologians interpret the phrase "Behold! The Lamb of God who takes the sins of the world" to mean, "There is the Lamb of God who takes the original sin." They say that Jesus took the original sin of all people, and therefore, the personal sins we commit in this world must be washed away by offering the prayers of repentance. That is a misinterpretation of the Scripture verse. They have added interpretations from their own minds, which are not recorded in the Word of God, giving believers confusion and misunderstanding.

Dear fellow believers, Jesus took all the sins of the world by receiving the baptism at the Jordan River and He bore all those sins onto the Cross. Jesus completely took all the sins that we commit in this world. This is the biblical basis that enables us to receive our salvation through our faith. There is no place in the Bible where it says that Jesus took only the original sin. Rather, the Bible says that when Jesus received the baptism from John the Baptist, He took all the sins of the world onto Himself once and for all.

We, all humanity, commit sins throughout our lives in this world. These sins are called the sins of the world. By the world, we mean the world from its first moment of creation until the end of the world, and all the sins that people commit from their birth to their death are called the sins of the world. The sins of the world include from the sins that were committed by Adam, the first human being, to the sins that will be committed by the last human. Everyone commits sins. Yet, Jesus took all the sins of the world by being baptized by John the Baptist and He paid all the wages of those sins by shedding His blood on the Cross. This is how He has delivered us from all the sins of the world.

We believe in the written Word of God as it is, while the theologians believe that Jesus has taken only the original sin. But, what they believe is utterly nonsense and merely a groundless thought that came out of their own heads. They argue, "How could Jesus have taken sins that have not been yet committed? Jesus must have taken those sins that we have committed until the moment of our conversion and the sin we inherited from our mothers' wombs." Because they try to comprehend the intricate Truth of God with their limited intelligence, they make these inane claims. Claiming that Jesus only took our original sin and not all of our sins through His baptism is the most unintelligent interpretation a person could make.

Dear fellow believers, let's think about ourselves. Because we help but commit sins in this world until we die, Jesus had to take every single sin of the world once and for all through His baptism. Hence, Jesus fulfilled all righteousness of God just as the Scripture records, *"It is fitting for us to fulfill all righteousness" (Matthew 3:15)*. In order to do the righteous work of eliminating all the sins of the world, our Lord received the baptism from John the Baptist and bore all those sins onto the Cross, where He was crucified and left to bleed to His death. The baptism Jesus received and His bloodshed on the Cross were of the very righteousness of God which was given to us to revive us from our destined condemnation. By receiving the baptism from John the Baptist and at the same time receiving the judgments of death for all our sins in our place, Jesus blotted out all the sins of the world without any exceptions. This is the gospel of the water and the Spirit through which God has delivered us from all our sins. Dear fellow believers, do you believe this? Surely, you do.

Dear Fellow Believers! Are You and I the Beings of This World?

Because you and I live in this world, while we live here, we commit sins. How much sin do you and I commit in this world? People commit sins in this world until the day they die. The Lord is telling us that the sins we commit in the world are as countless as the clouds covering the entire sky. Let's look at Isaiah 44:22 together.
"I have blotted out, like a thick cloud, your transgressions,
And like a cloud, your sins.
Return to Me, for I have redeemed you."
Truthfully, if we were to count all sins we commit during our lives in this world, how numerous would our sins be? Do we commit much sin living in this world or not? We commit as much sin as a thick cloud. Some religions say that even opening our eyes is a sin. We commit sins even while we have dreams. Being awake is sin. All in all, our entire living being is

sinful in itself. How much sin do you think the world has, since we start sinning as soon as we open our eyes? There is so much sin in this world that it is described as a thick cloud.

We commit so much sin in this world that the Lord described it as "a thick cloud." The Bible refers to the sins we commit in this world as transgressions. He said, "Your transgressions are like a thick cloud," and He said that He had blotted out all these sins once and for all by the gospel Truth of the water and the Spirit. While people commit so much sin living in this world, our Lord blotted out all those sins in one instant through His baptism by John the Baptist and His bloodshed.

Thus, Jesus said, *"I have blotted out, like a thick cloud, your transgressions, and like a cloud, your sins. Return to Me, for I have redeemed you."* Our God the Father sent the Lord Jesus into this world and redeemed us in order to deliver us from all our sins. Our Lord has atoned for all our sins by accepting them through His baptism and paying the wages of them with His bloodshed. By receiving the baptism on His body, our Lord took all of our sins of the world onto Himself. By offering His body to be crucified on the Cross, He bled to His death. Thus, He delivered us from our sins through His baptism and bloodshed. Jesus has delivered us from all of our sins once and for all by blotting them out completely through the gospel of the water and the Spirit. On the third day after He died in our place vicariously, He rose from the dead and became our Savior.

The Lord says, *"I have redeemed you" (Isaiah 44:22).* We have been delivered from all of our sins by believing in the gospel of the water and the Spirit. The gospel of the water and the Spirit is relevant to everyone who believes in Jesus. Strictly speaking, this gospel of the water and the Spirit is necessary for everyone who lives in this world, and its relevance is not limited only to the believers.

Since we are constantly committing sins in this world, Jesus came to this world and took away all of our sins by His baptism and bloodshed. Through the baptism, Jesus took all the sins of the world and bore those sins onto the Cross at Golgotha. This gospel of the water and the Spirit has eliminated all the sins of everyone living in this world. To those who have received the remission of sin and to those who have not yet received the remission of sin, this gospel is a necessity. Jesus brought us salvation by taking all the sins of the world onto His own body through His baptism and crucifixion on the Cross. This gospel declares that Jesus has resurrected from the dead and brought us salvation, and therefore it is a gospel that everyone needs. This is truly blessed and good news. The gospel of the water and the Spirit is the only gospel by which our Lord delivered us by coming to this world.

This gospel of the water and the Spirit has power like dynamite. People constructing a highway use dynamite when a mountain is blocking the path. They drill a hole into the rock and put the dynamite inside, and then they detonate it from a safe distance. Next, they would lie flat to the ground and shield themselves. A moment later, there is a huge explosion. A rock bigger than this podium flies up to the sky and falls back to the ground. And a rock bigger than this church is broken to pieces. After the dust fills the air and the noise subsides, we see an entire mountain reduced to small rocks like cookie crumbs. Bulldozers and huge dump trucks come to load and take away all the small rocks. After all this, the rocky mountain disappears by dynamite without leaving any trace.

The sins we commit in this world are as numerous as

those rocks. The sins we commit before God are like a thick cloud. The Lord came to this world and had to be baptized by John the Baptist in order to abolish all our sins. And He carried all those sins onto the Cross and was crucified to death. When He was baptized, all the sins people committed and will commit until the day they die were transferred onto Christ. The huge mass of sins of more than 6 billion people in this world were completely blown up and abolished in one instant by the gospel Truth of the water and the Spirit. By receiving the baptism and the judgment for all our sins, Jesus has paid the price of all the sins of the world—all the future sins that will be committed by the coming generations in this world as well as all the past sins committed by everyone who has lived in this world until now since the days of Adam and Eve—and brought us salvation. Those who know and believe in Jesus Christ as their Savior who came to this world by the gospel of the water and the Spirit, have no more sin in them. This is the power of the gospel of the water and the Spirit by which our Lord has delivered us from all the sins of the world.

Because the gospel of the water and the Spirit has the amazing power to blot out all the sins of the people in this world, whoever believes in it has been completely cleansed of all his sins once and for all. This is the Truth that applies to everyone of this world without exception. Yet, some people believe in this and some still do not. Those who believe in the gospel of the water and the Spirit have no sin, but those who still do not believe have their sins for eternity. Since you and I have accepted in our hearts the love of God revealed in the gospel of the water and the Spirit, we have received the salvation from all of our sins.

All sinners are in need of the gospel of the water and the Spirit. It is necessary both to those who have not yet received the remission of sin and also to those who have received the remission of sin by their faith in the gospel of the water and the Spirit. Those who have received the remission of sin cannot help but commit sins in this world because of their weaknesses and deficiencies. Still Jesus the Lamb of God took all the sins of the world once and for all through His baptism from John the Baptist. He has taken every single sin committed by people during their lives without exception.

When you hear this gospel of the water and the Spirit, you should believe in your hearts that all the sins of the world have already been expunged completely by Jesus' baptism by John the Baptist and His bloodshed on the Cross. We must live victoriously, reminding ourselves daily that Jesus has taken all the sins of the world—even those that are committed after we have received the remission of sin by our faith.

Jesus is the Lamb of God who took away all the sins of the world. Jesus has washed away all the sins of the world through the baptism He received. Dear fellow believers, were all your sins—the sins you have already committed and the sins that you will commit in the future—taken away by Jesus through His baptism and bloodshed or were they not? If you believe in this, you no longer have any sin. Jesus received the baptism and then went to the Cross.

Then, should you intentionally commit more sins? Dear fellow believers, are you going to commit sins if I told you to do they were already washed away? If I said, "People! Commit these sins today in this place," would you, without a guilty conscience, commit these sins? That is nonsense. We do not commit sins because we are told to do so or told not to do so by someone. We are always committing sins because we live in the human flesh. Hence, we should always believe in the gospel of the water and the Spirit and profess our faith in it. We should meditate the Truth of salvation in our hearts.

Do you commit sins intentionally, through your thoughts or actions, because you believe that Jesus has already taken all your sins that you commit while living in this world? Not at all. Because we know the wage of sin, we increasingly love the righteousness of God in gratefulness and faith toward Jesus, who bore all our sins in our stead. Jesus has taken all of our sins—both those we have committed intentionally or unintentionally. All our sins were transferred to Jesus once and for all when He received the baptism from John the Baptist.

We have to check daily whether there is sin in our hearts by comparing our hearts to the light of the gospel of the water and the Spirit. Did Jesus take away the sins you have committed in this world or not? If all of our sins were transferred onto Jesus when He was baptized by John the Baptist, we are without sin. If that is not the case and our sins were not transferred onto Jesus, we would still have the same sins. Did your sins transfer onto Jesus or not? Were all your sins transferred onto Jesus when He was baptized by John the Baptist? The Lord declared, *"For thus it is fitting for us to fulfill all righteousness" (Matthew 3:15).* By receiving the baptism, which was the most appropriate process, all our sins were transferred onto Him. In the Old Testament times, the High Priest Aaron transferred all the sins of the Israelites onto the sacrificial lamb at one time. Likewise, when the representative of all humanity, John the Baptist, baptized Jesus, all the sins of the world were transferred onto Him once and for all. Did all of your sins transfer onto Jesus then or not? They were all transferred completely.

Let's look at the Word of God in Leviticus. *"Aaron shall lay both his hands on the head of the live goat, confess over it all the iniquities of the children of Israel, and all their transgression, concerning all their sins, putting them on the head of the goat, and shall send it away into the wilderness by the hand of a suitable man. The goat shall bear on itself all their iniquities to an uninhabited land; and he shall release the goat in the wilderness" (Leviticus 16:21-22).*

Aaron was the first High Priest to the Israelites. The job of the High Priest was to transfer all sins of Israel once a year on the 10th day of the seventh month on their behalf. They would bring two goats and offer one to God to take away all of the sins of the Israelites at once by the laying of the hands of the High Priest.

Once he laid his hands on the sacrifice, he cut the sacrifice and made an offering to God. The Old Testament priests were always tired. They had to remain standing all the time and offer sacrifices without any time to rest. A sinner would bring a flawless sheep to the priests and say, "Priest! I have committed a sin today." Then, the sinner would lay his hands on the sacrifice and transfer his sins onto it. Then, the priest in charge would take that sacrifice and cut it and offer it to God. As you can imagine, many priests were needed to atone for the sins of every Israelite. But, on the 10th day of the seventh month, the High Priest alone would perform a sacrificial ritual to transfer all the sins of all of the Israelites at once.

On the Day of Atonement, before the High Priest performed a sacrifice for the Israelites, he would transfer his own sins and the sins of his family to a bull (Leviticus 16:6). Only after he had performed that sacrifice would he perform the sacrifice for the sins of his people with two goats (Leviticus 16:15-23). He would lay his both hands on the head of the first goat and pray, "God! The Israelites have committed grave sins against You. They have served other gods before You, and committed murders and adultery. They were jealous and arrogant. They stole from each other and fought with one another." The high priest would transfer all of their sins and then cut the throat of the goat, drawing its blood. The blood of the sacrifice was sprinkled on the East side of the Ark of the Covenant inside the Holy Place.

The High Priest would say, "Oh God! The Israelites have received their judgments through this sacrifice. All the sins of the Israelites were transferred onto the sacrifice. I have transferred all those sins. And the blood of the sacrifice, which took all sins of the Israelites, is here present before You. See this blood." While saying these things, the High Priest would sprinkle the blood seven times. There were golden bells attached to the hem of his robe, so when he sprinkled the blood seven times, they made a ringing sound. People outside the holy place could listen to this bell sound seven times. Seven is the number of God, which implies "perfection." The blood of the sacrifice covered the horns of the altar, and it was also sprinkled on the ground East of the Ark of the Covenant.

He who has committed even a single sin must die before God. There is no forgiveness of sin without proper atonement before Him. There could be forgiveness between equally weak people, because both sides would have committed sins at times in their lives. Yet, before the Absolute, there can be no forgiveness. Before the Absolute God, you must die if you have sin. This is God's justice. But, there was one way that the Israelites could receive the remission of their sins. If one of them were to receive the remission of his sins, he had to bring a scapegoat and lay his hands on it and transfer all his sins onto it. The Israelites in the Old Testament times avoided the death due to their sins by transferring their sins onto a scapegoat by laying their hands on it and then killing it. By this method, the Israelites received the remission of a day's worth of sin.

These days, people can receive the remission of their sins if they believe in the gospel of the water and the Spirit, which states that Jesus took all the sins of the world through His baptism and death on the Cross. There is no leniency when it comes to sin. Therefore, we must receive the remission of sin, by believing in the Truth through which God has taken care of our sins.

The Sacrifice for the Eternal Redemption

However, the daily sin offering was imperfect and inefficient, requiring too many sacrificial lambs. Hence, God has granted us a better method for our salvation. It was to have a sacrificial ritual on the Day of Atonement once a year on the 10th day of the seventh month (Leviticus 16:29), when the High Priest would lay his hands on one scapegoat and transfer all the sins of the Israelites on their behalf. Thus, a year's worth of the sins of the Israelites would be transferred onto the scapegoat. And in a ceremonial manner, the scapegoat would be led to the wilderness.

Dear fellow believers, once the scapegoat, upon which all the sins of the Israelites were transferred, is released to the wilderness, it eventually dies of thirst. Jesus has come to this world as such a scapegoat, the promised Lamb of God. Jesus came to this world and received the baptism from John the Baptist at the Jordan River, so that He became the Lamb of God who took all the sins of the world. John the Baptist was the greatest among those born of a woman and he was also a High Priest, a descendant of Aaron. Now, Jesus, the scapegoat, and the High Priest John the Baptist completed the remission of sin that has blotted out all our sins for eternity.

By receiving the baptism from John the Baptist, Jesus took all the sins of the world once and for all. When Jesus was being baptized He said to John the Baptists, "For thus, it is fitting for us to fulfill all righteousness." When Jesus was baptized, not only were all of your sins and mine transferred onto the head of Jesus Christ, but all the sins of the world as well. Jesus is the Lamb of God who took all the sins of the world. By receiving the baptism, Jesus bore all the sins that we commit in this world. By doing so, He has delivered us from all the sins that we commit in this world. Our Lord has delivered us from all the sins of the world through his son Jesus.

Then, do we have sin or not? Although we live in this world, we have no sin now. We have received salvation from all the sins of the world. Because Jesus has taken the sins of the world through His baptism, we now do not possess the sins of the world. Through our faith, we have received salvation from all the sins of the world.

How do we feel now that we don't possess any sins of the world? What is the result of having faith in this Truth? We have come to be born again of water and the Spirit (John 3:5). We have received our salvation by hearing and believing in the gospel of the water and the Spirit. Also, we can share this gospel with those who have not yet heard it. We have now gained such a desire and responsibility. Because we have received the remission of all the sins we commit in the world, we want to devote our lives to the gospel.

Now, we want to be the servants if the gospel because we have the desire in our hearts to share the gospel of the water and the Spirit to those who have not yet heard this news. Only those who believe in the gospel of the water and the Spirit are qualified to share the Word of God. Thus, it is a task appointed to us. If you all believe in the gospel of the water and the Spirit, you have also become people with such qualifications. Those of us who have been born again by believing in the gospel of the water and the Spirit want to do the works of God and will do those works.

Dear fellow believers, I would like to conclude with the Scripture passage, *"Behold! The Lamb of God who takes the sin of the world!"*

Have you not committed sins in this world? Yes, we all have. Did Jesus take all of your sins that you commit in the world—whether they were committed in the past, are committing now, and will be committed in the future—or not? Jesus has taken them all. Were they or were they not transferred onto Jesus? They were all transferred onto Jesus. Then, do we possess the sins we have committed in this world in our hearts or not? Because all of our sins have been transferred to Jesus, we do not have any sin in our hearts.

Dear fellow believers, if we are tied down by our own sins, we are unable to do the works of the gospel and follow God. Jesus has already taken all the sins of the world. Then, what sins could we still have? We have no sin, because Jesus has taken all the sins of the world. Hence, you and I have received our salvation by our faith. Although we have committed many sins in this world, we are free from sin at this time. Now, we have become able to serve the gospel of the water and the Spirit as God's sinless people. Truly, this is the love of God, the salvation from God, the grace of God, and the blessing of God.

Dear fellow believers! Do you feel weak and deficient? Jesus has delivered you in the perfect way. Then, we must possess the concrete faith that we have received our salvation. We must live according to the Word of God with the conviction that we no longer have any sin in our hearts.

Although this spirit in our heart is invisible to our naked eye, if we know and comprehend the Word of God, we are freed from sin and made able to participate in the precious works of God. The Lord said, "You shall know the Truth, and the Truth shall set you free." God's Word of Truth has emancipated you all from all sins and made you into sinless people. This is the very gospel of the water and the Spirit.

Our Lord has made us into sinless people. Jesus has delivered us from all of our sins by taking all the sins of the world. I give thanks to God. Furthermore, He has adopted us as workers of God so that we may dwell together in His Church.

I hope that God will keep our faith until the last days and help us witness Jesus, who has taken all the sins of the world. I give thanks for the gospel Word of the water and the Spirit, which God has given to us from above. ⊠

The Faith of Believing Only in the Word of God

< John 1:1-8 >

"In the beginning was the Word, and the Word was with God, and the Word was God. He was in the beginning with God. All things were made through Him, and without Him nothing was made that was made. In Him was life, and the life was the light of men. And the light shines in the darkness, and the darkness did not comprehend it. There was a man sent from God, whose name was John. This man came for a witness, to bear witness of the Light, that all through him might believe. He was not that Light, but was sent to bear witness of that Light."

It is written in John 1:18, *"No one has seen God at any time. The only begotten Son, who is in the bosom of the Father, He has declared Him."* Jesus who was in the bosom of God the Father came to this world in the flesh of man to save us from the sins of the world. Not one human being has seen God with the eyes of the flesh. However, God appeared and showed Himself to us through His Son. God the Son came to this earth wearing the flesh of a human being and revealed Himself as the Son of God to be seen in the eyes of the people.

The Lord said to us, *"Nor is there salvation in any other, for there is no other name under heaven given among men by which we must be saved" (Acts 4:12).* God is saying that no other name can save us from the sins of the world except the name Jesus that God gave to His Son. Is Jesus Christ the only One on earth who has the name of the Savior who can save all the sinners from their sins? That is true. Jesus Christ is the Savior of our mankind, and He stayed on this earth for 33 years to save all of mankind from all sins. No one except Jesus has the power to be the Savior who can save mankind from the sins of the world.

In the world nowadays, there are people who pretend to be a savior. Don't these people have something wrong in their heads? There can be no true Savior in this world except Jesus. Only Jesus is the true Savior to mankind, for He is the only One who took our sins once and for all through His baptism from John the Baptist, and then cleansed all the sins of mankind. Only Jesus took our sins and shed His blood on the cross to receive the punishment for our sins, and gained a victory rising again from the dead. Therefore, all the people who say that they are the saviors, instead of Jesus, are liars. The Bible declares that Jesus is the only Savior, but there are crazy leaders of some religious sects who say that they themselves are the saviors. One of them claimed that he had read the Bible over 3000 times. When I heard of this, he was in his late 40's. People under him testified that he had read the Bible 3000 times during about 10 years of believing in Jesus. If he has read 3000 times in 10 years, it means 300 times a year then, a year is 365 days, so it means that he had to read the whole Bible about once a day. Such false prophets are deceiving the people declaring impossible things as fact.

We should never be deceived by such people. Now, if the last age comes, it is recorded that many people will appear and declare themselves as the savior (Matthew 24:5). I know that those who call themselves the saviors are relatively handsome in the flesh, and they claim to make fire fall down from the sky and make wonders and miracles happen with their faith. According to them, there is another savior besides Jesus. However, there is no other true Savior except Jesus.

John the Baptist and Jesus worked together to fulfill the salvation of mankind by fulfilling the righteousness of God. Then, was John the Baptist another savior? No, he was not. John the Baptist merely had played an assistant role to Jesus while He took the sins of the world. Jesus came to this earth and took all the sins of mankind once and for all through the baptism that John gave to Him. Jesus took the sins of the world through the baptism that He received from this John, and with the precious blood that He has shed on the Cross, He accomplished the gospel of the water and the Spirit.

Those who believe only in the blood of Jesus say that John the Baptist has failed. They argue that John was so radical that the authorities of his days could not tolerate him. However, they misunderstood the main mission of John the Baptist. They teach such absurd nonsense out of their ignorance of the Scriptures.

Therefore, we must know the mission of John the Baptist correctly. Only then, can we realize and understand the gospel Truth of the water and the Spirit. The entire Bible is the Word of God that reveals the Truth that Jesus saved mankind from sin by receiving the baptism from John and by being crucified. Who are the people of proper faith? They are the people who believe in the fact that Jesus Christ has come by the water and the blood. The faith that believes in the gospel of the water and the Spirit is the correct faith.

John 1:1states, *"In the beginning was the Word, and the Word was with God, and the Word was God."* The Word that in the beginning created the entire universe and all the things in it was God. It was also Jesus who created the universe at the time of the Creation of the world because Jesus is fundamentally God. Jesus is God the Son among the God of Trinity—the Father, the Son, and the Holy Spirit. This Triune God each has their own Person, but all of these three are the same God to us.

It is written in Genesis that Jesus created this world. And, it is written in the Gospel According to John that Jesus was God who saved us from the sins of this world. Jesus was God Himself who came to this earth wearing the flesh of man and saved us from the sins of the world once and for all.

It is written in John 1:4, *"In Him was life, and the life was the light of men."* "The light of men" here refers to the position of Jesus and His mission through which God saved us from the sins of the world. And the "light of life" represents the love of Jesus that saved mankind from sin. All creatures were destined to die for their sins, but our Lord came to this earth and gave new life to the people who believe in Him. He sent Jesus, who was baptized by John the Baptist, and then shed His Blood, and rose again from the dead. The Lord was the Savior who gave us new life. Jesus was the light of salvation to all people. Our Lord is the light of salvation. He came to this earth and took the sins of this world once and for all by receiving the baptism. Then He received the judgment for all sins by being crucified in our stead and then rose again from the dead through the righteousness of God, wiping away all our sins once and for all. *"The life was the light of men."* Our Lord saved us from all sin by giving us His life with the water and the blood. Jesus became the true life for us, and the baptism that Jesus has received from John and the shedding of the blood completed the righteousness of God.

Jesus Introduces Himself as the Bread of Life

Jesus introduces the will of the Father. *"And this is the will of Him who sent Me, that everyone who sees the Son and believes in Him may have everlasting life; and I will raise him up at the last day" (John 6:40).*

After Jesus performed the miracle of the five barley loaves and two small fish in the wilderness and fed all the gathered people, He said that He was the bread of life from Heaven (John 6:32-35). There were a lot of bread on earth, but there is only One who came from heaven. He told us that the bread of true life or the living bread is Jesus Christ. To blot your sins out, all you have to do is to eat the bread of life. We have to believe in Jesus, who is the bread wiping out the sins, the true bread that makes us earn eternal life. Jesus is telling us by coming as the bread of life: "Those who eat the flesh of Jesus receive the remission of sin and earn eternal life."

Our Lord wanted to eliminate the sins of the people by coming to this earth, and so he did as a man. Jesus wanted to give His flesh and blood to all the people on earth in order to save their souls that were dead from sin before God. Jesus came to this earth out of His own accord wearing the flesh of man and gave the gospel of the water and the Spirit to let the people in the world receive new life, the eternal life, and the remission of sin.

Jesus was God fundamentally. It is exactly our Lord Jesus who made the trees on that mountain, the grass, the great sun in the sky, that huge Milky Way, this ocean, all the animals, and He made you and me. I am stating that our Lord Jesus Christ, who is God, came as the Savior. God created man according to His image, and when these people fell into sin, God Himself was born into this earth wearing the flesh of man through the body of the Virgin Mary, giving up His seat of glory to take away the sins of these people. The Lord came to this earth out of His own accord and let the people receive the remission of sin and eternal life by giving His flesh and blood.

My fellow believers, let us examine why Jesus gave us His flesh and blood. The Lord said, *"Whoever eats My flesh and drinks My blood has eternal life, and I will raise him up at the last day. For My flesh is food indeed, and My blood is drink indeed" (John 6:54-55).* Let us examine what did Jesus mean by this passage.

First let us take a broader look at John 6:52-57. *"The Jews therefore quarreled among themselves, saying, 'How can this Man give us His flesh to eat?' Then Jesus said to them, 'Most assuredly, I say to you, unless you eat the flesh of the Son of Man and drink His blood, you have no life in you. Whoever eats My flesh and drinks My blood has eternal life, and I will raise him up at the last day. For My flesh is food indeed, and My blood is drink indeed. He who eats My flesh and drinks My blood abides in Me, and I in him. As the living Father sent Me, and I live because of the Father, so he who feeds on Me will live because of Me.'"*

What did the Lord Jesus give all humanity to save them from their sin and allow them to live? First, Jesus gave His flesh to save the people from sin. It means that Jesus has given His body to us. Second, Jesus also gave His blood. Therefore, if we eat the flesh and the blood of the Lord, we abide within the Lord, but if we do not eat the flesh and the blood of the Lord, we do not abide in the Lord. Do you understand what I am talking about?

Our Lord came to this earth in the flesh. Then, our Lord gave His flesh to us to save us, all humanity. What does it mean that He gave His flesh? Did He actually give us His flesh by cutting it from His body? During the Last Supper, Jesus took bread, blessed and broke it and said, *"Take, eat; this is My body."*

Let us read Matthew 26:26. *"And as they were eating, Jesus took bread, blessed and broke it, and gave it to the disciples and said, "Take, eat; this is My body.""* The Lord gave blessing with the bread and said, *"Take, eat; this is My body."* Our Lord has set this Holy Communion by His Word, and we are celebrating this in remembrance of His righteous act for our salvation. The Lord took the bread, blessed, broke and gave it to the disciples saying, "Take, eat; this is My body." He saved us by giving His flesh, and allowed us to receive eternal life by giving His blood to us. My fellow believers, do you understand? Our Lord did not only say, "Take, drink; this is My blood" but He also said "Take, eat; this is My body" when He practiced the first Holy Communion.

When our Lord came to save us from sin, He came by wearing the body of man, the flesh. If the Lord did not come to this earth with the flesh and the blood, He could not save us humans. Our Lord, in saving us, had to come by the same body as us, that is, in the flesh and the blood. Where is our life? It is in the blood. This blood is our life (Leviticus 17:11). And, where do we commit sin? We commit sin with the body. We also commit sin with the mind, but we also commit sin with our bodies during our whole lifetimes. So, our Lord had to come to this earth wearing the flesh to eliminate the sins committed by mankind. It was to give us His flesh. It was to bear all the sins of the world onto His body by receiving the baptism from John the Baptist, the representative of all mankind.

And He gave us His blood. The Lord gave us eternal life, and fulfilled the remission of sins by giving us His flesh and the blood. Our Lord has saved us by taking all the sins onto His own body. So, our Lord said, *"Take, eat; this is My body."*

What did Jesus have to do in saving us from all the sins? First, Jesus had to give us the flesh. We can receive salvation only when the Lord has given us His flesh. If the Lord didn't give us the flesh, we could not be saved. So, our Lord came to this earth wearing the flesh of man to save us, and gave us His flesh by receiving the baptism at Jordan River, when He became 30.

Jesus is the Savior who came to this earth wearing the same flesh as ours.

It is written in John chapter 1 verse 14, *"And the Word became flesh and dwelt among us, and we beheld His glory, the glory as of the only begotten of the Father, full of grace and truth."*

What are the "grace and truth" mentioned here? This means that Jesus has become our Savior by giving us His flesh and blood; that He gave us the remission of sin by receiving the baptism from John, dying on the Cross, and rising again from the dead. What we have to know is that the Son of God came to this earth wearing the flesh of man according to the prophesies in Old Testament. Namely, the Son of God came to this earth and saved us from the sins of the world. It is important for us to know and believe this.

You must know that Jesus is God, the One who created the heavens and the earth. Do you know that Jesus Christ is our God and Savior? Our salvation is guaranteed when we know and believe that Jesus is the true God and our Savior. Jesus not only created the heavens and the earth with the Word, but He also came to this earth as the Savior wearing the flesh of man (Genesis 1:1-2, John 1:1-14). God came to us wearing the image of man by through the body of the Virgin named Mary to save us from sin. Jesus is the true God of the universe who came to save us from the sins of the world by wearing the body of man.

The Lord lowered Himself to save us from sin and He experienced the weaknesses of man. He knows how weak and evil we are, and how Satan the Devil is so conniving. We may think that it will be okay if the Lord drives out the Devil once with His authority and power. But, the Lord did not do that. Mankind had fallen into the sin by being tempted by Satan the Devil, and The Lord wanted to save mankind fairly with His justice. Therefore, He took all of our sins onto His body by receiving the baptism from John the Baptist, and then bore the judgment of all those sins once and for all by shedding His blood on the Cross. This is the love of God and God's truth and justice. If we believe in the gospel of the water and the Spirit, we are able to follow the bright Light of the Truth, because our Lord so loved us and saved us completely and properly from sin with His law of justice.

We do not praise Him admiring only His power. We cannot praise Him just because of His power. He did not lie to us. And He did not use all of His divine power. Rather, He became the same being as a creature of flesh and blood, and saved us from sin and judgment, by properly satisfying the law that states that the wages of sin is death. Human beings were destined to die, to go to hell, and to suffer for their sins, but Jesus took all of our sin and bore all the condemnation vicariously by sympathizing with our situation. Jesus saved our humanity justly and fairly by taking the death and suffering of all human beings, in order to save them. This is God's grace of glory. The reason that we call Jesus, God, and believe in Him as God is because Jesus created the heavens and the earth, and He is our Savior. This is also the reason that we praise Jesus.

In Old Testament times, God set His law of atonement: If a sinner laid his hands on the sacrifice, saying, "God, I have murdered today, and I committed adultery," his sins would be passed onto it. Thus, God had established the law of passing of sins onto the sacrifice by confessing the sins to God and laying their hands on it. God then received the sacrifice in place of the sinner, and judged that sacrifice instead of those sinners, and gave him the remission of his sins. The burnt offering in Old Testament was the promise that God would give the eternal remission of sin like this in the future.

Inside the courtyard of the tabernacle there was the altar of the burnt offering, which was where God received the burnt offering of meat of the sacrificial animal. God's law states, *"The wages of sin is death" (Romans 6:23)*. Those who had sin had to pay for their sins with the corresponding wages, the death of their lives. This was why they had to offer the blood of the sacrificial animals in place of themselves to be spared before God from His judgment.

As the sinners in Old Testament could receive the remission of sins by laying hands on the sacrifice, drawing the blood of sacrifice, and giving God the fragrant scent of burning it on the fire of the altar, mankind could also receive the remission of sin by believing in Jesus Christ who came to this earth as the Lamb of God, received the baptism from John the Baptist and shed His blood to death on the Cross. This is the very gospel of the water and the Spirit that makes us sinless when we believe in it wholeheartedly. If we do not believe in the gospel of the water and the Spirit, we will be condemned, because we cannot receive the remission of sin, but if we do believe in it we will go to Heaven without fail. Those who have already been pardoned from their sins by believing in the gospel of the water and the Spirit shall be able to enter the

Kingdom of Heaven.

God has set this sacrificial system to save mankind, and promised to save us if we would believe in Him according to this promise. My fellow believers, this is the promise of God. What I mean by following the light is not that we must see some sparkling light in a mirage. We must follow the Light of the Truth in our minds.

The reason why Jesus received the baptism in the Jordan River was to save mankind completely by taking all of our sins by grace and fulfill to complete salvation. We can be thankful that God had come in a flesh of man and received the baptism to give mankind the great gift.

While reading this book you will truly understand who Jesus Christ is and you will receive the remission of sin and eternal life by coming to know the gospel of the water and the Spirit. ✉

We Couldn't Be Happier
Than This

< John 1:29-31 >
"The next day John saw Jesus coming toward him, and said, 'Behold! The Lamb of God who takes away the sin of the world! This is He of whom I said, 'After me comes a Man who is preferred before me, for He was before me.' I did not know Him; but that He should be revealed to Israel, therefore I came baptizing with water.'"

You are so tired, aren't you? I am very tired too. I know that we are weary because we work hard serving God's righteousness everyday. All of us truly have hardships, and we are serving the Lord in spite of these hardships.

Anyways, we have converted some precious souls that are more valuable than the universe during the evangelical meeting this week. I am sure that the souls received the salvation during this time because of all the spiritual works that took place at this evangelical meeting. I am very thankful that each of you have served in many ways and at every opportunity, leading souls, sharing newspapers, praying, attending meetings, and so on. We cannot thank God enough, for we have won some souls that are more precious than the entire universe! The evangelical meeting is really worth to having! We also are grateful to God whenever we hear the good news from our readers who have read our spiritual growth series. We really give thanks.

It would be much easier for us to preach the gospel of the

water and the Spirit if there were not the false teachers in this world. Today, preaching the gospel of the water and the Spirit is very difficult because there are lots of Christians who oppose the Truth of salvation. Furthermore, preaching the gospel of the water and the Spirit these days is getting more difficult than ever because of those who propagate the pseudo-gospels, which are similar to the true gospel. They make people fall into confusion with such fake gospels. They are the ones who cause people to sin. Woe to such false preachers, because the Lord said, *"It would be better for him if a millstone were hung around his neck, and he were thrown into the sea, than that he should offend one of these little ones" (Luke 17:2).*

Those who have not yet been born again from their sins cannot discern the true gospel from the false one. So, they are prone to deception by the false preachers. They are merely the prey of such predators, the spiritual wolves. I was told that a certain pastor in our city has plans to gather the offerings from his congregation up to 10 million US dollars to build a huge chapel. That preacher has collected 4 million until now. The congregation of that church number about 500; some say that he did not hesitate to mortgage the houses of the members of the congregations to raise the 10 million US dollars.

Frankly speaking, those who preach false gospel similar to the gospel of the water and the Spirit are using their ministry with the plan to extort money from their congregations. That is why they say every person in their church looks like money. It is the same with the taxi drivers saying all the people standing at the roadside look like money. They are very different from the servants of God who are preaching the gospel of the water and the Spirit. To those who have received the remission of sins by believing in the gospel of the water and the Spirit, each soul looks more precious than the entire universe. But to the people who are not yet born again, they are seen as precious because of money. Therefore, we have to thank the Lord who made us the soldiers who can preach the gospel of the water and the Spirit.

John said looking at Jesus, *"Behold! The Lamb of God who takes away the sin of the world!" (John 1:29)* The happiest thing for me in my religious life was that I realized that our Lord took our sins once for all by receiving the baptism from John the Baptist and shed His blood on the Cross. I could not express the joy in words when I realized the gospel Truth of the water and the Spirit. There was nothing in my spiritual life that gave me greater pleasure than the gospel of the water and the Spirit. Even now, the pleasure I felt at that time when the gospel of the water and the Spirit came to me is still taking place in my mind.

Why am I so happy? My mind is happy because Jesus blotted out all my sins absolutely once for all by receiving the baptism. Our Lord by His grace has spared the judgment of all my sins through His baptism. There is nothing better for every one than believing in this gospel of the water and the Spirit. How can there be more joyous gospel than this?

We did not have true joy before we knew the preciousness of the gospel of the water and the Spirit. However, there does not exist a more joyful salvation than if we know and believe in the gospel power of the water and the Spirit. When we listened to the gospel of the water and the Spirit at first, we just came to recognize that this is plain and simple truth. But, we feel happier as times passes while we listen to the gospel Truth through every meeting in God's Church. There is really no other joyful gospel for each of us than this gospel of the water and the Spirit. There is no other joyful gospel than the news that Lord took all the sins of this world when He received the baptism from John the Baptist, and so He saved us from the sins of the world.

We are truly joyful because of this gospel of the water and the Spirit. Where can there be more joyful news to us who were sinners? The laughter springs up from the depth of the hearts of those who have received the remission of sins by believing in the gospel of the water and the Spirit. If there are not sins in our mind, the joy springs up and the peace comes. It is true. If we do not have sins in our mind, the laughter springs up naturally in our mind because there is joy in our heart. Is it the same to you, or not? Yes, I am sure it is the same to all of you.

We cannot express how thankful we are because we are so happy because we do not have sins. There was a famous movie titled "Sound of Music." I remember that the story and the sweet songs of this movie gave me great joy and make an impression on my mind for a while after I saw the movie. But, the joys from this world do not last long.

The praise of faith that we give to God is greater than the pleasure of this world. The pleasure of salvation that our Lord has given us by blotting out our sins is so great that it cannot be compared with the joy of this world. Even if you spend your vacation at the beach of Waikiki pitching a tent under a coconut tree watching beautiful girls and scenery, in the hearts of the born-again, there is still a greater joy, a joy greater than anything we can get from this world. The blessings of being born again with the gospel of the water and the Spirit cannot be changed with any blessing in this world.

When the Lord was about to receive the baptism from John the Baptist, He said to John, *"For thus it is fitting for us to fulfill all righteousness" (Matthew 3:15).* And, the next day, John testified, *"Behold! The Lamb of God who takes away the sin of the world!" (John 1:29)* If these verses were not recorded in the Bible, all the people living on earth would die hopelessly in sin. We receive the salvation if we believe the promise of salvation that our Lord blotted out our sins by taking it with His baptism and the shedding of the blood. We clearly had sins before we believed in the gospel of the water and the Spirit, but now the sin has been blotted out.

Whether the people believe in the gospel of the water and the Spirit or not, the Lord has already blotted out all the sins of this world. Because our Lord has taken the sins of the world and He has fulfilled all the righteousness of God once for all, we received the remission of sins by the power of the gospel of the water and the Spirit that He gave us. We have true hope because the gospel of the water and the Spirit is in this world. Though there are many people in this world who have not yet received the remission of sins, they can be cleansed of their sins if they listen to this gospel of the water and the Spirit and accept it with their heart. This is why there is still hope.

We are happy living in the gospel of God and the in the guidance of the Holy Spirit. Those who have received the remission of sins live praising God because of the joy that they are sinless. That gospel is that our Lord has blotted out all the sins of mankind by receiving the baptism from John in the Jordan River (Matthew 3:15). Why did Jesus blot out our sins? It is because He loved us so much. The Lord came to this earth and saved us completely from the sins of the world by receiving the baptism from John at the Jordan River, because our Lord so loved all of us, the mankind in this earth. Jesus Christ cleansed the sins of this world once and for all by taking them through the baptism received from John the Baptist to follow the will of God the Father.

There are many people in this world who do not know the

fact that Jesus is God. Even among Christians, there are many do not truly know him. Especially, some Christian sects even do not mention the fact that Jesus is God. They themselves deny the divine nature of Jesus. Even some of the saints of my church do not have a clear understanding of this truth. When they heard from me, "Jesus is God," they said that they understand that Jesus is the Son of God but they do not understand that Jesus is God. It is all right. It is because they have not learned it yet. It is all right if they learn, know and believe that Jesus is God and the Son of God now and in the future. God the Father and His Son Jesus Christ are omnipotent, omniscient, omnipresent, eternal, ubiquitous, and almighty God. He is God who made this spacious universe.

Why did Jesus Christ who is God come to us? It was for Jesus Christ to have personal association and love with us. Jesus could not share true fellowship with the sinners. To have fellowship with God, we have to become the believers of the gospel of the water and the Spirit. So, God sent His beloved Son to this earth wearing the features of a man, for God so loved the world. Jesus came to us through the body of a human being. As it is written in John 1:14, *"The Word became flesh and dwelt among us,"* He came to this earth with flesh, but He was God fundamentally. Jesus Christ is the very God who made this boundless universe.

That God the Creator had to come as our Savior. God the Savior came to this earth having the same flesh as ours, experienced the same pains and sorrows of ours, received the baptism from John the Baptist, and saved the believers in the gospel of the water and the Spirit by rising again after dying on the Cross. The Lord became our Savior, our true God. That is why we are calling Jesus our Lord the Savior.

Jesus is God fundamentally (1 John 5:20). So, we are to

live wearing and feeling the love of God in Jesus by believing in Jesus as the Lord and Savior. Jesus took the sins of this world once for all by receiving the baptism from John, and He went to the Cross and received the judgment of the sins that the sinners supposed to receive. Now, we believers in the gospel of the water and the Spirit became sinless because of the Lord. We can become the people of God when we are saved from all the sins by believing in Jesus Christ with our hearts. Our salvation is all because of the love of God.

Therefore, what must be the true content of the sermons of the Christian preachers? The people who have received the remission of sins say that Jesus took the sins of the world by receiving the baptism, and that He has blotted out all sin through His death and resurrection. All we have to preach is that the Lord blotted out our sins once and for all with the gospel of the water and the Spirit and became eternal Savior to us.

Is this Truth of salvation engraved in our mind? The gospel of the water and the Spirit does not end even if we preach it forever, and we have to believe in this because it is the Truth that blotted out all our sins. The gospel Word of the water and the Spirit is the Truth of salvation that is good whenever we listen to it. This gospel of the water and the Spirit is really the blessed gospel, the love of God, and also the Truth of salvation. So, one receives great blessings in the mind whenever he listens to this gospel Word.

When we listen to the gospel of the water and the Spirit, we have to throw away our own thoughts and our fixed ideas. It is written in Colossians, *"Beware lest anyone cheat you through philosophy and empty deceit" (Colossians 2:8)*. We must not be cheated by the faith of the philosophy and empty deceit. We have to throw away our human thought and believe in the gospel Word of the water and the Spirit according to this admonishment.

You have heard through the written Word that Jesus took the sins of the world through the baptism received from John the Baptist. Jesus came to this earth as the Lamb of God. When the High Priest of the Old Testament laid both his hands on the head of the sacrificial lamb, all the sins were passed onto the Lamb. Then, the sacrificial lamb was killed for the sake of the sins of his people. Likewise, Jesus also offered a spiritual burnt offering by giving His body. Jesus remitted all our sins in "the same way as the laying on of hands in the Old Testament," receiving the baptism from John the Baptist (Matthew 3:13-17).

People consider philosophy as a high form of thought that is held in high regard. They consider it great for the human beings to have the ability to think. This is why there is a saying, "Man is a thinking reed." However, if you walk the side streets in Korea, you can find not a few philosophical centers. Philosophical centers sound like a place where the common people cannot approach boldly. But, the philosophical centers in our country are the place in fact where the fortunetellers earn their living. Such places are the irrational places in fact, but this phenomenon is supporting evidence that people give generous points to the word 'philosophy' without reason.

However, philosophy is nothing special. Philosophy is simply the system of thought of man. But, God said, *"The wickedness of man was great in the earth, and that every intent of the thoughts of his heart was only evil continually" (Genesis 6:5).* Therefore everything which comes from the thoughts of man are false, and the half gospel of the Christianity which is from and made out of man's thoughts will never be the same as the true gospel of the water and the Spirit, no matter how proudly it argues its history and tradition. No matter how hard we believe in half gospels, our sins would not be blotted out. What is so great about the half gospel? It is nothing.

Only the Truth and the true gospel of the water and the Spirit states that Jesus took the sins of the world through the baptism He received from John. John 1:29 is the clear evidence of this fact. Therefore, it is silly to substitute the gospel of the water and the Spirit with the half gospel and to console the heart with the thoughts of man while trying to fit the salvation according to one's own thoughts. What is the use of having ministry after studying the theology for 10 years, and then going for more study abroad? If they try to construct parts of a sermon, aren't they busy collecting piece by piece, little by little from the books of philosophy, literature, theology, annotation, the Bible, and all the dictionaries spread all over the room over several days? How tiresome is that work? Those kinds of sermons give suffering to people everyday, instead of giving the remission of sins.

We have to throw away the philosophical faith, which comes from the thoughts of man. Here is the gospel of the water and the Spirit that declares that Jesus has blotted out all of our sins. *"Behold! The Lamb of God who takes away the sin of the world!" (John 1:29)* We receive the remission of sins truly in our mind by believing in Jesus according to the evidence of Bible passages such as Matthew 3:15 and John 1:29.

It is true when it is written that Jesus took the sins of this world to the Cross once and for all by receiving the baptism from John. There is nothing for us to say but to believe it, if the Word of God states that Jesus bore all our sins once for all when He received the baptism from John the Baptist. It is really silly that we do not believe in the gospel Truth of the water and the Spirit because of our own fleshly or philosophical thoughts. The will and actions of God say that He saved us with the gospel of the water and the Spirit. If we cannot believe the true gospel with our own thoughts, then we are stupid and foolish.

My fellow believers, if war broke our in our country and you became the captives of the war, what then are you going to say to your enemies? As a prisoner, how can you dare to say to the enemy as follows? "I am a battalion commander in our force! Do you fail to recognize me? What is this, why aren't you shining my shoes? You kids must have no shame." What happens if he speaks roughly like that? He will be killed.

"Whether you are a battalion commander or a division commander of your army, if you cannot grasp the situation even now, wake up man! You are now captured by the enemies. Do you get it? Recover your senses, you son of a bitch! It is all right for me to shoot you a rifle or a gun. You are so noisy, and you seem to be out of your mind not knowing if we are friends or foes, if it is feces or urine." If the situation goes like this, the Geneva Conventions, which tries to uphold the human rights of captives in times of war, is of no use. It is the captive who does not have any power and the enemies will put him in excremental water up to his neck without giving him something to eat.

My fellow believers, if the Bible said that Jesus took the sins of the world by receiving the baptism from John, then, it is true. Being a captive of sin, what could a sinner do or say against the gospel Truth of the water and the Spirit and God? We simply have to believe if it is written in the Bible that Jesus has taken the sins of the world by receiving the baptism instead of shouting useless words. There is nothing for us human beings to be proud before Jesus no matter how smart we are or how much we have learned. Is there anything for you to be proud of?

We cannot boast of ourselves before Jesus even we have hundreds of Doctor of Divinity decrees. But then, there are so many ridiculous people in the Christian community. The personal records or resumes of some pastors reveal that they have attended several theological schools. They have gone here and there, but they have graduated from only one school. It is recorded that they have accomplished some subjects here and other subjects there, but they do still not know this Truth that Jesus took the sins of the world. They have sins everyday because they do not know this. Even though Jesus has taken the sins of the world, they still have sins because they do not know about the true gospel. Therefore they inevitably will remain as the captives of sin. It is silly for them to be fascinated in philosophy of the world because of their ignorance about the Truth of the water and the Spirit.

Philosophy and theology have come out of the thoughts of man, and therefore, they are no more than waste. The Apostle Paul also regarded philosophy as waste (Philippians 3:8). Those who dig into the field of philosophy know this fact well. Those who studied casually in this world might think the worldly studies are great, however those who studied the worldly studies properly know full well that there are limitations in the knowledge of mankind. So, as someone once said, "the more learned, the more confused."

Therefore, if it is said in the Bible that Jesus took the sins of the world, it is simply true. There is nothing more to say against it. Who testified that Jesus took the sins of the world? John the Baptist passed the sins onto Jesus and he testified for Him like this: "Behold! The Lamb of God who takes away the sin of the world! That Person is the Messiah to come, and He is the Savior who has taken all the sins of mankind. Jesus is your Savior. Believe in Him. Jesus has taken all our sins."

I mean to say that John the Baptist has testified like this. Of course, there were many people who asked for forgiveness of their sins everyday because of the sins in their hearts. Didn't John the Baptist say the very shocking words to them? *"Behold! The Lamb of God who takes away the sin of the world!"* It was very shocking that he called Jesus 'the Lamb of God.' Up until the moment John testified in this way, who among them believed in Jesus as God? Who among them believed in Jesus as the Messiah? His testimony might be very shocking to the people of his days, because no one knew who Jesus was yet. *"Behold! The Lamb of God who takes away the sin of the world!"* It is very shocking if we take the situation at that time into consideration.

"Behold!" They were asking for the attention. *"The Lamb of God who takes away the sin of the world!"* Namely, these words mean that Jesus is the Messiah. It means that Jesus is the Savior so to speak, or God. When John the Baptist testified, "That Person is precisely the Messiah who has been prophesized by Isaiah in the Old Testament," then the people were shocked and doubtful, likely saying, "Then, is He the One? But then, is He that shabby? He looks like a countryside man. Is He the Savior who looks like a stem from the dry ground?"

When we look into below passage of Isaiah, it is evident that the appearance of Jesus was nothing to admire.

"Who has believed our report?
And to whom has the arm of the LORD been revealed?
For He shall grow up before Him as a tender plant,
And as a root out of dry ground.
He has no form or comeliness;

And when we see Him,
There is no beauty that we should desire Him" (Isaiah
53:1-2).

It is usual for us to think Jesus as very handsome Jesus, but the Scripture said that there was no beauty that we should desire Him. But, the Words from His mouth were very precious. They were very rare and precious. The glory and preciousness of Jesus were without comparison.

My fellow believers, how wonderful were these words that John the Baptist has testified? *"Behold! The Lamb of God who takes away the sin of the world!"* It declares, "Jesus has blotted out all the sins of mankind." We also spread the same Word that John the Baptist did, as it is great news. However, there are many people who do not believe in this marvelous testimony. Some people just argue the doctrines of their denominations without learning or knowing them properly. They do not believe in the gospel of the water and the Spirit even though it is the Word written in the Bible.

It is frustrating that most Christians today do not believe in the gospel of the water and the Spirit because of their ignorance of it. They cannot know and believe in the gospel Truth of the water and the Spirit because they believe in their religious body, their power, their own thoughts, and even their own emotions. The Christian leaders of this world are prone to boast of themselves, but they do not have anything to boast in reality. They might be proud of their powers to calm evil spirits by touching the lower end of the possessed person's. But, they become dumb when they are asked to interpret God's Word, such as *"Behold! The Lamb of God who takes away the sin of the world!"*

Dear fellow believers, no matter how smart and talented you are, you can only be saved and receive the remission of sin if you believe the Word in the Bible which says, *"Behold! The Lamb of God who takes away the sin of the world!"* Why is it so hard to believe that John the Baptist passed the sins of the world onto Jesus and then testified that He is the Lamb of God who takes away the sin of the world? Just as the sacrifices of the Old Testament involved the passage of sins by laying hands on a sacrifice, Jesus has received and then blotted out all the sins of the people through His baptism. What then is more to say before the testimony of John? You would still be living as sinners if you did not believe in this Word.

The reason that our mind is peaceful now is because our Lord took the sins of this world with His baptism and blotted out our sins once for all on the Cross. That is why our mind is sinless and peaceful. However, there are countless Christians who have sins because they do not believe in the gospel Word of the water and the Sprit. There is no assurance of being saved from sin in them; their mind is always insecure, and they are very tired from showing off by endlessly doing virtuous deeds.

Some people go to hell even though they believe in Jesus wholeheartedly, and some people go to Heaven because they believe in Jesus according to the Truth. In fact, it seems that there are many Christians who should go to Heaven, but this is not the case. They know that they have sin and will be destroyed for their sins, and therefore, they try to escape from that destruction by doing good deeds in their own ways. They assume that they will go to Heaven by living virtuously, but they are going to hell.

God the Father appointed the Son of God as the Savior of this world, and decided that no one can be saved from his or her sins without having the faith in the baptism that the Son received and the blood of the Cross. We go to Heaven because of Jesus and the gospel of the water and the Spirit. Even if we live virtuously in this world, if we do not believe in Jesus who came by the gospel of the water and the Spirit, we cannot be saved from destruction, and we would go to hell. Originally, it was decided for everyone to go to hell because of sins in his or her heart, but there are the people who go to Heaven receiving the salvation because Jesus has saved them.

If a Christian does not know the way to be saved, he would go to hell, no matter how fervently he believes in Jesus. If people received salvation by living virtuously, many people in the world who are living kindly and ethically would go to Heaven. However, in spite of these false expectations, the law of God's salvation is the gospel of the water and the Spirit. We receive the salvation by believing in Jesus, who came by the gospel of the water and the Spirit. Philosophical people, very smart people, and intelligent people in this world will go to hell because of their sins because they do not believe in the gospel of the water and the Spirit.

I really thank our Lord that He blotted out our sins with His baptism and blood. I thank Him very much. If the Lord asks us of what we are most thankful for, we cannot help but to say that we are thankful that our Lord has blotted out our sins. I really want to proclaim this forever. Do you also want to say that you are thankful and grateful that the Lord has blotted out all your sins? I am sure you do. Do not have thoughts other than this; let us think most joyously that the Lord has blotted out all our sins in this world by faith. Such a person is clearly very wise.

What is more precious than the gospel of the water and the Spirit? We can do the works of God acceptably with the faith of believing in this gospel. We can serve and preach this true gospel, do good and live for others when we have the faith of believing in the gospel of the water and the Spirit in your mind. We have to live by the correct faith which enables us to receive the remission of sins. We can do good works with the faith in a mind that is grateful to our Lord for His blotting out our sins. We have to do this and that if the Lord wants. We have to thank God with faith. We always have to keep the faith in our mind and be thankful that the Lord Jesus Christ has taken and blotted out our sins. Do you believe now?

Those who do not have the gospel of the water and the Spirit in their mind at this point have to believe in the gospel of the water and the Spirit before the day the Lord returns.

We who have this beautiful gospel in our heart are giving thanks to the Lord forever because He has taken the sins of the world by receiving the baptism from John the Baptist in the Jordan River. Because of His righteous act, we are sinless even though we are too weak and insufficient to live without committing sins. Halleluiah! ✉

With What Kind of Look Did Our Creator Visit Us?

< John 1:1-13 >

"In the beginning was the Word, and the Word was with God, and the Word was God. He was in the beginning with God. All things were made through Him, and without Him nothing was made that was made. In Him was life, and the life was the light of men. And the light shines in the darkness, and the darkness did not comprehend it. There was a man sent from God, whose name was John. This man came for a witness, to bear witness of the Light, that all through him might believe. He was not that Light, but was sent to bear witness of that Light. That was the true Light, which gives light to every man coming into the world. He was in the world, and the world was made through Him, and the world did not know Him. He came to His own, and His own did not receive Him. But as many as received Him, to them He gave the right to become children of God, to those who believe in His name: who were born, not of blood, nor of the will of the flesh, nor of the will of man, but of God."

Who is Jesus? Jesus is the Master who has created the entire universe and everything in it with His Word. Who is Jesus to us? Jesus is our Savior. Jesus is the Lord and Savior who came to this earth as our Redeemer and saved us from all the sins of the world with the gospel of the water and the Spirit.

It is written in John 1:3, *"All things were made through Him, and without Him nothing was made that was made."* Jesus created the universe. When God said in Genesis chapter 1, *"Let there be light,"* there was light; and God said, *"Let the earth bring forth grass, the herb that yields seed, and the fruit tree that yields fruit according to its kind, whose seed is in itself, on the earth,"* it was so. All the plants, people, and all the things in the universe came to exist through the creation of Jesus Christ.

The amazing thing is that this Creator God came to this earth. The reason that Jesus came to this earth was to allow each of us to receive the eternal life of the remission of sins by giving us the gospel of the water and the Spirit, which is the true light of salvation. So, John the Apostle testified about Jesus, *"That was the true Light which gives light to every man coming into the world. He was in the world, and the world was made through Him, and the world did not know Him. He came to His own, and His own did not receive Him. But as many as received Him, to them He gave the right to become children of God, to those who believe in His name" (John1:9-12).* In other words, in order to blot out all our sins once and for all, including those that were inherited from the ancestors of the mankind, our Lord came to drive away the darkness of all sins by giving us the gospel of the water and the Spirit that is true light to this world.

Why People Refuse to Accept Jesus in Their Mind as the Savior?

Jesus, the King of kings did not come to this earth with attractive looks that would be welcomed by people. Many people refuse to accept Jesus Christ as their Savior because they do not throw away their fixed ideas. People live without knowing that they are still sinners and therefore are beings destined to hell. They have lived without realizing why they must believe in Jesus as their Savior and that they still don't know the gospel of the water and the Spirit. There are many people who don't know that Jesus Christ is the Son of God living on this earth. How ignorant are these people about the gospel of the water and the Spirit, and they do not even try to believe in Jesus who came by the water and the blood (1 John 5:6). They don't even recognize that they are sinners destined to hell for their sins. After all, they are not able to receive Jesus who came by the gospel of the water and the Spirit as their Savior because they do not know Him properly.

Jesus came to this earth as the Lord and Savior, but the Israelites and many sinners on earth did not accept Jesus Christ as their Savior. Though Jesus came to the land that He Himself created for His people, they still not accept and receive Jesus as their Savior. Jesus was born in Israel, in a small countryside village called Bethlehem. Jesus was born in a barn where the livestock were living; the reason He came was to save us, all of the lowly sinners of this world from sin. However, the sinners living in this world insisted to live in darkness by rejecting to receive Jesus and choosing to suffer for their sins. These people wanted to go to Heaven saved from their sins, but, because of their false knowledge and thoughts, they could not enter the line of people who received the salvation.

The Lord is the Savior who came to save all sinners from all the sins of the world. However, many people living in this world did not recognize that Jesus is the Savior. People in Jesus' time could not recognize that Jesus Christ was the Son of God and the Creator who created all the things of universe including them. That is why the Israelites and the Gentiles did not accept Jesus as their Savior.

So, we have to know the truth that Jesus Himself, at the age of 30, received the baptism to blot out the sins of mankind from John who was giving baptism at the Jordan River. We have to know why Jesus did so. Jesus had to receive the baptism to take all the sins of this world once and for all. His arrival on this earth was to cleanse all the evils and wrongdoings committed by all the sinners of all time.

Jesus commanded to John the Baptist at that time, *"Permit it to be so now, for thus it is fitting for us to fulfill all righteousness" (Matthew 3:15)*. This passage is the evidence that Jesus took the sins of the world by receiving the baptism from John the Baptist.

These words mean that it is ordained for Jesus to take the sins of all people by receiving the baptism and blotting out their sins once for all. Jesus said to John the Baptist, "I have to be baptized from you in order to take all the sins of the sinners and to save them. I must take all the sins that people are committing because of their weaknesses by receiving the baptism—the sins of the present, of the past, and all of the sins of the people who will be born until the day this earth stops to exist. Then, you John the Baptist obey my commandment and lay your hands on My head." So, to take the sins of mankind, Jesus received the baptism from John the Baptist, the representative of all mankind. Therefore, Jesus could cleanse the sins of mankind once and for all by receiving them through the baptism.

The baptism that Jesus received was as follows. It was performed in the same manner as the laying on of hands in the sacrificial rules of the Old Testament. God has set up this sacrificial system, and if its statutes were followed correctly, people of those days could pass their sins to a sacrificial animal, by the placing their hands on the animal's head. Then, the sacrificial animals had to be killed to draw their blood, and the people would burn their meat and fat on the altar and give it before God in place of their own death. This was how the people of the Old Testament could receive the remission of their sins.

Likewise, Jesus received the baptism from John the Baptist in order to take all the sins and the curses of all the people in this world. This is the Truth of Jesus' baptism that was revealed in the Word of the New Testament. Jesus received the baptism from John the Baptist to take all the sins of the Israelites once and for all like the Lamb in the Old Testament. That is why we had to be enlightened with Jesus' saying, *"Permit it to be so now, for thus it is fitting for us to fulfill all righteousness" (Matthew 3:15).*

Jesus is the true Savior to all mankind. Jesus has given the light of salvation with the gospel of the water and the Spirit to all mankind. The Lord is God of power and salvation. The Lord is God of mercy. Jesus has the power to save all the mankind from sin.

Jesus came to this world and shed the light of salvation on our minds. All of us cannot help but live in the dark world because of our sins. The Lord shed the true light of salvation in our minds with the gospel of the water and the Spirit. Jesus tells us, "I have taken your sins through the baptism. I have borne all the judgment of all the sins instead of you by shedding My blood on the Cross. I am your Savior. I have blotted out all your sins."

The Lord God lets us hear this beautiful and blessed news by shedding the true light in our dark minds. Jesus brightly illuminated our dark minds by giving us the delightful news of salvation that enables us to receive the remission of sins. Our Lord blotted out our sins clearly to transform us into sinless children of God. So, we can profess now, "Jesus became my Savior. Jesus blotted out all my sins."

Jesus gave the true light of salvation to all mankind. There is no true Savior in this world before or Jesus came. There has been no other Savior except Jesus Christ. No one could save the people in the world from the sins of this world. All people are unable to save themselves from their weaknesses, from their wrongdoings, from their sins, and from their eventual judgment. Therefore, it is only Jesus Christ who is able to save all the people from all their sins.

It is written in Isaiah 59:16,
"He saw that there was no man,
And wondered that there was no intercessor;
Therefore His own arm brought salvation for Him;
And His own righteousness, it sustained Him."

The Lord Himself planned the salvation of mankind, came to this earth to save all the sinners from their sins with the gospel Truth of the water and the Spirit. Thus, the Savior of mankind Jesus came as the Mediator between God and us, and He took all the sins of mankind on His body to break down the wall of sin that had separated God the Father from us. He took the judgment for all the sins of mankind by shedding His blood on the Cross, and then He rose again from the dead to give us new life. This righteous act was enough to give us the blessing to be called the children of God to all of us who believe in Jesus Christ as the true Savior. Our mind is pleased with the faith because our Lord came as the Savior with that kind of salvation.

We have to know that Jesus is our Savior through the gospel of the water and the Spirit. Jesus came to this earth to save us from the sins of the world. Jesus lowered Himself to human flesh, took all the sins of the world by receiving the baptism from John the Baptist, received the judgment by shedding His blood on the Cross, and therefore He fulfilled the salvation of mankind completely by rising again from the dead in three days. And, He is sitting on the right hand of the throne of God the Father still to this day. Now, whoever believes in the fact that Jesus is our Savior can become a child of God and enter the Kingdom of Heaven.

Now, whoever knows and believes that Jesus took our sins when He received the baptism from John the Baptist and that He has fulfilled all righteousness of God once and for all by shedding His blood, that person will receive the remission of sin, no matter how weak and deficient the person is, and no matter how many sins he has committed. It is the truth that you will be saved from all sin only if in your mind you believe in Jesus Christ who came by the gospel of the water and the Spirit.

We cannot enter the kingdom of heaven with money, but we can enter by believing in the gospel of the water and the Spirit. We become the righteous by believing in the gospel of the water and the Spirit in our hearts. By believing in the gospel of the water and the Spirit with our mind, we become the children of God and we can be blessed. That is why the only true Savior in this whole world is Jesus. The name Jesus means *'the one who will save His people from their sins' (Matthew 1:21)*. Therefore, the name Jesus Christ is most appropriate to He who is the Savior of mankind.

The same Jesus who came to this world, also is the very Lord who previously made man out of dust, and breathed into nostrils of Adam the breath of life to make him a living being. And the Lord also made Eve from a rib of Adam. Why did He make a woman and give her to Adam? It is to make us humans perfect.

I would like to teach you a funny thing. The Chinese character for person is "人(Ren)." This character is composed of two separated lines that imply two persons. If there is only one line "丿" in "人," it falls down. It cannot stand. Therefore, the fact that the Chinese character "人(Ren)" needs two lines means that two persons, a man and a woman, have to make one to become perfect. So, people say if a man marries a woman, he has become a complete person.

It is written, *"Therefore a man shall leave his father and mother and be joined to his wife, and they shall become one flesh" (Genesis 2:24).* This verse is talking about how a man and woman should marry and live happily together giving birth to their children. It is the standard that God has set for us. The Apostle Paul teaches us about the mystery of the marriage system, saying, *"This is a great mystery, but I speak concerning Christ and the church" (Ephesians 5:32).* God wants to cleanse us from all our sins to make us His bride and marry us. In short, God has set up the marriage system to help us understand His will toward us: He wants to make us righteous by blotting out all our sins so that we can live with Him in His Kingdom forever.

My fellow believers, can we go to Heaven our own actions? Can we go to Heaven by living virtuously? No. Even though these are complex questions, approach them as if you were a child. Children think in simple terms. That is why Jesus loved the children. Adults also must be simple like children to be blessed by God. Now, I ask you to be simple in answering the following questions.

My fellow believers, can a sinner enter Heaven? No. Whoever has sin in his or her heart will be cast down to hell. Is it possible for us not to commit sin even for one moment after we have born in this world? No. No person can prevent himself from committing sins. Then, is it possible for a person who committed a sin even one time to enter Heaven, or not? No, it is not possible. Then, it is only just that no one in this world should be allowed to enter Heaven.

Then, does that mean that there is no way to go to Heaven? No, it is does not. That is why the Savior is necessary for all of us. We can only go to Heaven through the Savior who saved us from all sins. So God made us, and He became a Man to blot out our sins after we had fallen into sin. Jesus is God Himself who came to this earth wearing the same body as us.

That Jesus has taken our sins, and the sins of all the people in this earth without any exception. Jesus was passed the sins of the world onto His body by receiving the baptism from John. Just as the High Priest of the Old Testament passed the sins of his people onto the scapegoat by imposing both his hands on the head of the sacrifice, John, the representative of mankind, laid his hands on the head of Jesus. Jesus commanded to John. "Permit it to be so now. I commend you. Pass the sins onto Me by imposing your hands on My head."

"The laying on of hands" means "to pass over." Jesus received the laying on of hands from John who is the representative of all mankind. The sins of the world passed onto Jesus at that exact time.

My fellow believers, even though you do not know what this thick Bible is all about, if you understand and accept the gospel of the water and the Spirit even in this short time, you can be saved from all your sins. I am preaching the core of salvation now with the gospel of the water and the Spirit. You will become the children of God by believing in the gospel of the water and the Spirit in your mind. Even if you have never given an offering, even if you have never done a good deed even once in your life you will go to Heaven by the faith of believing in the gospel of the water and the Spirit.

It is written, *"But as many as received Him, to them He gave the right to become children of God, to those who believe in His name" (John 1:12).* God gives the blessing of salvation to those who believe in the gospel of the water and the Spirit in their mind. God also blesses such people to be the children of God. We the sinners do not have any merits on our own; and it is just for me to go to hell after receiving the judgment. But God so loved us and He gave us His only begotten Son. His only Son came to this earth and took all our sins by receiving the baptism at the Jordan River and received all the judgment for our sins by shedding His blood on the Cross. And we are blessed to be the children of God by believing in this Truth. I wish for you to receive Jesus as your Savior by believing in the gospel of the water and the Spirit with your mind, and to be saved from the sins of the world.

How Do We Receive Jesus as Our Savior?

"But as many as received Him, to them He gave the right to become children of God, to those who believe in His name" (John 1:12). Have you received Him? Receiving someone is only possible when we know the visitor well. If someone knocks at the door outside, we say, "Who is it?" If that person is one of our acquaintances, we say and open the door widely, "What's up? Nice to see you. Come inside." This is how we receive our friends.

Even we haven't met Jesus personally, we can still receive Him in our hearts because we have come to know Him well through the gospel of the water and the Spirit. We know that Jesus has taken all our sins by receiving the baptism at the Jordan River. I can guarantee that you can receive the remission of your sins by doing so before God. I cannot guarantee things of this world, but I can guarantee your salvation, your going to Heaven, being blotted out of your sins, joining the righteous, becoming the children of God, receiving the eternal life, and receiving heavenly blessings. I can guarantee you all these wonderful things by believing in Jesus who received the baptism from John. With this faith, I can guarantee you that Jesus took not only your sins, but also the sins of your descendants, your ancestors, all the sins from Adam to the people who will be born until the last day of this earth.

Your heart is the most Holy Place where God can dwell. Receive the gospel of the water and the Spirit with the mind. Believe with your heart that Jesus is your Savior. I have nothing to be proud of by myself. However, the reason that I can bluster and be boastful sometimes is all because of the grace of Jesus and the gospel power of the water and the Spirit that Jesus has given me. Anyways, I truly wish for you to be the children of God today by believing in this in your own hearts.

You become a child of God only if you know and believe in the gospel Word of the water and the Spirit. You have to know the Truth of salvation correctly. If you believe in Jesus without knowing the Truth of salvation, you will end up becoming a hypocritical religionist. How many churches today are only intent on collecting money just like a corporate enterprise? There are rights and wrongs in Christianity doctrines. But, if you do not know the gospel Truth of the water and the Spirit but just believe in the doctrines of

Christianity, you cannot help but become a hypocritical religionist. I wish for you not to fall into these false doctrines of Christianity.

I am preaching the gospel of the water and the Spirit before God. I do not preach other things except the gospel of the water and the Spirit. It is clear that God wants to give; He does not want to receive from us. God gives us the salvation with the gospel of the water and the Spirit. He blots out our sins, allows us to be the children of God, gives the blessings of God, and He wants to give all these blessed things.

God blesses and saves us. We have to know this. I can guarantee your salvation before God without doubt. Jesus took all your sins when He received the baptism at the Jordan River, and He bore all the judgments and the punishments for the sins that you have committed in your lifetime on the Cross. And then He rose again from the dead in three days. He rose again from the grave and He sat at the right hand of the throne of God the Father.

My fellow believers, our Jesus is still alive. And He still looks for people to believe in Him by believing in the gospel of the water and the Spirit. Jesus is looking for the people who were born not of blood, not of the will of the flesh, or not of the will of man, but of God, and only of God. One cannot be saved because his father is an elder or a pastor. Even the son of a pastor cannot go to Heaven owing only to his faithful father. Anyone can be saved from sin and go to Heaven only when he believes in the gospel of the water and the Spirit in his mind and receives the remission of sins.

It is written, *"That was the true Light which gives light to every man coming into the world" (John 1:9).* If you receive the true Light, the darkness in your heart will fade away in no time, and you will become the children of Light. If you believe in your mind that Jesus came by the gospel of the water and the Spirit, you will be saved from all your sins without fail. I mean to say that Jesus came by the Savior for each one of us. Even though you do not know much about the Scriptures, you can be saved from your sins by believing in the fact that Jesus has taken all the sins of the world and thus He has fulfilled all the righteousness of God by receiving the baptism at the Jordan River. God remits our sins because we believe in the gospel of the water and the Spirit. I wish for you to believe in the gospel of the water and the Spirit. When Jesus was dying on the Cross, He said, *"It is finished!" (John 19:30)* I wish for you to believe this Word. He surely has completed all our salvation with His baptism and blood on the Cross.

We cannot see Jesus with our physical eyes. But we can believe in Him with our minds. Clearly before, there was pitch darkness in our mind. However, we came to escape from the darkness because someone has shined the true Light in our mind. This giver of Life is Jesus. We have to accept Jesus in our hearts knowing that fact.

And we also have to remember that we cannot live forever in this world. It is written, *"And as it is appointed for men to die once, but after this the judgment" (Hebrews 9:27).* We live for 70 to 80 years on average, and will die someday. Moses also declared,

"The days of our lives are seventy years;
And if by reason of strength they are eighty years,
Yet their boast is only labor and sorrow;
For it is soon cut off, and we fly away" (Psalm 90:10).

We will die someday. But it is not the end for us after that. There is God's judgment after our death and Heaven and hell await us after. Therefore, we have to receive the blessing of salvation while we are living on this earth by believing in Jesus and receiving Him with our mind. Only then, will there be no bad judgment for us on that day. And we will also be able to enjoy lots of blessings in this world. It is because God will change your mind and your family.

Someone might say, "Not me. I can't do it. I am not a person who will believe in Jesus. Why? A person like me must not be allowed believe in Jesus because I was born with the human nature of committing sins. The church will be ruined." Don't worry about it. Only if you believe in the fact that Jesus took all your sins and received the judgment for those sins, then Jesus will enter into your mind and change your sinful mind to the righteous and virtue-loving mind.

My fellow believer, I wish for you to entrust all your sins to Jesus. I wish for you to entrust God with your evil and weak mind that you cannot do anything about. If you entrust Him, He will take all your iniquities and weaknesses. It is because our Lord is an all-powerful God to whom nothing is impossible.

All of us have to live preparing in our mind to go to Heaven at any time while we are living in this world. After we have received the remission of sins with the gospel of the water and the Spirit we have rightly prepared to go to Heaven. And if we believe in Jesus, we will receive the heavenly blessings, not only the blessings this world, but also the blessings of the coming world. I also wish for you to know that God's grace does not end at your generation but it will be endowed to your children. If we believe in God, He protects us as our Shepherd. He protects us from the evil spirits so that they cannot touch us (1 John 5:18).

I thank Jesus that He became my Savior as well as your Savior. ✉

Who Is John the Baptist?

< John 1:19-42 >

"Now this is the testimony of John, when the Jews sent priests and Levites from Jerusalem to ask him, 'Who are you?' He confessed, and did not deny, but confessed, 'I am not the Christ.'

And they asked him, 'What then? Are you Elijah?' He said, 'I am not.'

'Are you the Prophet?'

And he answered, 'No.'

Then they said to him, 'Who are you, that we may give an answer to those who sent us? What do you say about yourself?'

He said: 'I am

'The voice of one crying in the wilderness:

'Make straight the way of the LORD,'

as the prophet Isaiah said.'

Now those who were sent were from the Pharisees. And they asked him, saying, 'Why then do you baptize if you are not the Christ, nor Elijah, nor the Prophet?'

John answered them, saying, 'I baptize with water, but there stands One among you whom you do not know. It is He who, coming after me, is preferred before me, whose sandal strap I am not worthy to loose.'

These things were done in Bethabara beyond the Jordan, where John was baptizing.

The next day John saw Jesus coming toward him, and said, 'Behold! The Lamb of God who takes away the sin of the world! This is He of whom I said, 'After me comes a

Man who is preferred before me, for He was before me.' I did not know Him; but that He should be revealed to Israel, therefore I came baptizing with water.'

And John bore witness, saying, 'I saw the Spirit descending from heaven like a dove, and He remained upon Him. I did not know Him, but He who sent me to baptize with water said to me, 'Upon whom you see the Spirit descending, and remaining on Him, this is He who baptizes with the Holy Spirit.' And I have seen and testified that this is the Son of God.'

Again, the next day, John stood with two of his disciples. And looking at Jesus as He walked, he said, 'Behold the Lamb of God!'

The two disciples heard him speak, and they followed Jesus. Then Jesus turned, and seeing them following, said to them, 'What do you seek?

They said to Him, 'Rabbi' (which is to say, when translated, Teacher), 'where are You staying?'

He said to them, 'Come and see.' They came and saw where He was staying, and remained with Him that day (now it was about the tenth hour).

One of the two who heard John speak, and followed Him, was Andrew, Simon Peter's brother. He first found his own brother Simon, and said to him, 'We have found the Messiah' (which is translated, the Christ). And he brought him to Jesus.

Now when Jesus looked at him, He said, 'You are Simon the son of Jonah. You shall be called Cephas' (which is translated, A Stone)."

Through today's Scripture passage, especially verses from

20 to 31 John the Baptist bore witness to himself and Jesus. Before baptizing Jesus, John the Baptist testified, *"I baptize with water, but there stands One among you whom you do not know. It is He who, coming after me, is preferred before me, whose sandal strap I am not worthy to loose" (John 1:26-27)*. He also witnessed that his ministry was to reveal Jesus Christ to Israel by saying, *"I did not know Him; but that He should be revealed to Israel, therefore I came baptizing with water."*

In order to witness that Jesus Christ was truly the Messiah, the Savior whom all the people of Israel had been waiting for, John the Baptist gave people the baptism of repentance, and he also baptized Jesus at the Jordan River. After giving the baptism to Jesus, he also testified that Jesus is the Son of God, saying, *"I did not know Him, but He who sent me to baptize with water said to me, 'Upon whom you see the Spirit descending, and remaining on Him, this is He who baptizes with the Holy Spirit.' And I have seen and testified that this is the Son of God" (John 1:33-34)*.

Actually, John the Baptist knew about Jesus from the beginning. When the priests and Levites were provoking a quarrel with him, John the Baptist bore witness to Jesus Christ. He witnessed that "Jesus Christ, He is the Savior that all the people of Israel have been waiting for, and He is the Savior of all humankind." Also, he gave witness to them about Jesus Christ by saying, "Having seen the Spirit descending upon His head, I knew He is the Son of God."

But, among the Pharisees, there wasn't anyone who could understand the things that John the Baptist was preaching about. It was because these people fundamentally thought that Jesus was neither the Son of God nor the Messiah. However, whether they did or did not believe, John's witness about Jesus continued on. The next day of Jesus' baptism, as John the

Baptist was standing with two of his disciples, upon seeing Jesus passing by, he witnessed by saying, *"Behold! The Lamb of God who takes away the sin of the world!" (John 1:29)* His account was true because he had transferred all the sins of humankind by baptizing Jesus Christ. When Jesus came to John to be baptized, John was at a loss about what to do at first. But, Jesus ordered him, *"Permit it to be so now, for thus it is fitting for us to fulfill all righteousness," (Matthew 3:15)* and John then laid his both hands on the head of Jesus to pass over all the sins of the world according to His command. Then, he bore witness to Jesus Christ as the Savior of humankind who has taken on the sins of the world. This means that he is the servant of God who had transferred the sins of the world to Jesus Christ. Through this witness given by John the Baptist, we have come to know that Jesus is the Lamb of God who has taken all the sins of the world.

As such, John the Baptist bore witness to Jesus and His ministry for us as well as to himself. When John the Baptist was willing to bear witness to Jesus, it happened to be that Jesus was about to pass by John the Baptist, who was standing with two of his disciples. Then, he witnessed to them saying, *"Behold! The Lamb of God!"(John 1:29)* He testified that this man, Jesus Christ, is precisely the Lamb of God. Due to his witness, two of John the Baptist's disciples followed Him and became disciples of Jesus.

After that, Andrew brought his brother Peter to Jesus, and Peter also became a disciple of Jesus. And the following day, Jesus met Phillip who also became one of His disciples, then Phillip went to Nathanael and said, *"We have found Him of whom Moses in the law, and also the prophets, wrote—Jesus of Nazareth, the son of Joseph."* And Nathanael said to him, *"Can anything good come out of Nazareth?"* Philip requested

Nathanael to *"Come and see" (John 1:46)*.

As Nathanael was coming toward Him, Jesus spoke of him, *"Behold, an Israelite indeed, in whom is no guile!" (John 1:47)* Nathanael was surprised to hear these words. He said, "Well, who would know everything inside of me? How do you know me? You truly are the Son of God. And, you are the King of Israel." Then, Jesus said to him, *"Most assuredly, I say to you, hereafter you shall see heaven open, and the angels of God ascending and descending upon the Son of Man" (John 1:51)*.

As such, John the Apostle also went on to say that Jesus is Messiah the Savior, as was written by the prophets of the Old Testament. Because God had the Savior of humankind born from the body of a woman and also, because he had sent Him to us as promised, Jesus Christ was more than sufficient to be proclaimed as the Savior of humankind, the Son of God, and the Creator who created the entire universe and all the things in it. Jesus Christ was the Son of God and the Savior of humankind.

Therefore, even if we has nothing else in our hearts, there has to be the faith of believing in the baptism that Jesus Christ received from John the Baptist and the blood of the Cross. Even if we don't have any material, power, or prestige of this world, we must have the faith of believing in the baptism that Jesus had received and His blood shed on the Cross. Why is this so? It is because by believing that Jesus Christ received the baptism by John the Baptist and shed His blood, we attain the faith which brings true cleansing of our sins.

When our Lord came to this earth, He was born in a barn and laid at the manger of a stable, but why was He born there? It was because there was no place to stay, for there were too many guests at places like hotel or inn where people usually eat and sleep. This means that if people keep so many things in their hearts, they actually lack room in their hearts to receive Jesus. Jesus has to be seated at the center of everyone's heart, but people usually fill their hearts with the things of this world. Therefore, they have no place in their hearts to invite Jesus to stay.

Dear fellow believers, do you think we could be well off without Jesus in our soul? If we have some necessities of life, we could go on living in this world on a basic level. However, if we did not have the faith of believing in the baptism that Jesus Christ has received and the blood shed for your life, as well as mine, what would happen? If this were the case, your life, as well as mine would be nothing. Even if we have everything that is needed for our flesh, our souls will wither away and die if we do not have the faith in the baptism that Jesus had received and the blood that He has shed on the Cross.

Jesus Christ is God, the Son of God, the Creator of all things of the universe, and our Savior. He has saved those of us who believe in the gospel of the water and the Spirit from worldly sins by taking our sins once and for all by receiving the baptism, going to the Cross, and vicariously dying on the Cross. Jesus is our Savior who has carried away the sins of this world. We must go on living by faith embracing Jesus Christ who came by the water and the Spirit in our hearts. Even if you and I have nothing else, we must go on living with one single Person in our hearts, Jesus. If we go on living our lives with Jesus Christ in our hearts, then He will provide us with things that we lack. Just as our Lord did miraculous works at a wedding in Cana, He will provide you with the Word of truth and other necessities that you need to live. But, if you go on living without the Lord within your hearts, He will not be able to help you when you are in a time of need.

Therefore, through the work of John the Baptist, we must learn how we must live before God by faith, and also how to believe in Jesus Christ. Although we are living in this declining and complex world, we must go on living by having faith in the gospel Word of the water and the Spirit. We must know what kind of life is wise and blissful to live before God. God wants us to live with the gospel of the water and the Spirit in the center of our hearts.

Through the witness of John the Baptist, you and I now are able to believe that Jesus has become our Savior by fulfilling the gospel of the water and the Spirit. If we were to disregard John the Baptist's role and his ministry, would we have been able to know the great secret of salvation hidden in the gospel of the water and the Spirit? Have we ever seen Jesus with our bodily eyes? Are you able to see Jesus taking on your sins once and for all by receiving the baptism with your eyes of the flesh? We have not been able to see these physically. Nevertheless, by the written Word of God, we are able to fully see that Jesus is our Savior.

Let us read the Gospel of John chapter 1 verses 6 and 7: *"There was a man sent from God, whose name was John. This man came for a witness, to bear witness of the Light, that all through him might believe."*

By these words, John the Baptist bears witness to the truth that Jesus is our Savior. The Bible had foretold John the Baptist as the one who would properly bear witness to Jesus. People today who believe in Jesus as the Savior are able to find out the true salvation through the ministry of John the Baptist and the account of the baptism that Jesus received from John the Baptist. Therefore, we have to know the ministry of John the Baptist and the account of the baptism that Jesus had received from John the Baptist as it is written in the Scriptures. And so, we must believe in the fact that the Lord has remitted us from all sins by the gospel of the water and the Spirit.

Unfortunately, most people continue to be unaware of the power of Jesus' baptism and His blood. We see people putting efforts into boasting of their own righteousness, without even knowing the significance of Jesus receiving the baptism from John the Baptist. They only try to raise their own righteousness. Sometimes, with Jesus as the pretext, they try to exalt their righteousness even higher. Therefore, they become separated from God even when they profess Jesus as their Savior.

"There was a man sent from God, whose name was John. This man came for a witness, to bear witness of the Light, that all through him might believe" (John 1:6-7).

God the Father sent a servant who would witness that His Son Jesus is the One who would save all the sinners, and that servant was John the Baptist. John the Baptist was the witness to salvation who could bear witness to Jesus as the Savior. We, who have received the witness of John the Baptist, are the disciples of Jesus who also have to witness to others that Jesus is the Savior who came into this world by the gospel of the water and the Spirit.

However, many people still say that John the Baptist was a failure. The reason is they misinterpret the context and meaning of Matthew 11:2-3, by concluding that John the Baptist doubted Jesus was Messiah. Did John really doubt Jesus when he sent his disciples to Jesus? No, absolutely not. John the Baptist was eager to send his disciples to Jesus, saying, *"He must increase, but I must decrease" (John 3:30),* and he actually sent his disciples to Jesus one by one. Then, who were those who still remained beside him until he had finished his ministry? They were followers who were reluctant to believe his witness about Jesus to the end.

If we were to disregard the witness of the baptism that John the Baptist had given to Jesus, how would we be able to realize the gospel Truth of the water and the Spirit? Without the gospel Truth of the water and the Spirit, how would we be able to believe in Jesus as our Savior? If we are to believe in the gospel of the water and the Spirit, we must first believe that John the Baptist is the servant of God who was promised to precede the Messiah in the Old Testament. With this faith, we can believe in all the testimony of John the Baptist. Only then can we believe in the Savior by seeing the baptism to Jesus, the vicarious death of Jesus on the Cross, and the resurrection of the Lord.

Dear fellow believers, if so called servants of God today were to refuse the witness of John the Baptist and Jesus, their followers would never be able to know the gospel of the water and the Spirit. We see that certain ministers today try to fulfill their own objectives by emptying the pockets of their church members. Such places where people gather should not be called a true church. These people do not know the true ministry of John the Baptist or that of Jesus. Yet, how could they know about the gospel Truth of the water and the Spirit? These ministers today are liars if they do not believe and bear witness to the truth that Jesus has come by the gospel of the water and the Spirit.

We have to know about John the Baptist well. In Matthew 11:11, it is said, *"Assuredly, I say to you, among those born of women there has not risen one greater than John the Baptist."* Truly, Elijah, who was prophesized in the Old Testament to come again before the Lord, is John the Baptist in the New Testament era (Malachi 4:1-3, Matthew 11:14). This is because John the Baptist completed the mission of Elijah of the Old Testament. Such a faithful servant of God was John the Baptist, and he had the true heart of a servant of God. John the Baptist, the servant of God, did the good work of giving Jesus a baptism, that is, the work that Jesus had to bear in order to save sinners from sins by the gospel of the water and the Spirit (Matthew 3:13-17).

Let us read together the Gospel of John chapter 1 verses 9 through 11. *"That was the true Light which gives light to every man who comes into the world. He was in the world, and the world was made through Him, and the world did not know Him. He came to His own, and His own did not receive Him."*

The true Light, that is, the light that shines upon every man by coming into the world refers to Jesus. It is said that Jesus is the true God, who came to this earth in human flesh, and He is the true Light of salvation. These words, "the true Light," means that Jesus is God, Jesus is the God of salvation, Jesus is the Master of life, and Jesus is the Savior who has saved us from the sins of the world.

John the Apostle continues to witness, *"That was the true Light which gives light to every man who comes into the world. He was in the world, and the world was made through Him"* *(John 1:9-10).* This universe was made by Jesus. This universe wasn't made through human beings. It didn't appear naturally, contrary to the evolutionists' claim. Never did this universe come into being in an evolutionary manner.

People of Israel did not believe in Jesus as God, the Son of God, or the Savior who came by the water and the Spirit. Of course, it is not the case that everyone did not believe, but many people did not believe in Jesus Christ as their Savior. Thus, God abandoned them for some time because they did not believe in the Savior of humankind. And because of their sins, they were put to death, and they had to live in agony as international orphans for nearly two thousand years. Captured by German Nazis, millions of Jews had died in gas chambers. It was because of just one reason that they did not believe in Jesus to be their Messiah, as well as God.

Because they did not know or believe the true identity of Jesus, not only did they not accept Jesus, but also they captured and handed over Jesus to Roman soldiers to crucify Him. All the more, they cried out to crucify Him. "Crucify Him! Crucify Him! He says that He is God. Such a man must be crucified!" At the time, when Pilate, the governor of Jews, tried Jesus, he found no guilt in Him. Even so, people shouted out loud to crucify Him. Just as the crowd shouted out those words, the governor Pilate washed his hands and said, *"I am innocent of the blood of this just Person" (Matthew 27:24)*. Pilate meant, "I have no choice but to crucify this innocent Jesus, for you request the crucifixion of Him obstinately." Because the people of Israel, in a voice even louder asked for Jesus' death, and said, *"His blood be on us and on our children," (Matthew 27:25)* they received the consequence of their actions in the future.

According to those words, the land of Israel was burnt to the ground completely and the people were sold as slaves in AD 70 by Titus, the Roman general. Although they resisted the Roman Empire and started independence movements during those times, General Titus of Rome took his army there and killed many people, regardless of age or sex. Also, he destroyed completely all the buildings of the Temple of God, and he even dug up and scattered the foundations of the Temple. In doing so, he destroyed the faith of all Israelites and eliminated every single ritual that they once performed. Furthermore, he scattered the people of Israel all over the Mediterranean world. And that is why the Jews have been living scattered all over the world.

Due to their sins of standing against God and not

believing in Jesus as God and their Savior, they suffered massacre by the Nazi army, and they have lived so miserably, scattered all over the world. This is because of the sin they committed of not accepting Jesus Christ, who is the true life, as their Savior. Even now, those who do not accept the true Light will suffer from the same consequence.

Even among the Christians, there are those who have been ruined. Why have they become so? It was because they did not believe fundamentally in Jesus who has come by the gospel of the water and the Spirit. Also, they have suffered such exploitation and have fallen into a truly blind faith because they did not believe in the witness given by John the Baptist, and they had professed that John the Baptist had failed. Most importantly, they have suffered because they did not believe Jesus to be the true Savior who blotted out our sins completely with the gospel of the water and the blood.

We must believe that Jesus is the true God, the true Savior, and the One who gives true life. We must surely know and believe the fact that the number of Saviors of sinners in this universe is only one, Jesus. No matter how great and competent a person may be, that person can never be able to save anyone from all sins. No matter how holy a pastor may be, without the gospel of the water and the Spirit, the pastor cannot save even a single person from sin. You can receive salvation only by believing in Jesus who has come by the gospel of the water and the Spirit. And you can believe this Truth only when you accept the witness of John the Baptist to Jesus Christ. It means that there is no other way to salvation, except through the gospel of the water and the Spirit.

Let us read the Gospel of John chapter 1 verse 12. *"But as many as received Him, to them He gave the right to become children of God, even to those who believe in His name."* Jesus has saved those of us who believe in Him, that He came to this earth in the flesh of man, took on all the sins of humankind once and for all through the baptism received from John, shed all His blood having both of His hands and feet nailed to the Cross, and gave up His life on our behalf as the judgment for our sins. To those of us who believe in Jesus, God gave us the right to become His children. But you have to pay attention to the words, *"But as many as received Him."* Whoever accepts Jesus and believes in Him with thanksgiving can be a child of God for free, but if anyone does not do so, the person will be condemned.

For you to be able to hear the Word of God is something truly great. It is a great blessing before God for you to be able to hear the Word of God in this hour of service. There are great many treasures within this Bible Word. The Word of God is so beautiful that nothing can compare with it. Even masterpieces such as the works of Shakespeare of England are not comparable to it. When we eager to listen to His Word with a believing heart, these Bible scriptures can fulfill our ears, our thoughts, our hearts, our souls, and even our bodies. However, in believing the gospel of the water and the Spirit, there is this provision, 'only those who receive Him.'

Then, what does it mean to receive, that is, to accept Jesus Christ who has come by the gospel of the water and the Spirit? It means for us to believe and accept in our hearts that Jesus is God, the Creator, the Savior who has saved us from sins, and the Lamb who has received and taken on the judgment for the sake of our sins. Our Lord gives the right to become children of God to those who accept the salvation of Jesus by believing in the Word of Truth, which says that our Lord has come to this earth and saved us by the water and the blood. Those who receive God's gospel of the water and the Spirit become filled with the blessing of the remission of all sins and other heavenly treasures.

The word, 'Jesus,' means 'Savior.' To those who truly believe the Truth that Jesus has saved us, our Lord gave the right to become the children of God. By believing in the name of Jesus, one is able to receive the right to become a child of God.

Now, let us read the Gospel of John, chapter 1 verse 12 and 13. *"But as many as received Him, to them He gave the right to become children of God, to those who believe in His name: who were born, not of blood, nor of the will of the flesh, nor of the will of man, but of God."*

Dear fellow believers, many people think that one would one would unconditionally receive salvation if the person believes in Jesus somehow. They hold fast onto the Bible passage, *"Whoever calls on the name of the LORD shall be saved" (Romans 10:13).* Others believe that they will be saved if they believe the doctrines of their denomination, and yet others argue that by relying on Calvin's doctrine of predestination one cannot be convinced of one's salvation until the person stands before God.

But, it is written, *"Who were born, not of blood, nor of the will of the flesh, nor of the will of man, but of God."* What people say is not important. What the Bible says is important.

"In the beginning was the Word, and the Word was with God, and the Word was God" (John 1:1). The Word itself is God. If we believe God's Word before God, we get to receive salvation. I mean that the Word itself is God, and therefore, if we believe in it as it is written, we are allowed to receive salvation from all sins before God. People who have received salvation from sins are not born of the will of a human. And, only those who believe in the Truth of salvation that was

spoken by God get to receive salvation. To be born of the will of man means to try to become born again by relying on one's own denomination or by provoking the will of one's own flesh and emotions.

Certain hair-raising feelings, the speaking of tongues, and vibrations in the body, are all things that you get when you pray, and are examples of human emotions. We receive salvation neither by desires of the flesh nor by blood lineage. It is never the case that we arrive at salvation on our own accord just because we are pastors or because we are the children of a pastor. No matter position, class, gender, or age, salvation is something individual, and no matter who you are, you have to accept the Word of God to receive true salvation. Only those who believe in the fact that Jesus is God, the Son of God, and their Savior and that Jesus has saved them by the water and the blood, receive the right to become the children of God.

Christianity today is moving in the direction of provoking the will of the flesh. People today who do not believe in the gospel of the water and the Spirit are like that. Thus, the hour of service gets very noisy. These people, speaking with tongues, only disturb others' ears. What do these people try to do with the gift of tongues and the abilities that they receive from God? They try to make money or exalt themselves. That is why, in this day and age, we must spread the gospel of the water and the Spirit in the language of people of every nation.

If one becomes a pastor, a deacon, or an elder, without the gospel of the water and the Spirit, it is the case that the person has believed in Jesus according to his desires of the flesh. They are proud of their duties and pretend to have received the remission of sin without knowing the gospel Truth. Even if your son were ordained, he would not be able to receive salvation from sins without the knowledge of the gospel of the water and the Spirit. It is absolutely useless to lead a life of faith without having first received the remission of sins by believing in the gospel of the water and the Spirit. Our true Truth of salvation comes only from the gospel of the water and the Spirit.

The salvation that God gives us is not of the will of the flesh nor of the will of man, nor of blood. It is only of the faith of believing in the gospel Word of the water and the Spirit, which is God's Truth. Is your faith based on the gospel of the water and the Spirit? These Bible scriptures testify that the gospel of the water and the Spirit is the only and original gospel. The Truth recorded in the Bible states that Jesus Christ has come by the gospel of the water and the Spirit and this Truth has not changed for thousands of years.

It is reported that over 90% of the remarkable scientists of the modern world history believe that these Bible scriptures are the Word of God. As you may know, Isaac Newton, one of the greatest scientists of world history, was a faithful believer in this Bible. If one wants to be a man of success or a man of value, the person has to know and accept the Word of God, for it is the Truth itself and it gives us wisdom and insight (Proverbs 1:2). Only through the Word of God, are we able to hear God's voice and know His will, and also, we are able to know and believe in the Savior who has come by the gospel of the water and the Spirit.

Let us look at John 1:14. It is said, *"And the Word became flesh and dwelt among us, and we behold His glory, the glory as of the only begotten of the Father, full of grace and truth."*

The fact that the Word became flesh means that God who had created us came into this world as a human being. And it means that all the people on this earth are able to meet Jesus through the Word of God. Upon seeing Jesus, John, who had seen and touched Him with his eyes and hands (1 John 1:1), said that He was full of grace and truth. It means that we get to see the glory of God through Jesus, who is the incarnation of the glory of God. We get to see the glory of God through Jesus. Through the Bible scriptures, we are able to see how Jesus has saved us from sins, and we see that He has saved us by receiving the baptism from John, then vicariously dying on the Cross, and finally resurrecting from the dead. We are able to see how righteous and full of love the grace of God is. Jesus Christ is the Master of love who has saved us from sins unconditionally. Through Jesus, God has shown us all the glory of His divine power and how just and merciful He is. Jesus Christ was full of grace and truth.

We have come to receive salvation from all sins by believing in the gift of salvation from Jesus Christ, who has come by the water and the Spirit. The truth that our Lord has saved you from sins is the greatest gift in the world. Just as the word 'grace' means to be thankful, the grace of salvation is a gift that God gave to us without price. Jesus Christ has saved us from the sins of the world once and for all by being born on this earth, receiving the baptism from John the Baptist, shedding His blood, and resurrecting from the dead. This is God's grace of salvation. God has given to you and me the gift of salvation from the sins of the world, which enables us to be born again. By spreading the gospel of the water and the Spirit throughout the entire world, God has bestows His grace of salvation to all living creatures.

The gospel of the water and the Spirit is the only Truth of salvation in this world. This Truth blankets the world with salvation and fills it with the grace of God. This Truth of salvation, which has not left us the least bit in want, is something that was accomplished according to the promises of the Old Testament. And, it has allowed anyone that believes in their heart in Jesus Christ, who has come by the gospel of the water and the Spirit, to receive full salvation from all sins. After believing in this gospel of the water and the Spirit, there is no concern for us to become a sinner once again due to our weakness. If we truly believe in this gospel Word of the water and the Spirit, we are blessed to receive full salvation through Jesus Christ and His Truth. Through this Truth, not only do we fully become the children of God, but also, we fully become just. And, we get to receive His abundant blessings.

Let us look at John chapter 1 verse 16. *"And of His fullness we have all received, and grace for grace."* You who believe in the gospel of the water and the Spirit are now complete in Jesus, and should feel no spiritual thirst. Jesus is your Savior. Jesus is the Son of God. Jesus is the Creator of the universe and all things in it. Would the One who has completely built the universe be in want of anything? Jesus, our Savior who came to save us from sins, is the One who has created the entire visible and invisible world; humans, animals, plants, angels and all spiritual beings.

"And of His fullness we have all received, and grace for grace" *(John 1:16)*. The entire Bible talks about no other Messiah other than Jesus. In the Bible, a great deal of Jesus' ministry is described, but only a little is shown about the ministry of God the Father, as well as the Holy Spirit. It is certain that people get to salvation from sins through Jesus, the Savior, and because of this, the Bible places relative importance on Jesus Christ. It is said that, through Jesus, God the Father made all creations and saved you and me from the sins of the world. Because Jesus is the Omnipotent God, it was sufficient enough for Him to save humans from sins. For us to receive salvation from the sins of the world is the gift of

salvation given to us from Jesus.

Now, let us look at the Gospel of John chapter 1 verse 17. *"For the law was given through Moses, but grace and truth came through Jesus Christ."* The Law that God gave to humankind was given through Moses. But, the true Life, the true Way, and the real Truth of salvation came through Jesus Christ. He said, *"I am the way, the truth, and the life. No one comes to the Father except through Me" (John 14:6).* The true Way to our salvation came through Jesus Christ.

Through Moses, God's Law entered into this world, but Moses could not save us with that Law. The Law shows us how lacking our actions are and what grave sinners we are. However, Jesus Christ came to this earth with the Truth, the true salvation, and the Life. The reason why Jesus Christ came to this earth was to save you and me, and He did save us. It is written that the law was given through Moses, but the truth came through Jesus Christ. There is no other true Savior, except Jesus. Except for God, there can be no one else who could truly be the Savior of humankind. There can be no one else.

In the future, our world will be under a situation where hostile policies against Christianity prevail. If that happens, people who believe in Jesus will be under great persecution. Even so, the fact that only Jesus is the God of salvation and the one true Savior and will not change, and our faith will therefore be unfailing. And yet, some "Christian authorities" say that there is salvation in other religions, but in fact they are wolves and robbers, who just exploit the money of their followers. Only Jesus has saved you and me from our sins and the sins of all humanity. Do you believe that only Jesus is our true Savior?

We must only believe in the one and only God, Jesus, and His Word. When we preach a sermon, we must deliver the

Word spoken by Jesus. People speak of what Socrates is like, what Hegel is like, what Kant is like, and what Confucius or Mencius said. But, do these figures have something to do with your salvation? No, absolutely not. If possible, it is better not to speak such things in the hour of sermon. This hour of sermon is a time to preach the Word of God, and it would be useless and even evil to preach anything else besides the Word of God. If others were to preach words or long to listen to words that stand against the Word of God in God's Church, these people would be going against God, and they would become enemies of God.

We have received salvation by believing in Jesus. And many people who haven't yet received salvation must listen to and believe in the gospel Word of the water and the Spirit. Our thoughts and hearts become clean only when we believe in the Word of God. If we were to interpret the Word of God in a worldly perspective, there would be no benefit for us at all. Humans can tolerate people's words, but when we view it in connection to our souls, such human thoughts we cannot simply tolerate. It is because human thoughts can block or degrade Jesus' Words.

Dear fellow believers, although we may change, the gospel of the water and the Spirit given by Jesus will never change. Jesus is the absolute Savior, and the Word spoken by Jesus will stay forever until the end of the world. The Lord said, *"For assuredly, I say to you, till heaven and earth pass away, one jot or one tittle will by no means pass from the law till all is fulfilled" (Matthew 5:18).* And for this reason, we must believe in the Word of God, and believe and spread the gospel Word of the water and the Spirit. Also, we must cherish this Word of the water and the Spirit within our hearts.

We must not keep a single piece of dirty dreg, which is of

human thought, inside our heads and hearts. We have received salvation by believing in the gospel of the water and the Spirit and the truth that Jesus is the true Savior and that Jesus is the true God. We believe that Jesus is the true God and the true Savior. We must continue to believe in the gospel of the water and the Spirit until we meet the Lord. ✉

CHAPTER 2

We Are Happy If We Accept Jesus into Our Hearts

< John 2:1-11 >

"On the third day there was a wedding in Cana of Galilee, and the mother of Jesus was there. Now both Jesus and His disciples were invited to the wedding. And when they ran out of wine, the mother of Jesus said to Him, 'They have no wine.' Jesus said to her, 'Woman, what does your concern have to do with Me? My hour has not yet come.' His mother said to the servants, 'Whatever He says to you, do it.' Now there were set there six waterpots of stone, according to the manner of purification of the Jews, containing twenty or thirty gallons apiece. Jesus said to them, 'Fill the waterpots with water.' And they filled them up to the brim. And He said to them, 'Draw some out now, and take it to the master of the feast.' And they took it. When the master of the feast had tasted the water that was made wine, and did not know where it came from (but the servants who had drawn the water knew), the master of the feast called the bridegroom. And he said to him, 'Every man at the beginning sets out the good wine, and when the guests have well drunk, then the inferior. You have kept the good wine until now!' This beginning of signs Jesus did in Cana of Galilee, and manifested His glory; and His disciples believed in Him."

The One We Should Invite into Our Lives without Fail

There is a small town called Cana in the Galilees. Today's Scripture passage talks about a wedding that was held in Cana, Jesus performed the miracle of turning water into wine.

When we speak of weddings in our lives, it reminds us of the happiest moment of our lives. How does a newly married couple feel when a man and a woman come to marry each other? They surely feel happy. Today's Scripture passage describes an event during a wedding feast, and it teaches us what we need to believe in order to have true happiness in front of God. I would like to share what we need to believe in the correct things in order to be as happy as we are at weddings.

Among those who were invited to the wedding ceremony were Jesus and His mother. Now, what kind of faith do we need, if our lives are to be truly blessed?

First, we need to know how God has worked through Mary by His providence. We need to consider Mary in our faith. That is, because Mary had borne and given birth to the baby Jesus from her virgin body by earlier accepting the Word of God brought to her by God's angel. This means that the begotten Jesus is not a mere creature but the Savior God, who came to deliver sinners from all their sins. Mary was used as a means for God to come into this world in the flesh of a man. This was prophesized in Isaiah 7:14. *"Therefore the Lord Himself will give you a sign: Behold, the virgin shall conceive and bear a Son, and shall call His name Immanuel."*

We must know that Jesus is the Son of God, that is, God Himself. Thus, Jesus is not another human creature like us but God, who created the universe and everything in it. To deliver us all from all our sins, Jesus came to this world as the Son of

God, the true God, and the Savior. We must first have the faith that Jesus is not a simply man but God Himself.

Only when we believe in Jesus as God and the Savior can our souls be happy and delightful, free from the problem of sin. Therefore, we must acknowledge and believe that Jesus is our Savior and that He is the Son of God. Furthermore we should listen to and believe the gospel Truth of the water and the Spirit, which states that our Lord came to this world and blotted out all of our sins. Just as Jesus and His disciples were invited to the wedding, we need to invite the gospel of the water and the Spirit into our hearts.

Our lives are full of shame and unhappiness because of our sins. In this world and the world to come, sin is what makes a person most miserable. The sins people commit before God are the primary reasons for their unhappiness. As a matter of fact, because of the sins of people, all kinds of curses, illnesses, and other misfortunes befall on them. Therefore, we must believe in Jesus. In order to live our lives with blessings, we must believe that Jesus is our true Savior. We have to believe in our hearts the Truth that our Lord Jesus came to this world in order to terminate all sins of humanity. For that purpose, Jesus received the baptism and shed His blood. Through His baptism and bloodshed, all our sins are completely washed away.

Those who know that Jesus is God borne of Mary and believe in Him as one's perfect personal Savior are happy. The hearts of those who have truly received the remission of sin by their knowledge and faith in the Word of God are as though they are always present at a wedding feast. Also, they have become the children of God and have happiness in their hearts.

If a person wants to live a happy life and a joyful life, there is someone he must invite into his life. That person is none other than Jesus Christ, who came by the water, the blood, and the Holy Spirit (1 John 5:6-8). We need to have faith in our hearts that Jesus' gospel of the water and the Spirit is the Truth. We must believe that Jesus has indeed borne all our sins by the water and that He has blotted out all our sins completely with His blood. Our lives know happiness and joy, when we know and believe in that Jesus as our Savior.

Jesus Has Solved All the Problems of Our Life

In our passage today, all the wine was consumed by the middle of the wedding feast at Cana, and Jesus solved this problem. Just like the wedding could continue without a hiccup due to wine shortage because Jesus was invited to the wedding, our lives can be happy because Jesus is with us.

Those who have invited Jesus are the ones who have accepted Jesus and believe in Him. These people have happiness like guests at a wedding banquet. Our Lord has indeed blotted out all our sins completely. Jesus has sufficiently delivered us from all our sins by bearing all our sins by the water and the blood. Because Jesus has become our true Savior, those who believe in this Truth are happy. Thus, there is happiness in our lives and joy in our hearts. Also, we can keep our composure living in this sinful world. Out of happiness and joy, we can share the gospel with others and invite them to share the joy.

Isn't it because we have joy in us that we are able to invite others? If we weren't joyful and rather full of sadness, could we invite others? Truly, those who have met the Lord can invite others to the Lord. Also, those who are able to give something good are able to preach the gospel, which is a very good thing as well. Thus, for us to be happy, we need to first have Jesus in our hearts. We must believe in Jesus, who has blotted out all our sins by the water and the blood.

And if we truly desire to be happy, not only should we have Jesus in our hearts but also have His disciples there as well. Who else should we invite after meeting with Jesus? We must also invite His disciples. They are the followers of the Lord in the church of God. When those disciples are present, we are happy and joyful. Unless our hearts are with the disciples, we cannot be happy.

The host of the wedding invited Jesus, Mary, and Jesus' disciples. The host was able to take care of the all the problems through Jesus, Mary, and the disciples. If the host of the wedding had not invited these three kinds of people, this wedding at Cana might have become the most dreadful wedding ever. In my life and yours, we must also invite all three types of people.

Jesus is the Son of God. He is not a mere human. He is the Creator of the universe and everything in it. He who has created the mountains, the heavens and the earth, and all the animals in the nature was none other than Jesus. The word Jesus means the Savior, and the word Christ means the King of kings. Put together, this means that God has come as our Savior. To invite Jesus in our hearts, we must believe that Jesus is the Son of God, and that He is the Savior, who has blotted out all our sins. And we must be with the disciples of Jesus in order to be happy. In other words, we must have fellowship with the other born-again believers in God's Church. Only then can all our problems be solved.

There was much joy at the wedding banquet at Cana, but the party was threatened when they ran out of wine. The guests asked the servers to bring more wine but there was none. Wine symbolizes joy. As a matter of fact, a wedding brings joy to the bride and the groom, and the family of the bride and groom, to the friends, and even to the guests. It was a great disaster that the wine barrels had gone empty in the middle of this joyful feast. Guests were still coming and there was no more wine left. What would you do in this situation? This situation is symbolic of our own lives, as oftentimes there are many problems in our lives and it seems there are no options available to take care of these problems. In such a case, we can say that we have run out of blessings.

The servants came to the master in urgency. "There is no more wine. What should we do?" These days, we can go out and buy more wine as long as we have money. Back then, if you ran out of wine that you have fermented yourself, you had no way to supply more. Thus, the master was startled when he heard this. And he talked to Mary. "It is a huge problem since we are out of wine. This is absurd. I never expected this many guests. I was expecting fewer guests and thought I had prepared enough. I should have prepared even more. And there are still more guests arriving. What should I do?"

After hearing this, Mary talked to Jesus, "They say that the wine has run out in this house. Why don't you do something?" That is the point. Mary had heard and accepted the Word of God through the voice of an angel when she was still a virgin. Soon, she became pregnant and gave birth to a child. That child was Jesus. Mary conceived Jesus by the Holy Spirit. Although Mary is biologically the mother of Jesus, she told Jesus that the wine had run out because she knew the true nature Jesus. Mary had the right faith. Because Mary knew and believed that Jesus is the Son of God, the Savior of all humanity, Mary talked to Jesus about the problem and told the servants to obey Him. When Jesus said, "My time has not yet come," Mary told the servants. "Do exactly as He tells you." Mary believed in Jesus Christ as the Savior.

Then, Jesus told the servants to fill up six stone jars, and the servants did as they were ordered to do. As the servants were filling up those stone jars, Jesus told them to take the water and give it to the master of the feast. Those who tasted the water that was made wine praised the master of the wedding, "It is the custom to bring out the good wine first, and then the bad, but this wedding provides even better wine towards the end."

As a matter of fact, when Jesus speaks to us, we should believe and do exactly as Jesus tells us to. Only then will the Lord work in us and bless us. Mary, Jesus, Jesus' disciples, servants, and the guests are all symbols relevant to our lives. If we think of the guests as the problems in our lives, who would be the One to solve these problems? It would be Jesus. Then, who are the people who first tasted the power of that Jesus? They would be the servants. The servants did as they were told regardless of whether it made sense to them or not. Remembering Mary's admonishment, "Do as Jesus tells you," the servants obeyed Jesus' command to "Fill the jars." Even when they were told to give the water to the master of the feast, they did it without asking twice. As they obeyed, an abundant miracle took place.

I am most displeased while working with our fellow workers or brothers and sisters when they are hesitant to say "yes" or "no" and then don't do what they are told. If I ask why they are not doing so, they reply that they did not obey me because I have told them to do something that does not make sense to them, something they don't believe is possible. I am so frustrated when that happens. Maybe because they are afraid of being embarrassed, they answer, "Yes" with the appearance of obedience. But soon, they come up with an excuse for not following my instructions. Some workers attach so many excuses and problems that they eventually say that they won't do it. After trying something else with their own ability unsuccessfully, they eventually do as they were told.

Still, we should keep in mind that we can taste the power and blessings of God when we do as we are told just like the servants did at Cana. People like the servants, who did as Jesus told them to do, will be able to first taste the blessings of God. Our Lord is God. He is the Creator. He is the Lord who created the universe and everything in it. To deliver us from all our sins, He temporarily came in the flesh of man. And He delivered us by the gospel of the water and the Spirit. If we truly want to taste these blessings, we must obey Him just like the servants did. Whether it makes sense to our puny minds or not, we have to do as we are told in order to taste the blessings. When we obey, we will lead happy lives.

Dear fellow believers, do you want to live your entire lives happily and joyfully? If so, we need to have the attitude of the servants, Jesus' disciples, Mary, and Jesus, who appear in today's Scripture passage of John 2 in our hearts. The many guests are the many problems in our lives. We need to know that Jesus is the One who can solve these problems. We also need to know and believe that only those with the faith like that of the servants will receive the blessings of Jesus. Then, just like there was great joy at the wedding of Cana, there will be great joy in each one of us.

Dear fellow believers, whether each one of us is happy or miserable depends on whether we obey what Jesus tells us to do or not. True joy cannot be found anywhere else. People become happy and free from misery and despair when they receive the remission of sin by their faith in Jesus, when they accept Jesus as their Savior, and when they obey as He has told them to do. By believing in Him, everything turns out the way He has told us. Happiness will come upon those who believe. There will be abundant happiness and a blessed life not only to one's soul but also to one's entire life, one' family, and one's whole surroundings.

However, there are no blessings to those who do not believe that the salvation brought by Jesus Christ, or those who may have believed but do not accept and obey every Word of blessings that our Lord has given us. These people have no happiness in their lives. If we are truly to live a joyful life like the wedding guests at Cana, we must believe and obey as the Lord has told us. If we do as the Lord has told us with faith in Him, all of His Word will eventually come true and we will enjoy happiness during our entire lives. Happiness belongs to those who have received the remission of sin by our faith in the gospel of the water and the Spirit and those who live obediently to His will.

I can tell whether a person is going to live happily or not, when I observe him. It doesn't have much to do with whether that person has been happy so far in his life or not. What I am saying is that I can tell whether that person will live a happy life or not from now on. I am a prophet, that is, a preacher of His Word. I tell people nothing but the Word of God. But there are those who believe and others who do not believe. Those who believe in the Word of God will live happily, and those who do not believe will have miserable lives. When I watch them through the Word of God, I am able to predict their future lives.

To those who believe in the Word of God, I say, "You will live a happy life. You will have many blessings for sure." But I tell different things to those who do not believe. "You will receive eternal damnation if you do not believe in Him and live according to your faith in yourself. And you will be utterly poor. Later, you won't even be able to beg. You won't even be able to say, 'Please, can you spare me a penny,' because you will be so tired. And you will regret that you would have not been born at all. You will definitely end up living like that."

I have no power to bless someone myself, but I am just telling you that we should learn how God blesses or condemns someone through today's Scripture passage. As we have seen in the wedding at Cana, if you do as Jesus tells you to do, you will automatically have blessings and joy. On the other hand, if you do not believe and do not obey Him, you will receive no blessing at all. Just like people can be refreshed by wine, those who desire to have happiness in their lives must believe in the Word of God. Whether we believe and follow after the Word of God or not will determine whether we will receive the blessings or curses in our lives.

Who do you need to have in your hearts if you want your lives to be joyful? You need Jesus Christ as well as the faith the servants in your hearts. If you believe in Jesus and obey as He commands you, your lives will be blessed. Even if everyone in this world falls, you will lead a blessed life like a tree planted by the water, bearing fruits in seasons and having green leaves throughout the year. Dear fellow believers, don't you want to live such lives? Of course, you do.

Do you have Jesus, Mary, and His disciples in your hearts? Do you think of Jesus with the utmost importance? Jesus is God. The Father of Jesus Christ is also God. Then, who among people can be as exalted as Jesus and deserve to be worshipped as much as Jesus? Jesus has to become the most important person in our hearts. No matter how deficient we may be, we receive blessings when we serve no other gods before Him. No matter how insufficient we may be, Jesus is the highest God for me. He is the One who blesses me and the One who solves every problem in my life. If you have such faith, you will be a blessed person like a tree planted by the water, bearing fruits according to the seasons.

I am happy because of Jesus. I hope that you also will be happy because of Him too. Without Jesus, we humans are nothing. If Jesus had not come to this world, this earth would have been already totally annihilated. If you truly want to become happy, invite Jesus, Mary, and Jesus' disciples into your hearts. To do so, you have to receive the remission of sin by the gospel of the water and the Spirit and also serve your God well.

Dear fellow believers, the disciples are the people belonging to the church of God. Our happiness is eternal when we live with the disciples, when we learn and believe what they have told us, and then obey what the Lord tells us. Regardless of how you may have lived up till now, your misery will end and your happiness will begin if you accept Mary, Jesus, and His disciples into your hearts by receiving the remission of sin by your faith in the gospel of the water and the Spirit. However, if your hearts are different from the obedient hearts of Mary and His disciples, you will receive only condemnations.

I sincerely wish you to be happy. Thus, I have told you that I am happy because I have accepted Jesus into my heart. To become happy and blessed people before God, all of us have to believe in our hearts that Jesus Christ is our Savior, who came by the gospel of the water and the Spirit. Halleluiah! ⊠

We Can Taste the Blessings From God Only If We Obey the Word of God

< John 2:5 >
"His mother said to the servants, 'Whatever He says to you, do it.'"

Jesus Was Invited to a Wedding Feast

If we look at the Word in John 2, we see that Jesus was invited to a wedding in Cana, a town in Galilee. Jesus attended the celebration with His disciples, and Mary, His mother on earth. The wedding feast was most likely very crowded with guests, as the servants became distraught because they had run out of wine. "What should we do about this? There are so many guests here. What should we do?" At this moment, Mary said something amazing. She said to the servants, *"Whatever He says to you, do it" (John 2:5).* Mary is telling the servants this with Jesus in mind.

As you know, Jesus is not the Son of Mary in the spiritual sense. Jesus temporarily utilized the body of Mary as a means to come into this world. In Luke chapter 1, we see that an angel appeared to a Jewish virgin one day and said to her, *"Rejoice, highly favored one, the Lord is with you; blessed are you among women!" (Luke 1:28)* That virgin was Mary. "Blessed

Mary! A baby will be born through you. Name Him Jesus."
Obviously this did not make any sense in a worldly sense. So,
Mary replied, "How is such a thing possible? I do not know
men. How then can I give birth to a child?" However, Angel
Gabriel said, "Your relative Elizabeth has also become
pregnant through the Word of God. Through your body the
Savior baby Jesus will be born."

This was the fulfillment of the Word of God through Mary,
prophesized by Isaiah some 700 years prior to the birth of Jesus.
Thus, after hearing everything, Mary accepted the Word
delivered by the angel in her heart and said, *"I am a mere
servant girl of Yours. May it be done as You speak" (Luke
1:26-38).*

Mary gave birth to baby Jesus 10 months after the
Immaculate Conception. When the baby Jesus was born, the
three kings of the orients came as well as shepherds. The
angels from Heaven sang, *"Glory to God in the highest, and on
earth peace, goodwill toward men!" (Luke 2:14)* Mary
experienced many of God's wondrous works. Thus, Mary
knew that Jesus was the Son of God, although He was born
through her. Because of that, Mary said and believed,
"Whatever He says to you, do it" (John 2:5) when the wine
dried up. Mary could say this because she had faith in Jesus in
her mind and also because Jesus was sitting next to her.

"Whatever He Says to You, Do It"

Today, I am trying to tell you a very simple yet profound
message. I am trying to explain why Mary said, "Whatever He
says to you, do it" and how it was possible for Jesus to tell the
servants what He said.

Mary correctly knew the Messiah, who had come to deliver the entire humanity from all its sins. Put differently, she knew that this Jesus was not a mere human but God the Savior who had come in the flesh of man. She knew that He was God. Thus, she could say, "Whatever He says to you, do it," and at the very moment, Jesus heard what Mary had said.

The Palestine area where the Jews lived is a desert area. Because of this, they wore sandals and covered their faces and their heads with clothes and hats. They did so because there is a lot of dust in that area as well as strong sunlight. Because of the dust, every house of those days had water jars full of water in front of their entrance doors. When guests came, servants were sent out quickly to present a basket of water to wash their hands and feet.

At the front door of the house at Cana where the wedding took place were also six large water jars. After hearing Mary's request, Jesus commanded the servants as follows. "Fill the jars." Then, the servants filled up the jars as Jesus told them to do. With much effort, they filled up the six jars to the brim. Then, Jesus said, "Draw some out now, and take it to the master of the feast." The servants drew out some of it and took it to the master of the feast.

When the master of the feast had tasted the water that was made wine, he called the bridegroom and said, "The usual custom at feasts is to bring out the good wine first and then bring out bad wine later. How is it that the wine gets better at this house? How is this possible?" The only people who knew the answers to these questions were Jesus, Mary, and the servants. It is written that the master of the feast had tasted the water that was made wine, and did not know where it came from, but the servants who had drawn the water knew (John 2:9).

Dear fellow believers, what is God trying to tell us through this account? In our faith in Jesus as our Savior, it is important for us to know who Jesus really is. Who do you think Jesus is? What do you believe in Him to be true? This is the first step in our faith. We believe in Jesus. Yet, who is this Jesus? Do you know Him to be a mere human? Or is He one of the four sages of the world history? Or do you know Him to be merely a person with a great character? Is He a knowledgeable person? Or is He a patriot? Is He a revolutionist against the traditional religions? Is He a scientist, novelist, or an artist? Who is Jesus to you?

Today's Scripture passage of John chapter 2 is about the first incident in which our Lord revealed His divinity after coming to this world. Jesus had many discussions with the Pharisees and He had preached on many things after He received the baptism from John the Baptist, but only now did He reveal His divinity for the first time.

The servants filled the jars with water because our Lord had told them to do so. Then, they drew the water and took it to the master of the feast just as they were told to do. The master of the feast tasted the water that was made wine, and said, "Wow! This is great wine! Who kept this good wine till now and is only now giving it out?" In this way, our Lord has shown a miracle through the water.

What do you know about Jesus? The meaning of the name "Jesus" is the One who will deliver His people from all their sins (Matthew 1:21). Then, who is Jesus fundamentally? He is the Son of God. Whether He is the Son of God or the cousin of God, let's leave it at that from our limited human perspective. What I am asking is who Jesus is fundamentally.

When we look at something, don't we ask ourselves what it is at its fundamental level? Whether it is a plant or an animal, don't we have curiosity in our hearts to know its original nature? Just the same, we have curiosity about who Jesus is. Jesus is God. He is God the Creator of this universe and everything in it. He made not only me or you but also all plants, all animals, this earth, and the entire universe.

Jesus said to take the water to the master of the feast after filling up the six jars with water to the brim. The servants took the water to the master of the feast just as Jesus told them to do. Then, they came to find that the water had changed into good wine. Dear fellow believers, is it possible for such a miracle to take place? It is apparent that all magicians in this world use illusions. However, that Jesus turned water into wine is a matter of fact. Only Jesus can turn water into wine and give it to us. What I am saying is that there is no other Savior to us except Jesus Christ.

Who is Jesus? He is the true God who has created you and me and also delivered us from sin. If we look at the Scripture passage in John 1:1-3 carefully, it states who Jesus in very clear terms. *"In the beginning was the Word, and the Word was with God, and the Word was God. He was in the beginning with God. All things were made through Him, and without Him nothing was made that was made" (John 1:1-3).*

Who made this beautiful flower that is in front of us? All things were made through Jesus as it says, *"All things were made through Him, and without Him nothing was made that was made" (John 1:3).* The pronoun "Him" refers to Jesus Christ, who delivered you and me from all our sins and created the universe and everything in it. Without that Jesus Christ, everything that exists could not have come into being. Through Him, everything in this world was created.

Dear fellow believers, in Genesis 1, when our Lord said, *"Let the earth bring forth grass, the herb that yields seed, and the fruit tree that yields fruit according to its kind, whose seed is in itself, on the earth,"* and it was so (Genesis 1:11), it shows God's power and authority to do everything only through His Word. He created seeds, which bore vegetables, and then created trees that bore fruits. When God spoke His Word, "Let there be seed bearing vegetables," seed bearing vegetables came into being. It is as simple as that. It is impossible for us to do, but it is easy for God. As our Lord spoke, so it happened in the exact same way.

The power of the Word of our Lord that created the world is still in effect. That is why even now the grasses and trees do not cease to exist. Rather, they grow wherever each of them is habitable, whether it is in the mountains or in the fields. When man does construction, they go in with bulldozers to flatten an entire mountain. Yet, the next spring, new life comes up anew in the same place. And in another year, the whole place is covered with grass and trees, although no one has sown the seeds. There is great power in the spoken Word of God that His works are still taking in place throughout all the ages.

Hence, our Lord said that the world may disappear but His word will last forever without alteration. Because the spoken Word of our Lord is still with us, the living creatures in this world are still around. *"All things were made through Him, and without Him nothing was made that was made. In Him was life, and the life was the light of men. And the light shines in the darkness, and the darkness did not comprehend it. There was a man sent from God, whose name was John. This man came for a witness, to bear witness of the Light, that all through him might believe" (John 1:3-7).*

Dear fellow believers, last time I shared a message about John the Baptist. Today I tell you that Jesus is the life of this world. He came to give us new and eternal life by recreating and renewing the souls of those who were destined to die because of their sins. Jesus came to blot out all our sins and include us with the righteous according to the will of God the Father. Because John the Baptist witnessed about our Lord, who came with that purpose, we are able to meet Jesus by that witness of John the Baptist. We received our salvation because we believed in Jesus. John the Baptist was not the Savior. He was a servant of God who witnessed about Jesus.

In John 1:10-12, it says, *"He was in the world, and the world was made through Him, and the world did not know Him. He came to His own, and His own did not receive Him. But as many as received Him, to them He gave the right to become children of God, to those who believe in His name."* Verse 14 says, *"And the Word became flesh and dwelt among us, and we beheld His glory, the glory as of the only begotten of the Father, full of grace and truth."*

The God who had made the world through His Word in the beginning came in the flesh of man to deliver us from all our sins. As our Lord came into His own world, His own people did not receive Him. But, He gave whomever that accepts the Lord and believes in His name the right to become God's own children.

Who is this Jesus to us? He is God the Creator of the entire universe. Everything was made through Him. And the same God who created everything came to this world in the flesh of man to deliver you and me from all our sins. And when He received the baptism, He took onto Himself all sins of the entire humanity, and then, when he was crucified on the Cross, He delivered you and me. Thus, we have received the remission of sin through this Word of Truth.

Who is Jesus from our perspective? He is God. He is a God, who turned water into wine. When they did as God told them to do, it was done exactly as He intended. Mary Jesus' mother in flesh told the servants to obey Him, and Jesus Himself also told the servants what to do. The servants merely filled up six jars to the brim. Water was filled to the top of the jars. Jesus told them to draw from it and take it to the master of the feast. The servants took the water to him as they were told.

The master of the feast was amazed at the new wine. The guests were also astonished and must have said to the master of the feast. "Master! This is quite amazing. Master, you are doing a great job with this feast. Truly, I have never seen a master of a feast like you. Usually, people bring out their best wine first and then later inferior wines diluted with water. However, you bring out the better wine later. You are an incredible person. Quite precious." The guests were patting the back of the master of the feast in commendation. However, I'm sure the master was confused because he had no clue on what was going on. The master did not know where the good wine came from, but the servants knew exactly what was going on. They knew very well that a miracle took place when they did as Jesus told them to do.

Even Jesus' own disciples at first followed Jesus thinking that He was just an honorable man. Later, they realized that He is not an ordinary person, and that He had awesome power to solve every problem they had. The disciples started to believe from then on. All of us who have received the remission of sin believe that Jesus is God. And Jesus truly is God. Jesus Christ is the Creator God who made the universe and everything in it.

The word "Christ" means the King of kings, the God of gods. Jesus is the anointed One, the Prophet, the High Priest, and the King of kings. Who is the Creator of universe and everything in it? He is Jesus Christ. This very Jesus Christ came to this world in the flesh of man and delivered us from all

our sins. Thus, when we believe in that Jesus Christ, we receive
the complete remission of sin. Because Jesus who was God
came to this world in the flesh of man to deliver us from all our
sins, we receive the remission of sin when we believe in Him.
When we believe in the Word He spoke, we indeed believe in
Jesus.

Jesus revealed His divinity at that moment. There is
another thing we must come to recognize in our hearts and
know. That is, they received true joy when they did as
commanded by His Word. Although the command did not
make any sense to the servants, a miracle took place when they
obeyed as they were told in faith. God is telling us this very
Truth.

Dear fellow believers, we struggle day by day to survive
in this world until the day we die. That is life. Am I right or
not? Some people resist dying on their last breath, saying, "No,
I cannot die! I won't close my eyes!" They die with their eyes
open, and someone else has to close their eyes for them.
Regardless of how stubbornly a person protests his own death,
everyone stops breathing eventually. We can only live and die
naturally in this way. Still, if we believe and obey the Word of
our Lord, we are told that we will taste blessings of a life full
of joy.

Dear fellow believers, what does our successful life look
like? How can we succeed in our lives? We must know the
truth about Jesus Christ. And we must believe in Him. We
must believe in Jesus who is God, and we must be born again
by receiving the remission of sin in our faith in the gospel of
the water and the Spirit. By believing in the baptism Jesus
received and in the blood He shed, we will receive the
remission of sin. Only if you believe in the gospel Word of the
water and the Spirit, will God cleanse all of your sins away.

You must also listen and obey the Word of God, if you have received the remission of sin in your hearts by believing in the gospel Truth of the water and the Spirit. If you do so, you will taste the amazing blessings of God. If God is telling you thus, you should believe and follow it as such. Although you cannot realize the gospel of the water and the Spirit on your own, you can hear the Word of God preached at the church of God. When the Word speaks so, you should listen and believe and obey. When you do so, you will surely receive the remission of sin.

We now live righteous lives because we have received the remission of sin at the church of God. In the church of God there are saints. Although there are many saints in the church of God, not all of them taste the miracles of God. Then, who are the people that experience the blessings from God like the servants in the today's passage? Those who obey the Word of God and who believe and follow the instructions exactly experience the blessings from God. This is true even if the Word may not make sense at the time, like the servants who filled up the water jugs faithfully. God's followers will experience amazing miracles and blessings like the servants did, and they continue to experience this throughout their lives.

Dear fellow believers, don't you want to live in this world tasting the miracles at the church of God and receiving the remission of sin? I really hope that all of you can become like these servants. Although the servants really did not know anything, they experienced the miracle because they did as they were told. Because they did so, the servants found out who Jesus really was. Regardless of what Jesus tells us to do, we need to believe that if we do as He tells us, things will follow according to His plan. Even though the master of the feast did not know what had happened, the servants knew what was going on. We should have faith like that of the servants in today's Scripture passage.

Dear fellow believers, if we desire to live truly blessed lives, we need to become men and women of faith. What kind of faith? We need to have the faith in the Word of God. Believers in the gospel of the water and the Spirit must also be the people of obedience to God. Dear fellow believers, if you believe that the church of God shares the Word of God, listen and follow the instructions and preaching of God's servants, who are your predecessors of faith. If you believe and follow the Word of God, you will experience many blessings of God, both big and small. In order to teach us this lesson, our Lord recorded these events in the Bible.

Dear fellow believers, we need to believe that Jesus is God. Furthermore, we need to also believe that Jesus has become our Savior. We need to believe that Jesus is our Pastor. We need to believe that the Word of Jesus is Truth. We need to believe that these blessings are bestowed only upon those who believe and obey the Word of Jesus. I hope that all of you have such faith. Our acceptance of the remission of the sin is not the end of our spiritual journey. We must also receive the guidance of God in addition to the blessings from God after we have received the remission of sin. We must grow into such people of faith. I hope that all of you can become such believers. Dear fellow believers, I hope that you truly live your lives in true faith.

Look at the servants of the wedding feast. Although it did not make any sense in their own minds, they filled up the jars with water to the brim just as Jesus had told them to do. And they drew from that jar and took the water to the master of the feast just as they were told. Don't you think that the servants' hearts would have been uneasy? They could have doubted and said, "Damn! If this doesn't work there will be a lot of people making a scene today!" What would have happened if the guests really received water when they were expecting wine? If the water had not turned into wine for real, all the servants would have been in deep trouble that day. Jesus would have been embarrassed as well as His mother.

Dear fellow believers, our Lord was God of power and authority who took care of the problem of wine shortage with a single Word. I encourage you to believe in that Jesus as your God. We must live by our faith in God. What is impossible with human efforts can be solved if we are guided by the faith in the Word of God as we lead our life of faith in His Church. When we believe in and follow Jesus, we experience His blessings and power in our lives. I hope that God will give you the blessing of faith in the Word of God. I hope you will experience your spiritual growth and the amazing blessings of God day by day as we read this Word.

It is the human philosophy to live stubbornly without God. Regardless of how much a person relies on himself, all man is limited. Life is walking on four limbs when we are born, two when we are in our youth, and three when we grow old. There is no true progress in life. However, God did not work like that. The only true way prepared for us is to be born again by believing in His Word. To believe in God's Word of Truth is to believe in God. We should not believe in strange dreams, visions, or illusions. We sometimes hear odd sounds when our hearts grow weak. All are distractions and are useless.

Blessings come from our faith in the written Word of Truth. You will be born again when you believe in the written Word of God. You will be blessed according to the Word when you believe in the written Word. God recorded what happened in the past in order to meet with us through this Word. That's why God has recorded all of His Word through the prophets of the Old Testament times and the disciples of Jesus of the New Testament era. Throughout all the Scriptures, from Genesis to Revelation, Who appears? Throughout these entire 66 Books of the Bible, Jesus Christ appears. Every single Book of the Scriptures is connected to Jesus Christ.

We have to believe in the written Word of God. When we believe in the Word of God, we believe in God, we meet with God, and we receive the blessings from God. That is because our Lord has come to us through this Word. Our Lord is God of the Word. Dear fellow believers, do you believe this? Yes, you do. I exhort you to believe.

Dear fellow believers, keep your faith and pray for the nonbelievers while leading them to God. According to your faith, come to the church of God and listen to the Word as often as you can. You will taste and experience the amazing miracles when the Word abundantly fills you up to the brim of your hearts.

Dear fellow believers, the greatest blessing in this world is to be born again by the faith in the gospel of the water and the Spirit, which is the Word of God. The Bible says that we should not live by bread alone but by the Word that comes out of the mouth of God. There is nothing sweeter than listening to the Word of God. The second blessing to those who have received the remission of sin is the blessing to hear the Word of God.

When we listen to the Word of God, the Holy Spirit within us fills us in strong agreement with the gospel Word of the water and the Spirit, which is the Word of God. "That's right! Right indeed!" The Spirit is encouraging us to have faith in God's Word.

I hope that you will really believe in the Word of God and

truly obey Him like the servants did. When you do so, you will receive the blessings from God for the rest of your lives. ✉

CHAPTER 3

We Have to Be Born Again By Knowing and Believing In This Way

< John 3:1-6 >

"There was a man of the Pharisees named Nicodemus, a ruler of the Jews. This man came to Jesus by night and said to Him, 'Rabbi, we know that You are a teacher come from God; for no one can do these signs that You do unless God is with him.' Jesus answered and said to him, 'Most assuredly, I say to you, unless one is born again, he cannot see the kingdom of God.' Nicodemus said to Him, 'How can a man be born when he is old? Can he enter a second time into his mother's womb and be born?' Jesus answered, 'Most assuredly, I say to you, unless one is born of water and the Spirit, he cannot enter the kingdom of God. That which is born of the flesh is flesh, and that which is born of the Spirit is spirit.'"

Most Christians are trying their best to be born again. Still, there are many who use the term "being born again" without knowing the meaning behind these words. Although they often hear that they need to be born again because they are sinners, most people do not know the exact meaning of these words. Still they say, "I have been born again since I believe in Jesus," or "I am sure I was born again when I was praying fervently in the mountain, since I felt the fire inside of me back then." The problem is that people only rely on their emotions in this matter of Truth. Those people, who are disillusioned into believing that they are born again without knowing the Truth of salvation, must be born again only through the Lord-given gospel Truth of the water and the Spirit.

Being born again and being free from all of one's sins is possible only by having faith in the gospel Word of the water and the Spirit. If we are to be born again, we must believe in God's Word of Truth. To do so, we must carve the God-given Truth of the water and the Spirit into our hearts by listening to it over and over again. First of all, we must realize that we cannot replace the gospel of the water and the Spirit with miracles and signs that we may experience.

Let's listen to the Word of God that is given to us. *"Most assuredly, I say to you, unless one is born of water and the Spirit, he cannot enter the kingdom of God" (John 3:5).* This Scripture passage tells us that we must be born again to be free from all our sins by the water and the Spirit. I would like to share with you today what it means to be truly born again by the gospel Truth of the water and the Spirit.

Every Sinner Must Believe in the Gospel of the Water and the Spirit in Order to Enter the Heavenly Kingdom

Most Christians, when they first start believing in the Savior, do not know much about the Word of the water and the Holy Spirit. Instead of being born again by the water and the Spirit, they believe that Christianity as one of the religions in this world. We cannot truly be born again from all our sins by only believing in Jesus as our Savior just as people of the other religions believe in their gods. Therefore, we must realize the gospel Word of the water and the Spirit, which is the Truth that brings us the remission of sin. Whoever recognizes that he is a lowly sinner before God and believes in the gospel of the water and the Spirit can then receive the salvation from all his sins and become born again.

It is wrong to only believe in Jesus as our Savior without the knowledge of the gospel Truth of the water and the Spirit. The Bible tells us about the gospel Truth of the water and the Spirit, which enables every human being to be born again from the sins of the world. We must realize and believe in our hearts the gospel of the water and the Spirit.

However, if Christians believed mistakenly without knowing the gospel Truth of the water and the Spirit, how can we be sure of the salvation from our sins? If we believed in Christianity without the gospel Truth of the water and the Spirit, what would remain in our hearts? Only confusion, despair, and all our sins would remain in our hearts if such were the case. If the gospel Truth of the water and the Spirit is not in your hearts, you would still only have confusion, despair, and sins in your hearts. Although you may believe in Jesus as your Savior, because you have not known the gospel of the water and the Spirit, you would still live as sinners. Although you believe in Jesus, you would be legalistic religionists with sins still remaining in your hearts. Your souls would be saturated with sin in your hearts because you have not truly met Jesus Christ, who came by the gospel Truth of the water and the Spirit. When a person thinks of Christianity as another good worldly religion, he only has confusion and despair in his heart.

These days, although there are many people who have believed in Jesus for a long time, they struggle with the confusion and emptiness in their hearts. Most Christians are living as the grave sinners before God, because they do not know the gospel of the water and the Spirit, which is the Word of God. Because they have fallen into religious confusion, they think that they would be all right even if they still have sins in their hearts. Once they become a religionist, they often masquerade as true believers and then become strict legalists with time. They end up facing their own condemnation, unable to escape from all their sins.

The faith in the gospel of the water and the Spirit enables us to escape from all our sins, and we should likewise utilize it to escape from the empty religions of the world. We must become born again by knowing and believing in the gospel of the water and the Spirit.

The Lord Is Telling Us That Only Those Who Believe in the Gospel of the Water and the Spirit Will Be Completely Delivered from All Their Sins

The Lord said, *"Unless one is born of water and the Spirit, he cannot enter the kingdom of God" (John 3:5).* Here, it is said that the resources that enable us to be born again are "the water and the Spirit." For a person to receive the salvation from all his sins, he must be born again by his faith in the gospel of the water and the Spirit. The water refers to the baptism Jesus received from John the Baptist (Matthew 3:15). Whoever believes in Jesus, the One who took all sins of the world by receiving the baptism from John the Baptist and was then crucified on the Cross, will receive the remission of sin, become born again, and have the Holy Spirit in his heart. Put differently, when we accept and believe the Truth of salvation

in the Word of God, we receive the remission of all our sins
and are made into righteous people.

To be born again means to be born twice. We were born
once by flesh from our parents. And to be born again is to be
reborn spiritually. Although at first we might have believed in
Jesus only religiously, we can be truly born again by receiving
the remission of sin and receiving God's gift of the Holy Spirit
through our faith in the gospel of the water and the Spirit,
which is the true salvation.

Let's Find Evidence of the Gospel of the Water and Spirit in the Old Testament

Let's examine the gospel of Truth revealed in Leviticus 1
of the Old Testament first. How did the people in the past
receive remission of their sins? The Word in Leviticus reveals
how God will deliver all humanity in the future. Therefore, we
have to examine the gospel of the water and the Spirit in the
Word of the Old Testament and believe in it.

Leviticus 1:1-3 says, *"Now the Lord called to Moses, and
spoke to him from the tabernacle of meeting, saying, 'Speak to
the children of Israel, and say to them: 'When any one of you
brings an offering to the Lord, you shall bring your offering of
the livestock—of the herd and the flock. If his offering is a
burnt sacrifice of the herd, let him offer a male without
blemish; he shall offer it of his own free will at the door of the
tabernacle of meeting before the Lord.'''"*

A title is attached to each of the 66 Books of the Bible
according to the main theme of each Book. Genesis is the
record of God's creation of the universe and everything in it as
well as the life stories of the fathers of faith such as Abraham,

Isaac, Jacob, and Joseph. Exodus records about how the descendants of Jacob, the Israelites, were delivered from Egypt as well as about the Ten Commandments, the Law of God, and the Tabernacle system. Leviticus explains us how man and God can be united through the sacrificial system, which shows us in detail the God's method for delivering us humans from all our sins. The name of the book refers to Levi who was the third son of Jacob by Leah and the progenitor of tribe of Levites. The name "Levi" means "joined to" (Genesis 29:34). So, how to join with God is the consistent theme of the Book of Leviticus.

The Law of God is the collection of His statutes regarding the do's and don'ts in our lives. There are 613 statutes in the Law. Although God has given His Law to us, we humans lack the power to live according to that Law despite knowing that His Law is right and just. That is because we have inherited original sin from Adam. Because every person has inherited a total of 12 kinds of sins from Adam, every person is unable to conduct righteously due to the inherited sin. Therefore, we were born as beings who cannot help but commit the sins, even when we know it is wrong.

"But God demonstrates His own love toward us, in that while we were still sinners, Christ died for us" (Romans 5:8). While all people were destined to be born as sinners and die as sinners, God has set the sacrificial system to His people so that they would be able to receive the remission of sin. God established the sacrificial system and entrusted its administration to the tribe of Levites. In other words, He gave the priesthood only to the tribe of Levites, Aaron and his descendants (Exodus 29:9, Numbers 3:10). Aaron, the first High Priest, was a descendant of Levi.

It is easier to understand how we can be born again, when we examine closely the role of the Levite priests. When we listen carefully to the Word of God which describes the sacrificial system, we can better understand the blessing of the remission of sin through Jesus Christ, which in the Bible is the most important focus.

God called Moses, a Levite, to His tabernacle and appointed his brother Aaron as the High Priest, who would transfer all sins to the sacrificial lamb. When anyone of the Israelites, needed to bring the Lord an offering, he was directed to bring an offering of his own livestock—one of the herd and of the flock (Leviticus 1:2). This implies that God had already limited the types sacrificial offerings that could bear all their sins. If the Israelites were to receive the remission of sin before God, they required by God to sacrifice a sheep or a goat. And if the sacrifice was part of a burnt offering, it was necessary to bring a male animal without blemish to the front of the Tabernacle.

A burnt offering is a kind of sacrifice offered to God by being burned. Through this offering, the sacrificed animal is killed as a substitute for the person and the sacrifice receives the judgment vicariously that sinner deserved from God.

Then, how were the sinners required to make an offering before God so that God would accept it joyously? Leviticus 1:4 says, *"Then he shall put his hand on the head of the burnt offering, and it will be accepted on his behalf to make atonement for him."* We can find the solution in the passage, "Then he shall put his hand on the head of the burnt offering." We should pay attention specifically to the phrase "to put one's hands on the head of the burnt offering." It is written that when a sinner laid his hand on the head of the burnt offering, all his sins were transferred onto the sacrificial animal. Thus, the correct order to perform an offering was to transfer one's sins by laying one's hands on the burnt offering before the sacrifice was put to death in offering to God.

"Then he shall put his hand on the head of the burnt offering" (Leviticus 1:4). The first step in receiving one's remission of sin in the Old Testament is the laying on of hands. The laying of hands is the action applied to the sacrificial person or an animal. The phrase "laying one's hands on of" means that one's sins are transferred onto the scapegoat. This was the proper method to atone for one's sin before God established by God Himself.

"Then he shall put his hand on the head of the burnt offering, and it will be accepted on his behalf to make atonement for him" (Leviticus 1:4). Atonement means that sins are extinguished along with the scapegoat. Because that scapegoat has borne all our sins by receiving them with the laying on of hands, we receive the atonement, the termination of all our sins. Atonement means to receive the remission of sins by transferring one's sins onto a sacrificial lamb through the laying of one's hands. In this way, the sins of the people are atoned through a sacrificial lamb.

As such, in the Old Testament times, when people committed sins before God, they had to offer a goat, a sheep, a calf, or a dove without blemish. And in order to receive the remission of sin, they had to lay their hands on the scapegoats to transfer their sins onto them before they offered the sacrifices to God. Once their sins were transferred onto the scapegoats, the priests killed the animals and drew their blood and transferred it over the horn of the altar and then poured it onto the ground. This was the sacrificial system, which God had granted the Israelites so that they might receive the remission of sin. Thus, they had to offer sacrifices according to God's Law by transferring all their sins onto the sacrificial lambs by the means of laying on of hands.

It says in Leviticus 1:5, *"He shall kill the bull before the Lord; and the priests, Aaron's sons, shall bring the blood and sprinkle the blood all around on the altar that is by the door of the tabernacle of meeting."*

Dear fellow believers, there are four horns on the four corner edges of the altar of the burnt offering. After a sinner Israelite confessed his sins and transferred them to the sacrificial animal by laying his hands on its head, the person had to kill the animal and hand over its blood to the priest before he could return home without sins. Now the next stage was up to the priest: Then, the priest had to sprinkle the blood of the sacrifice on the four corners of the altar and pour all the remaining blood at the base of the altar to completely atone that person's sins (Leviticus 4:30). The blood had to be sprinkled on the horns of the altar because the horns represent the judgment. Sprinkling the blood on the horns clearly symbolized that the blood of the sacrifice bore the sins of this person in his stead. God accepted the sacrifice and did not condemn the person when He saw the person's laying of hands and the blood of the sacrificial animal.

Why did the sacrifice have to shed its blood? This is because the life of flesh is in the blood (Leviticus 17:11). Because an Israelite should die by God's justice when he committed sin, the blood of a sacrifice was sprinkled instead of his own blood. In place of the sinner, a sacrificial animal would be killed after the person's sins were transferred onto it by the laying of his hands. With the sacrifice's blood, he could satisfy the Law of God, which says that the wage of sin is death (Romans 6:23). That was why the sacrificial animal shed its blood and died in the sinner's place after it took all of his sins.

The priests in the Old Testament put the blood of the sacrifice on the horns of the altar of burnt offering. When we examine Jeremiah 17:1 along with Revelation 20:11-15, we can find out that the horn refers to the Book of Deeds. Hence, sprinkling the blood on the horns of the altar is analogous to sprinkling the blood on the Book of Deeds.

All sins people commit in this world are recorded in two different places. One is on the tablet of each person's heart, and the other is in the Book of Deeds before God. Jeremiah 17:1 says, *"The sin of Judah is written with a pen of iron; with the point of a diamond is engraved on the tablet of their heart, and on the horns of your altars."* Hence, it is not enough that the sins our own hearts are expunged, but our names and sins inside the Book of Deeds before God must be erased as well. Thus, the laying on of the hands on the sacrifice signifies the transfer of all our sins onto the sacrifice, and the consequent sprinkling of its blood on the horns of the altar represents the judgment for the sins.

The sins of each person were blotted out when that person laid his hands on the sacrifice, shed its blood to death, and offered it to God. The Israelites offered their sacrifices like this by saying, "Please accept the price of death of this animal and wash all my sins away completely." As such, they could be cleansed of their sins through sacrificial lambs without blemish through the ministries of the priests in the Old Testaments. The sacrificial animals had paid the price of death before God in their stead.

"And he shall skin the burnt offering and cut it into its pieces. The sons of Aaron the priest shall put fire on the altar, and lay the wood in order on the fire. Then the priests, Aaron's sons, shall lay the parts, the head, and the fat in order on the wood that is on the fire upon the altar; but he shall wash its entrails and its legs with water. And the priest shall burn all on the altar as a burnt sacrifice, an offering made by fire, a sweet

aroma to the Lord" (Leviticus 1:6-9).

Cutting the sacrifice into pieces and then burning it is called a burnt offering or an offering made by fire, because it is offered through blazing fire. When we humans committed sins before God, we were meant to die shedding our blood just like the sacrifice. Through the burnt offering, God is telling us that we should have received the judgment of being put into the eternal fire. This burnt offering was the just judgment of God. God satisfied two of His law through the burnt offering: God's law of justice and His law of love.

Because God is the holy and just One, He grants the remission of sin to the person only when he offers a sacrificial animal instead of himself. Because God is just, He has to judge us for our sins, but because He is God of love, He does not judge us directly and instead He judges the burnt offering by having us transfer our sins onto it by laying our hands on it and having the sacrifice burned.

Here is another example of sin offering, which was for the atonement of the sins of the common people: *"If anyone of the common people sins unintentionally by doing something against any of the commandments of the Lord in anything which ought not to be done, and is guilty, or if his sins which he has committed comes to his knowledge, then he shall bring as his offering a kid of the goats, a female without blemish, for his sin which he has committed. And he shall lay his hand on the head of the sin offering, and kill the sin offering at the place of the burnt offering. Then the priest shall take some of its blood with his finger, put it on the horns of the altar of burnt offering, and pour all the remaining blood at the base of the altar. He shall remove all its fat, as fat is removed from the sacrifice of the peace offering; and the priest shall burn it on the altar for a sweet aroma to the Lord. So the priest shall*

make atonement for him, and it shall be forgiven him"
(Leviticus 4:27-31).

Everyone is born with innate sin that is inherited from
Adam. Our inner persons are full of sins. We are a pile of sins,
such as evil thoughts, adultery, fornication, murder, theft,
jealousy, wickedness, deceit, lewdness, an evil eye, blasphemy,
pride, and foolishness (Mark 7:21-22).

How can a person who has committed sins come to realize
he is guilty? He can recognize his sin by shedding the light of
the Law on his heart. It is written, *"Therefore by the deeds of
the law no flesh will be justified in His sight, for by the law is
the knowledge of sin" (Romans 3:20).* We come to realize our
own sins through the Law of God. If it weren't for God's
instructions of do's and don'ts in the Law, we would not know
that we have committed sin even after committing it. Hence,
God made us realize our sinfulness first in order for us to seek
His salvation.

How Do We Come to Realize Our Own Sins?

We realize what sin is through the Law of God. We know
whether we have done right or wrong to God by reflecting
upon our deeds and the written Word of God, which states the
Do's and Don'ts established by God. Whether one has
committed sin or not is not determined by one's own
conscience but rather by the Word of God. Through the Law of
God established in the Word of God, we come to realize our
own sins.

In the passage above from Leviticus 4:27-32, the Word
discusses unintentional sin. We often commit sins
unintentionally rather than intentionally because we were born

as sinners. Unintentional sins includes those sins we have committed without knowing, those we have committed because of our own weaknesses, and those we have committed because of our deficiencies or mistakes. We call sins that we commit out of our weaknesses unintentional sins. We cannot help but commit unintentional sins because we are sinful by nature. A human being cannot be perfect. People in ancient times were as weak as we are now. They also committed sins unintentionally everyday by disobeying any of the commandments of the Lord.

We are meant to be put to death because of our trespasses and sins (Ephesians 2:1). The sin and guilt of a person is distinguished as follows. We call the innate evil in our hearts and thoughts "sin," and we call our wrongdoings "trespasses," that have been put into action because of our innate evilness. If someone committed sins unintentionally and recognized his sins, he then was required to bring as his offering a kid of the goats, a female without blemish, as an offering for his sin that he had committed. *"And he shall lay his hand on the head of the sin offering, and kill the sin offering at the place of the burnt offering" (Leviticus 4:29).*

In order for the Israelites to receive the remission of sin, they first had to realize that they were indeed sinners. Regardless of how desperately God wanted to grant them the remission of sin, it would be impossible for God to grant the remission of sin to those who didn't recognize their sins. Thus, the Israelites had to know which of God's commandments they had broken and also understand what the rightful judgment for their sins was. Then, they needed to offer burnt offerings to God to receive the remission of sin.

Everyone who has not yet received the remission of sin still has sin within him or her. Each and every one of the Israelites, who had sins in his heart, had to first bring a female goat and transfer his sins onto it by laying his hands on its head. And then the person had to offer its blood by cutting its throat. This was the proper way for them to receive the remission of sin. Of course, the sacrifice could be a goat, a bull, or a lamb. The condition of the sacrificial animal was that it has to be one approved by God without blemish. If the sacrifice limped, was scarred on its body, or has a diseased coating on its eyes, God would not accept that sacrifice. For a sacrifice to be acceptable sacrifice the animal had to be clean and without blemish. Clean animals are those that have cloven hooves and chew the cud (Leviticus 11:3). Therefore, among clean animals such as the lamb, the goat, and the calf, only those that were without blemish could be offered as proper sacrifices to God. Then, who in the world is without blemish? The only answer is Jesus Christ.

All sins of people could be transferred by the process of the laying on of hands. This was God's promise written in His Word. *"Or if his sin which he has committed comes to his knowledge, then he shall bring as his offering a kid of the goats, a female without blemish, for his sin which he has committed. And he shall lay his hand on the head of the sin offering, and kill the sin offering at the place of the burnt offering"* *(Leviticus 4:28-29).*

God told the Israelites that they had to lay their hands on the head of the sacrifice, which would then bear the sins in their stead, and become a sacrifice for them. The laying on of hands in the Old Testament was the means by which sins were transferred. All sins were transferred to another party, the sacrificial animal, by the laying on of hands. Put differently, every sinner had to transfer his sins by this laying on of hands. Before the sacrificial lamb or goat was to be killed, it first had to take the sins of the sinner by the laying on of hands. Only when the animal received the sin from the hands of the sinner and then was killed, could the sinner receive the remission for his sin. A person in those days could receive the remission of sin when he first transferred his sins to a sacrifice by laying his hands on it and then offering it to God with a heart acknowledging his sinfulness saying, "I am a sinner who should die bleeding like this sacrifice because of my sins."

Wherein does the life of flesh lies? It lies in the blood (Leviticus 17:11). In the blood of a person is his life. The life of all flesh is in the blood. Regardless of how healthy one's heart is, if blood is not provided to it to be pumped, that person will surely die. Then, why did God tell the Israelites to sprinkle the blood on the horns, when they were offering the sacrifices to God? It was to let them know that "This animal has died in the place of the sinner" after the blood was sprinkled on the horns.

The laying on of hands was the method by which all sins of a person were transferred. God has taught humanity His way of transferring all their sins. That method is the laying on of hands from the Old Testament and the baptism of Jesus in the New Testament. Hence, God delivered the sinner completely after seeing the blood of his sacrifice, proclaiming, "Yes! You no longer have any sin. You do not have to die now for all your sins were transferred by the laying on of your hands." The laying on of hands and the shedding of blood simultaneously fulfills the love of God as well as His righteous judgment.

When God creating us humans, He created us out of dust. For the remission of all our sins, both God's Book of Judgment as well as the tablet of each one's heart must be covered with blood. Complete remission of sin is possible only when both of them are covered with the blood. That is, for the remission of sin, all recorded sins must be blotted out before God as well as in our hearts. Dear fellow believers, do you accept the Word of God?

The last process of the sin offering is described in the following passage, *"He shall remove all its fat, as fat is removed from the sacrifice of the peace offering; and the priest shall burn it on the altar for a sweet aroma to the Lord"* *(Leviticus 4:31).* This says that all of the filthy parts of the sacrifice, such as the excrement, must be thrown away, and the separated fat from the animal had to be burned together with the rest of the sacrifice on the fire of the altar. This fat in the Bible refers in fact to the Holy Spirit.

Hence, in order for the Israelites to receive the remission of sin, they had to make offerings exactly as God had commanded to them. The sacrifice must be a clean animal without any blemish. Only when they followed God's rules for sin offerings exactly could they receive the remission of sin before God. If they had been filled with excessive passion so they thought it best to offer a big animal such as an elephant, they would have fail to receive the remission of sin. God has specifically ordered to bring a clean animal such as a lamb, a goat, or a calf. All three of these have cloven hooves and chew the cud. God is pleased with believers who ruminate over the Word of God and are set apart from the world.

The ultimate sacrifice to God without blemish is Jesus Christ, who was perfect without sin. The people in the Old Testament times received the remission of sin by bringing a lamb or a goat without blemish, by laying their hands on it to transfer their sins, and by the priest making an offering to God. This applies to the New Testament as well. Jesus received the baptism from John the Baptist, who transferred all our sins onto Jesus. Jesus finally delivered us by receiving the judgments for all our sins when He died on the Cross.

The last part of the passage about the conclusion of the sin offering of common people states that, *"So the priest shall make atonement for him concerning his sin, and it shall be forgiven him" (Leviticus 4:26).*

Let us reexamine the whole process of the burnt offering for the common people. What the common people had to do was to lay their hands on the sacrificial offering in order to transfer all their sin onto it, and then the throat of the sacrifice was cut to draw its blood. This was the whole task each individual sinner had to perform by himself. By doing this, they confessed that they were sinners who should have died like the animal sacrifices as God's judgment.

The rest of the job belonged to the priests, who acted on behalf of the people. The various jobs of the priest were to sprinkle the blood on the horns of the altar, to pour the remaining blood on the ground, to separate the fat, and to cut the flesh into pieces so that they could be burned on the altar. And on the Day of Atonement, the High Priest had to lay his hands on the scapegoats as the representative of his people, cut its throat, draw its blood, and sprinkle the blood inside the Holy Place.

Hence, the Israelites would not have been able to receive the remission of sin, if it had not been for the High Priests. On the Day of Atonement, all the priests had to leave the Tabernacle. The High Priest represented all the people and he had to minister the entire sacrifice ritual for the remission of yearly sins of the Israelites (Leviticus 16). The High Priest delivered them from God's judgment by transferring their yearly sins by laying his hands on the sacrifice on their behalf. As such, we can find that the laying on of hands was the only proper action to transfer the sins of Israelites onto sacrifices in both cases: the sacrifice for the remission of daily sins of the common people and the sacrifice for the remission of yearly sins of all Israelites on the Day of Atonement.

In the Old Testament times, the priests performed the job of blotting out all the sins of the Israelites. Not just anyone could perform the tasks of put the blood on the horns, pouring the rest of the blood on the ground, and burning the sacrifice before God after it had been cut into pieces. Saul, the first king of Israel, tried to do the task of a priest himself (1 Samuel 13:9), and that was a grave sin before God. No one except a priest could offer a sacrifice before God. Who had God chosen as His priests? He chose Aaron and his descendants.

Therefore, only a descendant of Aaron could become a High Priest. Not anyone could become a priest before God. God had appointed only the tribe of Levites, to become priests. A priest necessarily had to be a Levite. Was it acceptable if a person from Judah came and said, "I will make the offering to God since I am the king"? That kind of person would receive the curse of leprosy from God. God had created and established the rules for the sacrificial system, and the task of priest was appointed to the tribe of Levites only. God had determined that only a descendant of Aaron from the tribe of Levites could become a High Priest. That is to say that God had already determined on His own terms the sacrificial system of offering to Him. The Israelites of the Old Testament times received the remission of sin by transferring their sins through the laying on of hands and by atoning for them with the blood of the sacrifice.

We Must Know God's Law of Salvation and Our Own Weaknesses

We also have to offer the sacrifice according to the

sacrificial system God had established to receive our remission of sin because we cannot help but sin everyday due to our weaknesses. Because we know in our conscience that we have sins in our hearts and that we have not lived according to the Law of God, we must make an offering by the gospel Truth of the water and the Spirit.

In the Old Testament times, people had to make an offering by choosing a goat or a lamb without blemish. When the Old Testament people brought a lamb before God to make an offering because they had sinned, that lamb followed its master obediently without knowing its fate. The Israelites did not raise the lamb, the goat, and the calf for food but to receive the remission of sin through them. Hence, they raised a lot of young animals without blemish.

Remission of a Day's Worth of Sin in the Old Testament

In the Old Testament, Israelites could give offerings for the remission of a day's worth of sin. When the people of the Old Testament times committed a sin against God, each one of them had to bring a sacrifice without blemish before God daily, transferring his sins by laying his hands on its head, and then cutting its throat to draw blood, which in turn was handed to the priests. The priests would then put the blood on the horns of the altar and pour the rest on the ground. Also, they would cut the sacrifice into pieces, separating its fat, and offer it on fire of the altar before God. The people of the Old Testament times had to bring a sacrifice before God and offer it to God whenever they sinned. Also, since they had to bring a sacrifice every time they committed a sin, those who had a bad

conscience or could not live according to the Word of God had
to offer a lot of calves, goats, and lambs. Still, the number of
animals would not come close to the amount of sins a person
committed.

How much sin do people commit while they are alive in
this world? Since they always commit sins, the number of
sacrifices is proportionally much shorter. Thus, God knew that
it was too difficult for the Israelites to receive the remission of
their daily sins, so He granted them a sacrifice for the
remission of their year's worth of sins. If people realized that
they could not continue to offer sacrifices daily for the sins
they commit, they would become hopeless and give up in the
end. People are fundamentally such weak beings. People could
go to their limits to do what is in their ability. But if they fail,
they are disappointed and say, "Be as it may be." If people
have no way of completing a construction while it is still only
halfway through, many would declare bankruptcy and fall into
self-despair.

Dear fellow believers, although we try to live according to
the Law of God while offering prayers of repentance everyday,
we end up abandoning our faith in Jesus since we can never be
cleansed of our sins. Such people fall into a habit of despair
and live hopelessly for the rest of their lives. Regardless of how
well a person believes in God or how much a person repents,
one cannot blot out all one's sins with such actions. Or even if
he makes an offering according to the sacrificial system God
had established, it is useless. When people have no money or
material goods, they are unable to make an offering.
Sometimes, people cannot make an offering because of their
laziness. Because people have their dignity, it is not easy for
people to go to the Tabernacle daily to make an offering.

There is another instance when sinners are unable to make

an offering. This is when they have no recollection of their sins so they do not think to offer their sacrifices. A person should make an offering to God, if he has committed a sin against God. However, he cannot do so if he forgets immediately after he has committed a sin. It doesn't take much time for a person to commit another sin, even though he may be wondering, "When did I commit a sin?" For some people, it takes an hour. For others, it takes mere minutes. Once a person commits a new sin, he forgets his previous sins and it becomes hard to recall all of them accurately. Hence, it is a lie when a person says that he always offers the prayers of repentance appropriately. How could a person offer the prayers of repentance well when he forgets his sins so easily?

I was told that a fish has the short-term memory of three seconds. Tic tac, tic tac, tic tac. And its previous memories are all gone. For instance, let's say a fish takes a bite of bait a fisherman has put on a hook and gets stuck. The fish shakes and loosens the hook at the edge of its mouth, escapes and falls back into the water. The fish is in pain and says, "Wow, it hurts. I almost died. It hurts. Whew, I barely survived." Three seconds after thinking this, the fish swims toward another bait that is put into the water, although its mouth still hurts and it almost died an instant before.

"Wow, this one looks really delicious. It is strange. I'm not sure I have seen this one before." Hence, the fish goes to the bait and pokes it a few times with its mouth. "Wow, it really looks delicious." How delicious would this worm look to the fish while it was moving around the hook? To the fish, the worm appears to be saying, "Please eat me." "Oh, it's so cute. Where I should I begin eating it? Should I start from its head, or should I eat the whole body all at once? It's so cute and tasty looking." After stroking it a few times, the fish takes the whole worm in its mouth. When it realizes what just happened, the fishing hook has gone deep into its throat this time. When it is still in pain, it is brought up above the water. The same person holds it in his hands, but the fish does not recognize him.

The memory of a fish does not last three seconds. Hence, even if it falls back into the water a third time, if you put another bait on the hook and quickly drop it into the same point, the same fish will bite it again. Although humans have better memories than these fish, because of their hypocrisy and forgetfulness and because they have committed so many sins, they forget the sins they have committed only moments ago. Since we commit so many sins, it becomes impossible to remember them all. If people break the Word of God so many times, they tend to only remember those sins that are the biggest. They edit episodes of their own sins and remember only the few very big ones.

Thus, it was impossible to grant meaningful remission of sin by offering sacrifice for their daily sins in the system that God had established for the people of Israel. Because it was impossible to fulfill God's law of justice and His law of love by the daily offerings, God granted Israelites another sacrifice that could atone their sins for one year at once. This shows the love of God He granted us with His grace, because He knew our weaknesses. God granted people His grace of remission of a year's worth of sins at once.

The Shadow of the Eternal Remission of Sin and Its Reality

It said in Leviticus 16:29, *"This shall be a statute forever for you."* This statute refers to the rules God has established about how to offer the sacrifice of the Day of Atonement. As it said in Leviticus 16:29-31, *"This shall be a statute forever for you: In the seventh month, on the tenth day of the month, you shall afflict your souls, and do no work at all, whether a native of your own country or a stranger who dwells among you. For on that day the priest shall make atonement for you, to cleanse you, that you may be clean from all your sins before the Lord. It is a Sabbath of solemn rest for you, and you shall afflict your souls. It is a statute forever."*

Here, "you" refers to the entire Israelites. The Israelites gained great comfort in their hearts on the tenth day of the seventh month of each year, when all one-year's worth of their sins were blotted out. When the High Priest made an offering on behalf of the entire people of Israel, they received the remission of sin for the entire year. Hence, they gained great comfort in their hearts. The Israelites in the Old Testament times received the remission of sin in such a manner. It is similar to the way the spiritual Israelites of nowadays receive the remission of sin by believing in the gospel of the water and the Spirit.

The Sacrifice for the Remission of a Year's Worth of Sins

Let's look at how the people of the Old Testament times offered the sacrifice for the remission of a year's worth of their sins. This sacrificial system of the Day of Atonement is written in Leviticus chapter 16. God is holy. Because God is holy, the High Priest who administers the offering on that day must receive his remission of sin before he can make the offering on behalf of the entire Israelites. Any person who is unholy cannot go before God. Hence, the High Priest had to receive the remission of sin first.

If we look at Leviticus 16:6, it says, *"Aaron shall offer the bull as a sin offering, which is for himself, and made atonement for himself and for his house."* Aaron had to offer a male calf for his own sin offering. Before God, he had to first lay his hands on the head of the calf according to the sacrificial system. Then, in order to receive the remission of sin, he had to cut the throat of the sacrifice, draw its blood, sprinkle the blood on the horns of the altar, and then pour the rest of it on the ground. Then, the sacrifice was cut into pieces and burned before God. The death of the sacrifice was a symbol that Aaron should die as a sinner in the same manner. God accepted the death of the sacrifice in his stead and granted him the remission of sin. God had forgiven him for all his sins. God had delivered him from all his sins.

Aaron the High Priest offered a male calf first for himself and his household. On the tenth day of the seventh month, ordinary priests could not go into the Holy Place. Aaron alone ministered the sacrifices on that day.

Then, Aaron offered two goats for his people's sake. Leviticus 16:7-9 says, *"He shall take the two goats and present them before the Lord at the door of the tabernacle of meeting. Then Aaron shall cast lots for the two goats: one lot for the Lord and the other lot for the scapegoat. And Aaron shall bring the goat on which the Lord's lot fell, and offer it as a sin offering."*

On the tenth day of the seventh month, Aaron and his household first received the remission of sin, and then he took two goats for the remission of a year's worth sins of his people. Two goats were needed. Aaron had to cast lots for the two goats: one lot for the Lord and the other lot for the scapegoat.

For the one offered to God, the High Priest, as the representative of all Israelites, had to lay his hand on the head of the first goat to transfer all their sins onto it so that the people of Israel would become without sin before God. Next, he drew the blood of the sacrifice and took it before the Ark of the Covenant inside the Holy Place, sprinkling its blood seven times so that the year's worth of sins of all Israelites would be blotted out. Instead of the people of Israel dying in front of God, a goat, on which Aaron had transferred their sins, vicariously received the just judgments for their sins. In this way, the High Priest administered the offering of the Day of Atonement on behalf of the people of Israel.

We have to remind ourselves that a sacrifice as well as a High Priest was necessary in order for the Israelites to receive the remission of a year's worth of sin. These two conditions were absolutely necessary. They also had to follow the sacrificial system established by God. If the sacrifice had blemishes, then all ceremony would have been in vain. The sacrifice had to be without blemish, the High Priest had to lay his hands on the sacrifice, and its blood had to be sprinkled after it was killed. This was the task of the High Priest. Hence, if it had not been for the High Priest, each one of the Israelites would not have been able to receive the remission of sin. Through the High Priest, the Israelites received the remission of a year's worth of their sins. This is the mystery of our Lord. This was the plan of our Lord. So the Bible says,

"For unto us a Child is born,
Unto us a Son is given;
And the government will be upon His shoulder.
And His name will be called
Wonderful, Counselor, Mighty God,
Everlasting Father, Prince of Peace" (Isaiah 9:6).

Aaron received the duty as the first High Priest. Moses the servant of God was appointed as the administrator of the Law, the one who would receive and deliver the Law to the people and declare the Word of God to the people. On the other hand, Aaron was appointed as the High Priest among many priests. Aaron also received from God the duty of making an offering on the tenth day of the seventh month. The authority of the High Priest Aaron came from God.

On the tenth day of the seventh month, lots were cast for two goats. One would be offered to God and the other would be the scapegoat. On that day, all sins of the Israelites were transferred onto these two goats by Aaron's laying on of hands. Through the laying on of hands by the High Priest Aaron, the representative of the Israelites, God has established that all sins of the Israel in that year would be transferred onto the sacrifices.

We must first know the procedure of the offering on the Day of Atonement. Two goats were brought to be offered: One of them was offered before God. The other was offered outside the Tabernacle so that the people could see the High Priest transferring all the people's sins by the laying of his hands on the goat. Then the people could gain assurance of the remission of sin.

The first goat was offered as follows: Aaron first laid his own hands on it to transfer the sins of the Israelites before God. Then, its blood was drawn by cutting its throat, and was sprinkled seven times on and the east side of the Ark of Covenant inside the Holy Place. The blood was sprinkled seven times on the Mercy Seat on the east side. Aaron might have said in his heart, "God! This goat, on which all sins of the Israelites were transferred, died on the behalf of the Israelites."

The number 7 implies perfectness or completion as it is

used in the Book of Revelation. In the Bible 5 is a number designating grace. 6 is the number that implies humanity. 4 always refers to trials and hardships. The number 2 is related to the witness. Such meanings are implied within these numbers in the Bible.

Thus, if we look in the Bible, the number 4 appears wherever there is trials or hardship. 40 days prayer in the wilderness, 40-day fasting prayer, and 40 years in the wilderness are such examples. When talking of grace, the number 5 is necessarily applied. There were five porches by a pool called Bethesda, where Jesus healed a certain man who had an infirmity thirty-eight years (John 5:1-5).

The number 2 applies to witnesses. In order to receive the remission of sin before God, God had to accept the evidence of the people's offering, and also people needed to have in their hearts the assurance of their remission of sin before God. That is why two goats were needed on the Day of Atonement. One of the goats was taken before God and the other was taken outside the court of the Tabernacle so that the people could see Aaron's hands on the goat. Only if the High Priest, whom God had appointed, laid his hands on the goat in front of all the people on the tenth day of the seventh month would people accept that all their sins for that year were transferred onto the scapegoat. Thus, God prepared two goats for the offering.

One of the two goats was offered to God inside the Tabernacle. Aaron would say with his hands on the goat's head, "God! The people of Israel have gone against every statute of the Law that You have taught us. They have committed murder, adultery, and theft. They were jealous of one another and fought one another. They worshipped other gods, did not keep the Sabbath, and called Your Name in vain." As he lifted the hands that were laid on the goat, all sins were transferred immediately.

All sins of the Israelites were transferred onto the sacrificial animal by the laying of the High Priest's hands on its head. Then the High Priest cut the throat of the goat. He did so because the wage of sin is death. What did he do after they drew its blood by cutting the throat of the goat? The High Priest would then take its blood inside the Holy Place, where God resided. He would lift the curtains and enter the Most Holy Place and sprinkle the blood seven times on and before the east side of the Ark of the Covenant.

If the High Priest had forgotten to take the blood in there with him, he would have died. The reason why he would die if he did not take the blood or burning incense with him was because a person can approach God only after passing his sins onto a sacrifice for their judgments. Whoever desires to go before God must receive his judgments first. Otherwise, there is no way to approach the most holy God. Hence, even the High Priest had to take the blood of the sacrifice, which already received the judgments for his sins, as a sign of having been judged already and approach God with faith in the blood in order to live.

Now, one of the two goats was offered to God as a sacrifice. Let's look at Leviticus 16:18-20. *"And he shall go out to the altar that is before the Lord, and make atonement for it, and shall take some of the blood of the bull and some of the blood of the goat, and put it on the horns of the altar all around. Then he shall sprinkle some of the blood on it with his finger seven times, cleanse it, and consecrate it from the uncleanness of the children of Israel. And when he has made an end of atoning for the Holy Place, the tabernacle of meeting, and the altar, he shall bring the live goat."*

Aaron offered a perfect sacrifice to God with the first goat.

Then, he had to bring the other live goat. What would happen
to this goat? Let's look at the next few verses.

*"Aaron shall lay both his hands on the head of the live
goat, confess over it all the iniquities of the children of Israel,
and all their transgressions, concerning all their sins, putting
them on the head of the goat, and shall sent it away into the
wilderness by the hand of a suitable man. The goat shall bear
on itself all their iniquities to an uninhabited land; and he shall
release the goat in the wilderness" (Leviticus 16:21-22).*

Dear fellow believers, we humans need to receive the
remission of sin on two different levels. First, we need to
receive the remission of sin from God. Second, we need to
receive the remission of the sin in our hearts. In other words,
with the blood of the first sacrifice, the Israelites needed to
receive the remission of sin by covering their sins recorded in
the Book of Judgment in the Heavenly Kingdom. When God
saw that blood, He granted them the remission of sin, by saying,
"The people of Israel have received the judgments for all their
sins. They have received the remission of sin. They have
received the atonement for their sins. This sacrifice has died in
their place after all their sins were transferred onto it." We
must first receive this remission of sin before God.

If we look at the Lord's Prayer, it says, *"Our Father in
heaven, hallowed be Your name, Your kingdom come, Your will
be done on earth as it is in heaven" (Matthew 6:9-10).* The
phrase "Your will be done on earth as it is in Heaven" is
speaking about the salvation and emancipation we receive from
all the sins in our hearts when we accept that Jesus has taken
all the sins we have committed in this world.

Let's visit Leviticus 16:20-21 again. *"And when he has
made an end of atoning for the Holy Place, the tabernacle of
meeting, and the altar, he shall bring the live goat. Aaron shall*

lay both his hands on the head of the living goat, confess over it all the iniquities of the children of Israel, and all their transgressions, concerning all their sins, putting them on the head of the goat, and shall send it away into the wilderness by the hand of a suitable man."

Now, the sins recorded in Heaven were blotted out with the first goat, then, how did Aaron blot out the sins present in the hearts of the Israelites? God prepared another goat to be shown in front of the people, on which Aaron the High Priest laid his hands. Aaron laid his hands on the head of this second goat and prayed, "God! I transfer the sins of the Israelites. They have committed the sins of murder, adultery, theft, jealousy, and confrontation. They have served other gods, called Your name in vain, gave false testimony, did not keep the Sabbath holy, and offended each and every commandment of Your Law. All these sins I transfer onto this goat." The High Priest on behalf of the people laid his hands on the goat and transferred all sins of the Israelites as such. Then, the goat was sent away into the wilderness by the hand of a suitable man. The scapegoat bore all sins of the Israelites and wandered around the vast wilderness, where it died still bearing the sins of all the Israelites.

By accepting that by this method all the sins of the Israelites were transferred once for all to the scapegoat, they knew in their hearts that they had received the remission of sin and the assurance of their salvation. The scapegoat on which all of their sins were transferred wandered deep into the wilderness. The Palestine area is a vast desert. The place the Israelites offered their first sacrifices according to the Tabernacle system was the wilderness of Sinai. There was not even a single leaf or grass growing in this area. The goat that was abandoned there eventually died there. Because the scapegoat died bearing the sins of the Israelites in their place, the Israelites received the remission of sin in their hearts after seeing with their own eyes how Aaron had made on offering for them on the tenth day of the seventh month. This also tells us the process by which we can receive our remission of sin.

The remission of sin for people has to be done in two different places. The sins under the names of the people in the Book of Judgment in the Kingdom of God as well as the sins in our hearts must be erased. These two parts equal the true remission of sin. Dear fellow believers, God has blotted out all our sins completely. God's will has been completed in Heaven. What we have to do now is to receive the complete remission of sin in our souls by accepting that all our sins were already transferred onto the sacrificial offering. Accepting in our hearts this gospel Truth is what we need to do.

Hebrew 10:1 says, *"For the law, having a shadow of the good things to come, and not the very image of the things, can never with these same sacrifices, which they offer continually year by year, make those who approach perfect."* It says that the sacrifice of the Day of Atonement of the Old Testament tomes was a shadow of the good things to come, that is, the eternal redemption fulfilled by Jesus Christ, our Savior.

Now, let's look out how Jesus has fulfilled the remission of all our sins in the New Testament.

First of all, we have to know that Jesus Christ is the Son of God who came to this earth to deliver all humans. Matthew 1:21-25 states, *"'And she will bring forth a Son, and you shall call His name Jesus, for He will save His people from their sins.' So all this was done that it might be fulfilled which was spoken by the Lord through the prophet, saying: 'Behold, the virgin shall be with child, and bear a Son, and they shall call His name Immanuel,' which is translated, 'God with us.' Then*

Joseph, being aroused from sleep, did as the angel of the Lord commanded him and took to him his wife, and did not know her till she had brought forth her firstborn Son. And he called His name Jesus."

Our Lord Jesus came to this world as the God Immanuel as prophesized in the Old Testament. The Hebrew word 'Immanuel' means 'God with us.' He came to this world to be with us. And His name was called Jesus. The name 'Jesus' means 'the Savior.' Our Lord came in the lowly flesh of man in spite of His perfect divinity to become our Savior in this world. He delivered us from all our sins by blotting out all our sins for us, His people, who were created in His image.

Let's look at Matthew 3:13-17 to see what our Lord has done after coming to this world. *"Then Jesus came from Galilee to John at the Jordan to be baptized by him. And John tried to prevent Him, saying, 'I need to be baptized by You, and are You coming to me?' But Jesus answered and said to him, 'Permit it to be so now, for thus it is fitting for us to fulfill all righteousness.' Then he allowed Him. When He has been baptized, Jesus came up immediately from the water; and behold, the heavens were opened to Him, and He saw the Spirit of God descending like a dove and alighting upon Him. And suddenly a voice came from heaven, saying, 'This is My beloved Son, in whom I am well pleased'"* (Matthew 3:13-17).

The word "Then" signifies the time when Jesus would fulfill all righteousness by coming as the heavenly High Priest. Why did Jesus Christ receive the baptism at the Jordan River? Our Lord came to this world to pay off all wages of sins in the world. That is why Jesus came to this world and received the baptism from John the Baptist. Jordan River is the river of death. The river runs rapidly toward the Dead Sea. Thus at the Jordan River, Jesus received the baptism from John the Baptist.

Then, John the Baptist said, *"I need to be baptized by You, and are You coming to me?" (Matthew 3:14)* Jesus responded, by saying, *"Permit it to be so now, for thus it is fitting for us to fulfill all righteousness" (Matthew 3:15)*. Thus, the two High Priests came together and fulfilled all righteousness.

John the Baptist is the greatest among those born of a woman, as it is written in Matthew 11:11. Jesus, the representative of Heaven, was about to receive the baptism from John the Baptist, the representative all mankind. Jesus said, "You should baptize Me." Then, John asked back, "How could I dare baptize You?"

Jesus said to him in a stern attitude, "Permit it to be so now, for thus it is fitting for us to fulfill all righteousness. It is right for us to fulfill all righteousness in this way. I mean, it is right for you to baptize Me, as it is right for Me to fulfill all righteousness by receiving the baptism" (Matthew 3:13-17).

The word 'baptism' means to wash away. Therefore, all our sins were washed away completely when Jesus received the baptism from John the Baptist. Just as all the sins of the people of Israel were washed away from their hearts by the laying on of Aaron's hands on the scapegoat in the Old Testament.

Matthew 3:15 says that Jesus was baptized "to fulfill all righteousness." What then is this righteousness? It is said that the righteousness of God is revealed in the gospel and it leads us from faith to faith (Romans 1:17). The righteousness of God could mean the justice of God. The rightful deed God granted us humans was His blotting out all our sins through His Son. This was the very baptism Jesus received.

How can we humans receive the righteousness from God? We can receive the righteousness of God by believing that all our sins has been transferred onto Jesus when He received the baptism from John the Baptist by means of laying on of hands. Baptism has the same meaning as the laying on of hands in the Old Testament. The righteousness of God is for us to become His children as well as to become the righteous. We receive our salvation from all sins by believing and accepting in our hearts that Jesus Christ took all our sins when He received the baptism from John the Baptist. This is the righteousness we receive from God.

"'Permit it to be so now, for thus it is fitting for us to fulfill all righteousness.' Then he allowed Him. When He had been baptized, Jesus came up immediately from the water; and behold, the heavens were opened to Him, and He saw the Spirit of God descending like a dove and alighting upon Him" (Matthew 3:15-16).

When Jesus received the baptism, the Heavens were opened up and the Holy Spirit of God descended like a dove and a sound echoed from Heaven. *"This is My beloved Son, in whom I am well pleased" (Matthew 3:17).* Who just received the baptism? He was Jesus Christ the Son of God. He was simultaneously the Son of God as well as the God who created us. "This is My Son, in whom I am well pleased." God was well pleased with Jesus. God the Father had all our sins transferred onto Jesus, the Son of God. The Son of God obediently bore all our sins vicariously according to the will of the Father so that we may become the children of God.

The word "baptism" has the meaning of "to cleanse, to immerse, and to transfer." We use the word baptism to also imply the immersion. We can receive the remission of sin by accepting the salvation, which was possible because all our sins were transferred onto Jesus when He received the baptism.

Also, we believe that all our sins, which were recorded in the Book of Judgment in the Kingdom of Heaven, were washed away by Jesus' sacrifice on the Cross. All our sins that were recorded on the tablets of our hearts were also washed away completely when Jesus received the baptism. God's will was fulfilled on earth as it has been done in Heaven (Matthew 6:10). Both of these acts were fulfilled.

Dear fellow believers, this Word is the pairing of the Old Testament and the New Testament. Where the two merge together is the baptism that Jesus received. People ask how could their sins be transferred when Jesus was baptized, but, my dear fellow believers, the word "baptism" also means 'to pass over,' because it is administered by the action of "laying on of hands." Baptism also has the meanings of "immersion" and "burial." If Jesus was to be buried, He had to first bear all our sins. Jesus could die vicariously for us only after all sins of the world were transferred onto Jesus. That is why Jesus received the baptism. At that moment, all our sins were transferred onto Jesus. Thus, the Bible defines His baptism as the fulfillment of all righteousness.

Furthermore, the baptism of Jesus is analogous to the transference of one year's worth of sins of the Israelites in the Old Testament. Jesus received the baptism for our sake. The word "baptism" has the meanings of "to wash away, to bury, and to transfer." If we look it up in the theological dictionary, it has even more meanings. Dear fellow believers, all our sins were transferred onto Jesus when He received the baptism. The sins of those who accept that all our sins were transferred onto Jesus by His baptism can be washed away all at once.

Dear fellow believers, I urge you to accept this Truth into your hearts. If you do not accept this Truth into your hearts, you will not be able to receive the remission of sin. If there is any other way by which all our sins are transferred other than the baptism of Jesus, try to receive your salvation by believing in that. However, in reality there is no other way. I admonish you to become children of God by receiving the salvation by accepting and believing the gospel of the baptism of Jesus.

My beloved fellow believers, this is the gospel of the water and the Spirit, which God has spoken to us. This is the Word of Truth. Believing in this is the core of the true faith. By the baptism our Lord received at the Jordan River, all our sins in our hearts were washed away completely. By the death of our Lord on the Cross, all the sins of the world that were recorded in the Book of Deed in the Kingdom of Heaven were washed away completely. All sins we have committed in this world as well as the sins that the future generation will commit were completely washed away. By believing in Jesus, the Deliverer of our salvation, we have been rescued from all our sins. He has blotted out all our sins through His baptism (the laying on of hands), His blood of the Cross (judgment), and His death and resurrection.

Now, is there still any sin in your hearts? There is none. Are you still a sinner? No, you're not. You have become one of the righteous.

John 1:29 says, *"Behold! The Lamb of God who takes away the sin of the world!"* The very next day after Jesus had received the baptism, John the Baptist testified, *"Behold! The Lamb of God who takes away the sin of the world!" (John 1:29)* The fact that Jesus took and bore all sins of the world is the Truth.

Here are some diagrams for your understanding:

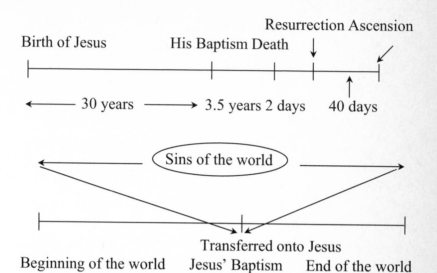

Jesus took all the sins of the world by receiving the baptism at the Jordan River. *"Behold! The Lamb of God who takes away the sin of the world!" (John 1:29)* He finished everything on the Cross by saying, *"It is finished!" (John 19:30)*

The sins, which you have committed from the moment you stepped out of your mother's womb to when you were 10 years old, are the sins of the world. Do you accept the truth that all those sins were transferred unto Jesus when He received the baptism? Did those sins transfer to Jesus? Yes.

You have also committed many sins in your teens, from 11 to 20 years of age. Were these sins transferred onto the head of Jesus as well? Yes. The same is true for the sins you have committed in your twenties. Were all the sins you committed so far transferred onto the head of Jesus as well?

The sins you might commit in the future are also included

in the sins of the world. Were those sins transferred onto Jesus as well? Yes, they were transferred. Dear fellow believers, do you believe that Jesus truly took all sins of the world by receiving the baptism? Yes, we believe. And do you believe that Jesus took care of all of the sins of the world and fulfilled all righteousness? Yes, we believe. With His baptism and bloodshed on the Cross, Jesus took care of all sins of the world and even all the sins that will be committed until the end of the world. Jesus fulfilled all of God's righteousness by taking the sins of the world through His baptism and by receiving the judgments for those sins on the Cross.

Do you still have sin or not? Now, there is no longer any sin in this world. If you believe in the Word of God and the Truth that Jesus blotted out all sins of the world by His baptism and blood, then you have no sin. That is salvation. That is God's gift of salvation. This is the gospel of the water and the Spirit, the very foundation of our faith. These are all the works of atonement that our Lord did to deliver us from all our sins through His baptism.

Dear fellow believers, do you now believe in the gospel of the water and the Spirit? To look to Jesus and to accept the gospel of the water and the Spirit is to believe in the Word of Truth. This is the Word of being born again. Only when we accept this Word can we become born again. Dear fellow believers, do you want to be born again by the water and the Spirit? If so, believe in the gospel of the water and the Spirit. This is true faith and true spiritual life. Christianity as a religion is to believe in Jesus whom people have created according to their own thoughts and to receive salvation arbitrarily. However, true faith believing that Jesus has delivered me out of His love for me and according to His promise, and that He has completed the salvation on only His own accord. His salvation is nothing to do with our own deeds.

God blotted out all sins of the Israelites in the Old
Testament times by the laying on of the hands of the High
Priest on the sacrificial lamb. In the New Testament, Jesus took
all of our sins by receiving the baptism from the High Priest
John the Baptist. We, who live in the New Testament times,
must accept and believe in the baptism of Jesus, which has
made us sinless. Since there would no transference of sins or
consequent bloodshed without the baptism of Jesus, there can
be no remission of sin without the baptism of Jesus. Jesus has
wholly delivered us by taking all our sins with His baptism and
by receiving the judgments for all our sins through His blood
shed on the Cross. Therefore, we the believers of the gospel of
the water and the Spirit will not receive the judgments for our
sins.

We must believe that Jesus wholly took all sins of the
world when He received the baptism and that He vicariously
received the whole judgments for our sins on the Cross. We
must accept into our hearts the gospel of the water and the
Spirit, which Jesus prepared for us so that we could receive the
salvation out of His love for us. We can avoid all judgments for
our sins by accepting the Truth that our Lord has redeemed us
completely in order to deliver us from all our sins and therefore
all judgments. Sinners can now be made into the righteous by
believing in the gospel of the Spirit in heart and confessing
with their lips, "Lord, I believe in You. Although I have no
merit, I believe in Your baptism, death, and resurrection." We
receive our salvation when we gratefully accept the works of
our Lord in our faith, looking up to Him. True faith is to
believe in Him and to accept His righteous acts like this. This
is the Word of being born again.

"And you shall know the truth, and the truth shall make

you free" (John 8:32). Don't we need to have some essential knowledge to carry out a certain important duty such as the mayor of a city? Don't we need to know the Truth to receive our salvation? We will truly receive our salvation only if we have the biblical evidence that Jesus became our personal Lord and Savior by the gospel of the water and the Spirit.

The Truth shall make you free (John 8:32). Dear fellow believers, have you received the freedom? Do you accept this Truth? Do you believe this? Are you and I religionists or people living genuine spiritual lives? We are people who live spiritual lives in the faith in our Lord. Still, there are still many religionists in this world.

Those who have genuine faith in Jesus Christ have no sin. However, religionists cannot help but remain as sinners because of their deficiencies even though they believe in the same Jesus as us. You and I truly have no sin in our hearts. Truly, there is no sin in our hearts. However, the faith of the religionists is wrong because they believe that they have no sin if they are good in their religious lives, but they still have sin they nonetheless commit regardless of their faith in Jesus.

Hence, they say that they have to wash their sins by prayers of repentance whenever they sin. But, in actuality, such prayers of repentance cannot replace the gospel of the water and the Spirit, which has blotted out all sins for our lifetime. No doctrine of the worldly religions can substitute for the true gospel of the water and the Spirit, which has blotted out all sins of those who accept—even sins not yet committed. The prayers of repentance cannot replace Jesus, who washed away all our sins with His baptism and His blood on the Cross. We cannot cleanse even a single sin in our hearts by our prayers of repentance alone.

God's gift of salvation is not given to us according to our

deeds. The gift we have received is our salvation through the gospel of the water and the Spirit when we believed in Him. This is the spiritual life, the true faith, and true salvation. Believing in the gospel of the water and the Spirit is being born again. Dear fellow believers, this is the Truth of being born again of water and the Spirit, which our Lord has told Nicodemus (John 3:5). Believing in two events from the Bible, Jesus' baptism and His death on the Cross, is the very salvation and the only way of being born again.

Dear fellow believers, how were you washed from all your sins and made born again? You have received your salvation from all the sins of the world and all your personal sins, because you believed in the baptism Jesus received from John the Baptist and His blood on the Cross. Am I not right? If we truly have received the whole remission of sin by believing in the gospel of the water and the Spirit, we must give thanks to God by our faith in the baptism and blood of Jesus.

Those who lead the true spiritual life believe in the very gospel Truth of the water and the Spirit and truly witness that gospel to others. All the righteous are the born again who have the biblical evidence of God's salvation in them. Even if a person leads a spiritual life, unless that person has the three beliefs in the Holy Spirit, the water, and the blood, he is not yet born again. We receive our eternal salvation by believing in the baptism, by which our Lord took all our sins Himself, and the blood on the Cross.

Who is the very Person that has done this righteous acts? He is Jesus Christ who is not a mere human being but God. Can you dig it? Those, who believe in the Lord who fulfilled the gospel of the water and the Spirit, are the born again. If you believe in the gospel of the water and the Spirit, you do not just believe in any religion. Just as our Lord cleansed commander

Naaman's leprosy completely when he dipped his body in the Jordan River seven times, we believe that our Lord cleansed us of all our sins. People receive the whole remission of sin by believing in Jesus' baptism and His blood on the Cross.

Dear fellow believers, I was born again when I believed in the gospel of the water and the Spirit. Hence, I no longer live a religious life but a life of spiritual faith. I believe that God has blotted out all my sins and became my Savior, my Shepherd, and my true God because He loved me. Because we did not love God first but God loved us first by grace, God delivered us from all our sins by the gospel of the water and the Spirit. I have received my salvation from all my sins and the eternal life by believing in this.

My beloved fellow believers, do you also have the assurance of your eternal life? The baptism Jesus Christ received washed away all our sins and blotted them out.

Have you not been born again yet? Do not be afraid of those who have not born again. All that you have to do is just believe in God, who will make you born again by the water and the Spirit. Look at the Truth of the water and the Spirit and believe in the Truth by which God delivered us from all our sins. And give thanks to God. Then, you will receive the eternal life and the everlasting blessings.

The Word in John 1:12-13 says, *"But as many as received Him, to them He gave the right to become children of God, to those who believe in His name: who were born, not of blood, nor of the will of the flesh, nor of the will of man, but of God."*

And The Word in Hebrews 10:9-18 says, *"Then He said, 'Behold, I have come to do Your will, O God.' He takes away the first that He may establish the second. By that will we have been sanctified through the offering of the body of Jesus Christ once for all. And every priest stands ministering daily and offering repeatedly the same sacrifices, which can never take away sins. But this Man, after He had offered one sacrifice for sins forever, sat down at the right hand of God, from that time waiting till His enemies are made His footstool. For by one offering He has perfected forever those who are being sanctified. But the Holy Spirit also witnesses to us; for after He had said before, 'This is the covenant that I will make with them after those days, says the Lord: I will put My laws into their hearts, and in their minds I will write them,' then He adds, 'Their sins and their lawless deeds I will remember no more.' Now where there is remission of these, there is no longer an offering for sin."*

Matthew 3:15 states, *"For thus it is fitting for us to fulfill all righteousness."* A person is born again when he believes in the baptism Jesus received. Jesus has delivered all people completely by receiving the baptism to take all the sins of all humanity. Jesus has received all judgments for all our sins by being crucified on the Cross, where He shed His precious blood. This is the gospel of the water and the Spirit, which makes us born again. The faith in the gospel of the water and the Spirit is the true faith and the Truth of being born again. ⊠

Do You Believe in The God-given Gospel of The Water and the Spirit?

< John 3:1-8 >

"There was a man of the Pharisees named Nicodemus, a ruler of the Jews. This man came to Jesus by night and said to Him, 'Rabbi, we know that You are a teacher come from God; for no one can do these signs that You do unless God is with him.' Jesus answered and said to him, 'Most assuredly, I say to you, unless one is born again, he cannot see the kingdom of God.' Nicodemus said to Him, 'How can a man be born when he is old? Can he enter a second time into his mother's womb and be born?' Jesus answered, 'Most assuredly, I say to you, unless one is born of water and the Spirit, he cannot enter the kingdom of God. That which is born of the flesh is flesh, and that which is born of the Spirit is spirit. Do not marvel that I said to you, 'You must be born again.' The wind blows where it wishes, and you hear the sound of it, but cannot tell where it comes from and where it goes. So is everyone who is born of the Spirit.'"

Nicodemus, a Religious Leader

Jesus is speaking clearly to Nicodemus in today's

Scripture passage, *"Unless one is born again, he cannot see the kingdom of God."* As Jesus said this, Nicodemus asked in return, *"How can a man be born when he is old? Can he enter a second time into his mother's womb and be born?"* Again, Jesus said to Nicodemus, *"Most assuredly, I say to you, unless one is born of water and the Spirit, he cannot enter the kingdom of God."*

We have to die to our sins in our faith and be born again by believing that Jesus Christ the Son of God has truly fulfilled God's righteousness by coming to this world, taking all the sins of the world onto Himself through the baptism He received from John the Baptist, and paying them off with His blood on the Cross. This is being born again. The Bible tells us that no one can enter into the Kingdom of God unless he is born again of water and the Spirit (John 3:5).

The Lord said to us, *"That which is born of the flesh is flesh, and that which is born of the Spirit is spirit"* (John 3:6). *"For to be carnally minded is death, but to be spiritually minded is life and peace"* (Romans 8:6). It tells us that no matter how fervently we believe Jesus in our flesh, we cannot be born again through such means. The Holy Spirit cannot reside in a heart that still has sin in it. If God were to administer His spiritual test, that person would fail that test. Whoever lives in this world can be born again only by the faith in the gospel of the water and the Spirit.

The Lord continued to tell Nicodemus, *"Do not marvel that I said to you, 'You must be born again.' The wind blows where it wishes, and you hear the sound of it, but cannot tell where it comes from and where it goes. So is everyone who is born of the Spirit"* (John 3:7-8). This Word tells us that we have been born again and freed from sin by believing in the gospel of the water and the Spirit. Such a faith enables us to know the will of God and allows us to be born again.

The Lord said, *"The wind blows where it wishes, and you hear the sound of it, but cannot tell where it comes from and where it goes. So is everyone who is born of the Spirit"* *(John 3:8)*. However, not a few Christians who don't know the way to be born again misinterpret this passage and say, "We don't know when we were born again of water and the Spirit. People are becoming born again unaware to themselves because they believe in Jesus fervently." Yet, Jesus did not say this with such an intention. He meant by this, "Nicodemus, you don't know anything. You do not know that God delivered you from all your sins by the gospel of the water and the Spirit. Still, believers in the gospel Word of the water and the Spirit know well how God has delivered them from all their sins. They can enter and see the Kingdom of God by being born again with their faith in the gospel of the water and the Spirit."

The Lord meant by this passage that we must believe in the gospel of the water and the Spirit. He wants to inform us that only when we believe in the gospel of the water and the Spirit do we receive the remission of sin, and that only those who have received the remission of sin can receive the gift of salvation from God and become His children. Isn't it true that only those who have become the children of God can enter His Kingdom?

Thus, the entire population in this whole wide world must become born again to be the children of God by believing in the gospel of the water and the Spirit. Furthermore, those who have become the children of God through their faith must spread the gospel of the water and the Spirit throughout the whole world according to the will of God. In today's Scripture passage, the Lord tells us clearly that those who are born again through the gospel of the water and the Spirit will enter the

Kingdom of God as they have become His children, and they will be blessed as God's own people even in this world. Jesus told clearly to Nicodemus, "You are not yet born again, because you don't know the gospel of the water and the Spirit yet." The Lord said, *"Most assuredly, I say to you, unless one is born of water and the Spirit, he cannot enter the kingdom of God" (John 3:5).* In this passage, we can understand the Truth to enter the Kingdom of Heaven by our faith.

Do you know why the Lord says that people can see and enter the Kingdom of God only if they are born again by the gospel of the water and the Spirit? Those who believe in the gospel of the water and the Spirit are the blessed saints who have been cleansed completely from all their sins. Our Lord said that being born of water and the Spirit is possible only when that person believes in the gospel of the water and the Spirit.

Then, why did He say that we are born again of "water and the Spirit," rather than to say that we are born again of "the water and the blood"? Actually, these two expressions are the same. By His choice of words, He meant that God the Father has delivered us by blotting out all our sins by sending His Only Son to this world. God's will was for His Son to receive the baptism which transferred all the sins of the entire humanity onto His body, and have Him pay for all those sins by bleeding to His death on the Cross. Jesus received the baptism from John the Baptist, by which He took all of our sins. He bore all those sins onto the Cross, where He died, and later resurrected from the dead. God Himself did all these works in order to blot out all our sins. By this passage, God the Father tells us that He has delivered all of us from our sins by the gospel of the water and the Spirit through His only begotten Son.

Thus, it is not important how long people have believed in Jesus. Our Lord has come to this world and delivered us by giving us new life through the gospel of the water and the Spirit, even before we came across Jesus Christ. The Lord asks us, while we are still sinners, "When did you hear the true gospel of the water and the Spirit? And when did you first believe?" We cannot help but hold tightly to this gospel Word of the water and the Spirit because this gospel Truth is better understood once we hear it through the Word of God. What I am saying is that we are not born again by holding onto a specific passage from the Word of God but first by holding onto the gospel Word of the water and the Spirit.

What did the Lord do after He had come to this world? He blotted out all the sins of the world by being baptized by John the Baptist and then shedding His blood on the Cross. He delivered us from all the sins of the world by the gospel Truth of the water and the Spirit. Our Lord had completed our salvation in this Word of Truth. Hence, the believers in this Word can show generosity to everyone because all their sins were transferred onto Jesus Christ, when He received the baptism. Only God determines the goodness or the badness of our faith. If He says, "Your faith is bad," you have to turn back from your current way of faith right now.

Psalms 51 is a Psalm of David that was written after he committed adultery with Bathsheba. He stated in this Psalm that even though he had committed grave sins, if the Word of God declared that he was righteous, then he was sinless. But, if the Word of the Lord declared he was guilty, then it is clear that he still harbored sin. Everything about us is determined by the judgment God makes. Therefore, if God tells us through His Word that we are sinful, then we indeed have sin. If He tells us that we are innocent, then we are without sin. Thus, those who believe that God has delivered you and me from all our sins have become people free of sin. Jesus has delivered us from all our sins by coming in this world and receiving the baptism, dying on the Cross, and resurrecting from the dead. If God says He has delivered us from all our sins in Jesus Christ by such means, it is so.

If we are told that we were delivered from all our sins in such a way, we have to believe this. And we need to have the true confession of our faith in the gospel of the water and the Spirit. To be free from our sins, we have to die once in the gospel of the water and the Spirit. And to claim our righteousness, we have experience our own resurrections by our faith in the gospel Truth. You and I have been born again by believing in the gospel of the water and the Spirit.

Therefore, if we do not truly possess the faith in the gospel Word of the water and the Spirit, we are not yet born again. It does not matter how many Bible passages you and I have read or believed. It does not matter how much hard work we have done for our Lord. And it does not matter what our current positions at our churches are. The only means by which God has made us born again from all our sins is the gospel Truth of the water and the Spirit. We have received the remission of sin and have been born again as the children of God only by our faith in the gospel of the water and the Spirit. Regardless of whether it came late or early, those who are born again by the water and the Spirit are the children of God, who will receive great rewards before God.

Yet, when we listen to some people's testimony about their salvation, they say, "Jesus, I give glory to God for delivering me from all my sins by Your dying on the Cross." These kinds of people have not truthfully transferred all their sins to Jesus. It is very hard for us to share the gospel with such people. And they are sharing a different gospel other than the gospel of the water and the Spirit. It would be an erroneous faith to claim that one gospel is as correct as another gospel, when we have clearly received the remission of sin by believing in the gospel of the water and the Spirit. If our faith is the only and true way to our salvation before God, there is no other faith but that of the gospel of the water and the Spirit. Only the gospel of the water and the Spirit is the true gospel. Any other gospel, although it may appear close to the gospel of the water and the Spirit, cannot be the true gospel.

There is another phenomenon we find among the Christians: Those who have not yet been born again hate those who have been born again. These people claimed a similar yet different gospel from the gospel of the water and the Spirit, when they first started believing in Jesus.

We have to approach our Lord with the faith in the gospel of the water and the Spirit. The Bible passage that says, *"You have cast all my sins behind Your back,"* is the confession of the king Hezekiah who had faith in the gospel of the water and the Spirit (Isaiah 38:17). Even when Jesus said on the Cross, "It is finished," He declared that He had completed the Truth in the gospel of the water and the Spirit (John 19:30). *"Now where there is remission of these, there is no longer an offering for sin" (Hebrews 10:18). "Behold! The Lamb of God who takes away the sin of the world!" (John 1:29) "Permit it to be so now, for thus it is fitting for us to fulfill all righteousness" (Matthew 3:15).* All these words take their full effect when we believe that all our sins were transferred onto Jesus when He received the baptism from John the Baptist.

Because Jesus took all the sins of the world onto Himself when He received the baptism from John the Baptist, all my sins were transferred then as well. Because I believe that, I have received the remission of sin. Moreover, Jesus bore all sins of the world onto the Cross, where He received the judgments for all those sins and died vicariously in my stead. I believe that. And Jesus resurrected from the dead. We believe that Jesus Christ has become our eternal Savior by resurrecting from the dead. We will be spared from the rejection by God, only when we offer the correct answers of our faith in the present tense.

Those who have been born again by the gospel of the water and the Spirit always talk about this gospel Truth. If a person has the precise faith in the gospel Word of the water and the Spirit in his heart, he can confess his faith truly at any time and in every circumstance. However, if a person does not believe in his heart the gospel Word of the water and the Spirit despite knowing it in his head, he would not be able to share the true testimony of his salvation. Still, as long as one believes in the gospel of the water and the Spirit, even an old grandmother would say when giving a testimony of her salvation, "I have no sin because all my sins were wholly transferred to Jesus when He received the baptism from John the Baptist. Jesus has delivered me from sin when He bore all my sins onto the Cross, died, and resurrected from the dead. Thus, I have been born again."

Once, many grandmothers enrolled in our gospel class during a retreat. When I asked them to give testimonies of their salvation after receiving the remission of sin through their faith in the gospel of the water and the spirit, one elderly lady said, "John the Baptist safely transferred all my sins onto Jesus. Thus, He bled on the Cross. And I have been born again because I believed this." The whole congregation gave a loud applause after hearing such testimony. Another elderly lady came up to give a testimony. She said, "I have no sin because

John the Baptist has safely transferred my sins to Jesus." About a total of ten elderly ladies gave their testimonies, but it took no longer than half an hour. It took them longer to go up the stairs to the pulpit and go down to their seats. The actual presentation of their testimonies took no longer than 30 seconds per each testimony. That was because the elderly ladies' testimonies of their salvation were as if it was a testimony of one and the same person. Still, these elderly ladies who had correct faith before God and had received the remission of sin were born again by the water and the Spirit at that time. We have helped them become born again by sharing the gospel of the water and the Spirit with them.

We have become born again only by the faith in the gospel of the water and the Spirit. Is there anyone who can be born again before God by his own efforts? Can we be born again by praying in the mountains? Can we be born again through fasting and prayers? Would God make you born again if you fasted for 10 days? How about if you fasted for 40 days? Never. God tells us that you can be born again only when you believe that He has blotted out all your sins by the water and the Spirit.

Jesus said to Nicodemus, *"The wind blows where it wishes, and you hear the sound of it, but cannot tell where it comes from and where it goes. So is everyone who is born of the Spirit."* This means that those people who do not know the gospel Truth of the water and the Spirit do not know how God has made us born again. However, the believers in the gospel of the water and the Spirit know correctly that they were born again by this gospel Truth. He said that all the born again are like this.

We must believe in the gospel Truth of the water and the Spirit now and in our hearts. Only then can we boldly say that today we are without sin in the present tense. When I gaze into my own heart, I am always sure of the gospel of the water and the Spirit. Some people may say, "That preacher must have memorized only the gospel of the water and the Spirit, because he always talks about that gospel whenever he opens his mouth. It comes out like a fountain spring whenever he opens his mouth." That is not true. I can continuously talk about the gospel of the water and the Spirit only because I still believe in this gospel even to this very moment. He who does not believe in the gospel Truth of the water and the Spirit cannot continuously witness it with joy.

Dear fellow believers, you have to believe in the gospel of the water and the Spirit in order to be born again. If you do not believe in the gospel of the water and the Spirit, you cannot receive the remission of sin. However, if you have received your salvation by believing in the gospel of the water and the Spirit now, you cannot deny that this gospel is the genuine truth of being born again. Both in the past and the present, all believers in Jesus have been born again by their faith in the gospel of the water and the Spirit. God gave the gospel of the water and the Spirit from above so that we the sinners can be born again into the righteous. The Lord has delivered us from all our sins and adopted us as God's children.

We now know that this gospel Truth brings us tremendous blessings from above. That's why we must believe in the gospel of the water and the Spirit, which has blotted out all our sins. There is no other way to be born again except believing in this Truth. God had His only begotten Son receive the baptism and die on the Cross so that all our sins might be blotted out completely. Regardless of who we are, we must all believe in the gospel of the water and the Spirit. We cannot wait until later to believe in this gospel Truth but we must believe in it right now. We must hold onto the gospel of the water and the Spirit by faith now.

Do you think that we do not need to talk about the gospel of the water and the Spirit although we may not know it? No. It must be mentioned now. It must be discussed now in the present tense. Believing in the gospel of the water and the Spirit must always take place in the present and cannot wait till tomorrow. It is a task for us to do right now. If you and I had not believed in the gospel of the water and the Spirit, it would have been impossible for us to receive the remission of sin no matter how many Bible passages we believed in.

When Nicodemus asked Jesus, "How can a man be born again?" Jesus replied, "One is born again by the water and the Spirit." The Truth that makes a person born again is none other than the gospel of the water and the Spirit. However, most Christians think and believe in their own ways about being born again, despite the reading of this Scripture passage. Some people even say that the water is not referring to the baptism Jesus received. They interpret the 'water' as amniotic fluid saying, "A baby is born from its mother with the amniotic fluid." Then, how do they interpret 'the water' in 1 John 5:6-8? I hope you remember John 3:6 that says, *That which is born of the flesh is flesh, and that which is born of the Spirit is spirit.* The water in John 3:5 refers to the baptism Jesus received, and the blood on the Cross means the judgment of all our sins. The gospel of the water and the Spirit is the gift of the remission of sin by God to humanity. This Truth is the key to Heaven.

Most Christians these days do not know what the gospel of the water and the Spirit is. They say that believers are born again one day without realizing it and not by the Word of the water and the Spirit. They interpret John 3:8 as such. They say that one can be born again suddenly at any moment—while you're praying, eating, dreaming, or even working. They say that people are born again suddenly by chance without their own recognition, as long as they believe in Jesus. How ignorant are they to say this? This is why there are so many believers in Jesus, but very few people are born again. As the Scripture says, *"For many are called, but few are chosen" (Matthew 22:14),* there are many people who are not yet born again despite believing in Jesus.

In short, most Christians believe in Jesus fatalistically. They believe that if God allows them to be born again, they will be born again as the chosen people, but if He does not allow them to be born again, they will suffer eternal condemnation even after having believed in Jesus all their lives. The common Christians believe fatalistically like this. However, the Bible has taught us that God has completed our salvation with Jesus' baptism and His bloodshed on the Cross, that we should believe in the gospel of the water and the Spirit to be born again, and that believing in this gospel or not is absolutely up to every person's free will.

I believe that our Lord has allowed us to be born again from all our sins by the gospel of the water and the Spirit. Thus, we have been born again free from all our sins. We believe in the gospel of the water and the Spirit. Thus, we have been emancipated from all our sins. Dear fellow believers, do you believe this? Yes, you do. You should not hold onto the religious faith of mainstream Christianity that believes only in the blood of the Cross, which is different from the gospel of the water and the Spirit. We can be born again only by our faith in the gospel Word of the water and the Spirit. Am I right or not? Dear fellow believers, all our sins were transferred onto Jesus when He was baptized from John the Baptist so that His blood on the Cross could deliver us completely from all our sins. We have received the Holy Spirit by the gospel Word of the water and the Spirit, became the children of God, and are now made sinless in our hearts now.

Those Who Believe in the Gospel of the Water and the Spirit Now Are without Sin

Dear fellow believers in the gospel of the water and the Spirit, do you have sin in your hearts? There is absolutely no sin in you. How is it possible that you have no sin? It is possible because you have believed in the gospel of the water and the Spirit that says God has blotted out all your sins by Jesus' baptism and His blood. What is the basis upon which we are able to do the works of God? We were able to do the works of God by believing in the gospel of the water and the Spirit. How have we become the workers for the gospel? How are we able to participate in the first resurrection and in the Millennial Kingdom? How can we go to the Kingdom of Heaven? It is all possible by believing in the gospel of the water and the Spirit. The key to all of these heavenly doors is the gospel of the water and the Spirit. He who does not enter through the door is like a thief or a robber.

What righteousness or good deeds could we possibly have in us? What righteousness could possibly be in us? We are born again in our faith in the gospel of the water and the Spirit because God has given us the Word to make us born again from above and sent His Son Jesus to do the works, which enables us to be born again. Otherwise, how could we be born again? What could we do to be born again? Would it be possible from the perspective of the flesh such as the way

Nicodemus asked, "How can an old man go back into his mother's womb?"

How can we be acknowledged before God as the righteous and say that we are without sin? How could we dare find the courage to say that we are without sin? It could never be possible for us to become sinless from a human perspective. It is impossible to be born again through fleshly means except the way God the Father has us born again through Jesus. Because Jesus Christ Himself has blotted out and washed away all our sins by His baptism and His blood on the Cross, we are born again by believing in the gospel of the water and the Spirit. Only our faith in the gospel of the water and the Spirit is accounted for as righteousness by God. Also, because God has given us the Holy Spirit, we can say that we are sinless by the Holy Spirit.

Now, the end of the world is approaching us. The world is becoming darker and colder. We cannot predict when a great war, famine, earthquake, plague, or massacre might occur. It seems like the calm before the storm. Because the whole world is experiencing prosperity now, people are acting like a frog in a well, not knowing that dark clouds and thunder storms are not far away for they can only see the clear sky above the well. Are the rotating neon signs still working in your life? Are people still acting the same? However, you have to know that this age is going through the calm before the storm. If you only knew the future to come, you would not hesitate but believe in the gospel of the water and the Spirit right now.

"God, I have been born again by believing in the gospel of the water and the Spirit." This is the kind of faith we should present to God whenever it is and wherever we are. We would not be able to avoid the judgments from God if we did not present our faith in the gospel of the water and the Spirit. When

God pours down tribulations and disasters, all our brothers, sisters, and ministers within His Church will be the most blessed people, just like the family of Noah during the time of the great flood.

We must reach out to those outside of the church that still do not believe in the gospel of the water and the Spirit. Those who do not believe in the gospel of the water and the Spirit now must realize that this gospel is the only Truth that makes them born again. Those who are inside the church of God but still do not believe in the gospel of the water and the Spirit must repent. The careers or abilities of those who do not believe in the gospel of the water and the Spirit are of no use before God. What is important is their present faith. Although they might have had good spiritual lives in the past, if they do not believe in the gospel of the water and the Spirit now, they are nothing.

Dear fellow believers, does your glorious career in the flesh deliver you from all your sins? It would be nice if you could be born again by fleshly means, but there is no way to be born again by such means. Only the gospel of the water and the Spirit can bring a new life to you and me and deliver us from all our sins.

We have been born again by believing in the Lord-given gospel of the water and the Spirit. Thus, I cannot but give thanks unto God and be humble before Him daily. We are always thankful for the present, for the future, and for the past. We have neither righteousness of our own nor any excellence of our own. We just need to believe in the Word of God with the pure and simple heart of a child and be thankful to Him. It is sufficient for us to serve and follow our Lord and teach and lead others at the church of God in our spiritual lives with the faith in the gospel of the water and the Spirit. Regardless of how long we have already believed, we should pray to God that we may keep our faith until the end. If you believe in the gospel of the water and the Spirit, you should be thankful because of it.

Do you believe in the gospel Truth of the water and the Spirit? We believe! Although this is an amazingly great Truth, the Truth is naturally simple. Actually, the Truth is so simple and precise that it can give us much assurance even though we are dull in our understanding. On the other hand, the man-made doctrines of worldly religions seem plausible, but they become more complicated the more we try to know them.

For example, there is an Buddhist doctrine called 'transmigrationism.' Those who believe in the Buddhist doctrine of transmigration of the soul say, "People who have done many good deeds will be reborn as human beings in wealthy families in their next lives. People who have done many bad deeds will be born as one of the lower animals in their next lives. If an animal behaves nicely, it will come back as a human being in its next life. If it does even more good deeds, it will be born in a better kingdom. Thus, every creature in this world might be a relative of mine. Hence, do not murder." If we look through the perspectives of the transmigration of the souls in Buddhism, a rabbit should be very important to us. Why? Because one of our ancestors may have become a rabbit after he had passed away. Therefore, Buddhism prohibits their believers from killing any lower animals. Why? It is because one of their ancestors may have come back as a bug.

Do people really become insects and rabbits when they die? If it were truly so, we won't have to worry about our next lives. We don't have any need to believe or worry about our next lives, because we will come back in the next life regardless of whether we live a good life or a bad one. If we are born as a wolf, we should go and feast on as much meat as we can find. We might come back as an eel and swim around the river till we die. This time around, we may come back as a fly. The next time, it will be something else. If the doctrine of transmigration were true, what need do we have to live morally? What fear do we need to have about death? Why would we need to agonize over our sins?

Humans are precious beings. God has made us humans in His profound Providence. Humans are fundamentally different from the other animals. Although animals don't recognize God and have no soul, a human being has the spirit of God within him. Animals are not eternal beings, but humans are eternal beings. God has created human beings so they can be born again and be adopted as His children.

Because God has given us the gospel of the water and the Spirit, we can be born again by believing in that gospel. Believe in the gospel of the water and the Spirit. Do not be stubborn but believe in the gospel of the water and the Spirit. If you obey this, you will become honored as it is written, *"A man who is in honor, yet does not understand, is like the beasts that perish" (Psalms 49:20).* If you reject the gospel of the water and the Spirit, you are the same as the beasts that perish.

Unfortunately, there are people who stand against their brother and sisters even though they have been in the church of God for a long time. Such people are not born again even though they have pretended that they have been born again. They only say that they believe in the gospel of the water and the Spirit. I knew a pastor of like this. I thought that he was born again just like I was born again by believing in the gospel of the water and the Spirit. I respected him because he seemed to preach the gospel of the water and the Spirit. I thought, "I cannot share this Truth actively because my situation limits me. But you are a precious person sharing this gospel of the water and the Spirit." And when people around me were speaking ill of him when he did unacceptable behaviors, I protected him saying, "Don't be so cruel to him. He is a servant of God and a good person. Do not insult the one who is sharing the gospel of the water and the Spirit." But I later found out that he neither believed in the gospel of the water and the Spirit nor had shared it with others. There was no reason to respect him any longer after I have found out the truth about him.

Dear fellow believers, if God made us born again by the gospel of the water and the Spirit, we must believe in it purely and be thankful. However, we have to recognize that there are people who do not believe in this gospel of the water and the Spirit and interfere with it instead. Those people cannot get along with believers in the gospel of the water and the Spirit.

Dear fellow believers, we should treat those who God treats as precious preciously, and hate those whom God hates. The faith of a believer in the gospel of the water and the Spirit is the correct faith. Being born again by the water and the Spirit entails that we are born again from all our sins by believing in this gospel Truth. This is how God has made us born again through His grace by the gospel Truth of the water and the Spirit. We have been born again from all our sins by believing in the gospel of the water and the Spirit. We give thanks to God by believing in this true gospel. ✉

What Makes It Possible for Us to Be Born Again?

< John 3:1-15 >
"There was a man of the Pharisees named Nicodemus, a ruler of the Jews. This man came to Jesus by night and said to Him, 'Rabbi, we know that You are a teacher come from God; for no one can do these signs that You do unless God is with him.' Jesus answered and said to him, 'Most assuredly, I say to you, unless one is born again, he cannot see the kingdom of God.' Nicodemus said to Him, 'How can a man be born when he is old? Can he enter a second time into his mother's womb and be born?' Jesus answered, Most assuredly, I say to you, unless one is born of water and the Spirit, he cannot enter the kingdom of God. That which is born of the flesh is flesh, and that which is born of the Spirit is spirit. Do not marvel that I said to you, 'You must be born again. The wind blows where it wishes, and you hear the sound of it, but cannot tell where it comes from and where it goes. So is everyone who is born of the Spirit.' Nicodemus answered and said to Him, 'How can these things be?' Jesus answered and said to him, 'Are you the teacher of Israel, and do not know these things? Most assuredly, I say to you, We speak what We know and testify what We have seen, and you do not receive Our witness. If I have told you earthly things and you do not believe, how will you believe if I tell you heavenly things? No one has ascended to heaven but He who came down from heaven, that is, the Son of Man who is in heaven. And as Moses

lifted up the serpent in the wilderness, even so must the Son of Man be lifted up, that whoever believes in Him should not perish but have eternal life.'"

Must One Enter into His Mother's Womb Twice to Be Born Again?

The Lord said to Nicodemus, *"Unless one is born of water and the Spirit, he cannot enter the kingdom of God" (John 3:5).* Then, Nicodemus asked Jesus in return, "How can an old man be born again? Can he enter a second time into his mother's womb and be born again?" Nicodemus was a ruler of the Jews and a Pharisee. But, he did not understand what Jesus said to him because of his carnal perspective. As a result, he thought that one had to be born again from his mother's womb all over again.

Everyone is born in this world once and dies once, for this is a law that God has set for every human being. After death, each person is to face the judgment of his sins once without fail. All humans are born with sin in this world from the parents of their flesh, and therefore, they will bear the condemnation of their sins if they die without obtaining remittance from their sins. Therefore, everyone must believe in the gospel of the water and the Spirit and be born again before he dies.

A while ago, I saw a fascinating TV program showcasing sea crabs, explaining how they hatch from the eggs and exuviate. Every larva lives a new life again by transforming itself into an imago. For example, a maggot transforms into a cicada. Similarly, for us humans, it is by believing in the gospel of the water and the Spirit that we are born again as righteous people from being sinners.

It is written in 1 Timothy 2:3-4, *"For this is good and acceptable in the sight of God our Savior, who desires all men to be saved and to come to the knowledge of the truth."* Therefore, it is never God's will for everyone to be born in this world once and then just die without being born again. It is not God's will that people should be born as sinners from their mothers' wombs and then die as sinners. Just as a larva becomes a cicada, so, too, must everyone be born again by believing in the gospel of the water and the Spirit. Through the gospel of the water and the Spirit, everyone must be born again from the status of a sinner into a righteous person.

In this world, there are those who have been born again from their sins by believing in the gospel of the water and the Spirit, and then there are those who have failed to do so. According to today's Scripture passage, this man named Nicodemus had lived in ignorance of the gospel of the water and the Spirit.

Nicodemus said to Jesus, *"Rabbi, we know that You are a teacher who comes from God" (John 3:2).* Although he pretended to know Jesus, Jesus said to him, "Unless one is born of water and the Spirit, he cannot enter the Kingdom of God," and with these words He left a puzzle in Nicodemus' heart to ponder upon. Jesus continued to say to him, "That which is born of the flesh is flesh, and that which is born of the Spirit is spirit. Do not marvel that I said to you, 'You must be born again.'" By this, He meant that just as the wind blows where it wishes, but we cannot tell where it comes from and where it goes, so is someone who is not born again from his sins unable to recognize those who have received the remission of their sins through the gospel of the water and the Spirit. By saying this to all those who are not born again yet, our Lord wanted to teach them what the Truth of being truly born again through the gospel of the water and the Spirit is.

But Nicodemus asked Jesus, "How can a man be born again?" and Jesus answered him saying, "How can you not know this as a teacher of Israel? For everyone, one can enter the Kingdom of God only when one is born again of water and the Spirit." In other words, everyone must enter the Kingdom of God by believing in the gospel Word of the water and the Spirit.

We should all remember what Jesus said to Nicodemus. By telling all of us, "If I have told you earthly things and you do not believe, how will you believe if I tell you heavenly things?" Jesus wanted to teach us about being born again through the true gospel of the water and the Spirit.

The Misconceptions That Many People Now Have about Being Born Again

Many people now have various misconceptions about being born again. They yearn to meet Jesus in their visions or dreams, or in their prayers, and they erroneously believe that they can be born again once they meet Jesus in these ways. That is why they tend to make outlandish claims. Saying that they saw Jesus in their vision while fasting, they claim that they are now born again. There are also some people who believe that they have been born again while dreaming. Someone even claimed that while he was dreaming, he saw Jesus in his vision, with His feet bound by iron chains and bleeding profusely, calling his name and telling him that He loved him. By claiming that the Lord told him, "I died for you like this. Can you see it now? You shall establish a prayer house here," he says that he was born again at that time, and that this is why he built a prayer house.

Like this, some people make false claims about being born again. They also go through mistaken experiences. Some say that while they were giving their prayers of repentance to God, something hot descended on them from above. As the Holy Spirit is said to have descended like fire, they claim that something like fire descended on them and went through them from the tip of their heads to their toes. They say that it was then that the Holy Spirit came to them.

Still others claim that while they were praying, they saw a vision, and in this vision they were reminded of all the sins that they had committed, even their childhood wrongdoings and disobedience to their parents, and that all these sins were displayed right in front of them as if they were watching a film. So they say that they beat their chests and wailed, confessing each and every one of these sins in their prayers of repentance. They claim that by the time they were done with all their prayers of repentance, two days had passed by. Spinning out such fantastic stories and claiming that what seemed only a moment to them was in fact two days, they say that at that moment, they were remitted from all their sins and born again.

Some say that while they were praying, the heavens split, and Jesus came through this opening, saying to them, "I love you," and entered into their hearts. So they say that it was then that they were born again. At any rate, speaking of their mystical experiences in various forms, people claim that they were born again by such experiences. But this kind of faith is not the faith that is based in the gospel Word of the water and the Spirit. These people instead end up having false beliefs.

However, Jesus made it clear in today's Scripture passage that it is only by believing in the gospel of the water and the Spirit that one is born again. Because people do not know

God's Word of the water and the Spirit, they yearn to experience some mystic phenomena instead. And they convince themselves that they have somehow been born again through such experiences. But this is not the Word of the Truth of being born again of water and the Spirit that the Bible speaks of.

Some people say that when they were offering their prayers of repentance, the Spirit of God came to them and made them repent. But this is not the Spirit of God. It is the spirit of the Devil. The Bible says that it is Satan who accuses us. To accuse is to point out someone's sins and to charge him before others. The Devil says to people, "You've sinned, haven't you? Of course you've sinned!" This is accusing. The Devil always points out people's sins, shows them their shame, makes them reach the condemnation of sinners, and destroys them through their sins. If anyone prevents people from realizing that it is through the gospel of the water and the Spirit that they can receive the remission of sin, and instead only points out their sins, then this is no more than the Devil's work.

God also points out people's sins, but He teaches them through His Law what their sins really are. Moreover, He also enables them to know the good news that Jesus has taken away all their sins with the water, the blood, and the Spirit. Therefore, if anyone claims to have been born again without the gospel Word of the water and the Spirit, then his testimony is all a lie.

What Kind of People Does the Holy Spirit Come To

Just as it is clearly explained in Matthew 3:13-17 and Acts 2:38, it is through the gospel of the water and the Spirit that one is born again, and it is only when one is saved from all his sins that he receives the gift of the Holy Spirit. The Lord said in John 3:14-15, *"And as Moses lifted up the serpent in the wilderness, even so must the Son of Man be lifted up, that whoever believes in Him should not perish but have eternal life."* When the people of Israel were bitten by fiery serpents and were dying, they were healed from all their wounds by looking at the bronze serpent that was raised up on a pole, like General Naaman was healed from his leprosy in the Jordan River. By telling us this, Jesus has made it possible for us to have hope for our salvation.

When we turn to Numbers 21, we see that when the people of Israel were passing through a region called Edom on their way to the land of Canaan, their souls became very discouraged on the way and they turned to speak against God and against Moses. They accused God, saying, "Is there no other place to put us to death that You have dragged us to this wilderness to die? Our God, the God of our forefathers, the God of Abraham, the God of Jacob! If You are indeed the true God of Abraham, of Isaac and Jacob, then why have You dragged us to this desert and placed us in such a desolate place with neither food nor water only to suffer freezing temperatures in the night and scorching heat in the day?"

As the people of Israel spoke against God, God sent fiery serpents among them, who were dwelling in tents, and had these serpents bite them. Bitten by these venomous serpents, the people of Israel were dying off. Moses then prayed fervently to God on their behalf. The people of Israel also confessed their wrongdoing and prayed to God to save them. Hearing Moses' prayer, God said, "Make a bronze serpent, and set it on a pole; and tell the people that everyone who looks at it shall live."

As a matter of fact, among the people of Israel, those who believed in the words of God's servant Moses—that is, those who looked at the bronze serpent—were indeed saved from the serpents' venom. This event is recorded in the New Testament also, as it is written in John 3:14-15, "And as Moses lifted up the serpent in the wilderness, even so must the Son of Man be lifted up, that whoever believes in Him should not perish but have eternal life." This means that Jesus, now that He was baptized to take upon all the sins of mankind, would have to be crucified to death to pay the wages of all our sins.

Just as Moses in the Old Testament raised up the bronze serpent in the wilderness, Jesus, too, was lifted up on the wooden Cross to save His believers from of all their sins by being baptized by John the Baptist and thereby accepting all the sins of this world that are like the venom of serpents. Jesus said that when He carries on His shoulders the sins of the world by being baptized by John the Baptist and is crucified to death, He would deliver those who believe in this Truth from all their sins.

Understanding the gospel Word of the water and the Spirit written in the Bible is like finding a hidden picture. It is like solving a jigsaw puzzle. Many children enjoy playing with jigsaw puzzles. A big picture is cut up into many pieces of different shapes, and when each piece is put together, the original picture is revealed. If any single piece is lost or misplaced while putting the jigsaw puzzle together, the original picture cannot be fully restored. But when a child puts together each jigsaw piece one by one, he comes to realize what the picture looks like.

As such, the Bible is also divided into the Old and New Testaments, but when all the pieces of the Word are put together, what ultimately emerges is the gospel Word of the water and the Spirit. The Word that makes it possible for us to be born again is this very gospel of the water and the Spirit. God's Word is the Truth that enables us to be born again from all of our sins through the baptism of Jesus and His blood on the Cross.

Once more, we need to examine one by one what the Word is that allows us to be born again. We need to reach the definitive understanding of the meaning of the Word of the water and the Spirit spoken in John 3.

Jesus said, *"As Moses lifted up the serpent in the wilderness, even so must the Son of Man be lifted up" (John 3:14).* Why, then, did Jesus have to be baptized by John before He was crucified? He said that it was because of our sins. It was because Jesus had accepted all the sins of this world by being baptized by John the Baptist before He was crucified, that He could carry on His shoulders the sins of the world and be nailed to the Cross.

Does this then mean that Jesus was crucified as punishment for our sins? Yes, this is precisely the reason for His crucifixion. Jesus was crucified because He had taken upon all the sins of mankind, and because He consequently had to suffer the punishment of death on the Cross for all the sinners of the world. Having accepted all the sins of mankind once and for all through His baptism by John the Baptist, He had to be crucified in accordance to the Law of God that declared the wages of sin to be death.

When Jesus said that He would be crucified and lifted up high, He spoke about the condemnation of sin from His Word of "the water and the Spirit." In other words, for everyone to be born again from his sins and to become God's own child, he has to realize and believe that both the baptism Jesus received from John and His Crucifixion have blotted out all his sins perfectly. It is through the gospel of the water and the Spirit that one is born again from his sins.

The Spirit refers to Jesus Himself, who is God. It tells us that Jesus is the Son of God and the true Savior who came to save sinners from all of their sins. Jesus was conceived by the Virgin Mary and became a Man. He accepted all our sins through the baptism that He received from John the Baptist, the representative of mankind, in the Jordan River (Matthew 3:13-17), died on the Cross while carrying the sins of the world, rose from the dead again, and by doing so He has delivered us from all our sins, thus becoming our true Savior. To save sinners from their sins, God Himself took upon all the sins of mankind through His baptism by John, and saved them from their punishment of sin, by bearing all the condemnation of sin on the Cross—through these righteous acts, He has saved them once and for all. All the acts of salvation fulfilled by Jesus clearly manifest that He is indeed the Savior who has saved sinners from their sins. In the gospel Truth of "the water and the Spirit," the water refers to the baptism that Jesus received, and the Spirit manifests that Jesus is fundamentally our Savior.

Jesus was baptized by John to accept the sins of mankind, and for Him to able to be crucified also. Put differently, it was not the case that Jesus could be crucified even if He had not been baptized by John. Jesus had to be crucified and lifted up from the earth precisely because He had taken upon all the sins of mankind once and for all by receiving baptism from John the Baptist in the Jordan River. Thus, He has fulfilled the righteousness of God once and for all. This is how He was able to bring salvation from all the sins of the world to those who believe in the gospel Truth of the water and the Spirit at one time. Jesus has washed away all our sins once and for all with the baptism that He received, and He bore the condemnation of all these sins on the Cross. Therefore, it is by believing in the baptism of water that Jesus received, and in the blood that He shed on the Cross, that we have been saved from all our sins.

Speaking to Nicodemus about being born again, Jesus said, *"As Moses lifted up the serpent in the wilderness" (John 3:14).* The serpent symbolizes those who stand against God. The serpent lifted up on a pole implies two meanings. One is that God had judged the sins of mankind, and the other is that Jesus Himself would bear the condemnation of all the sins of mankind.

Jesus is the Savior of all humanity. He came to this earth as a man, and when He turned 30, He took upon the sins of the world by being baptized by John the Baptist in the Jordan River, as the very first act of His public life dedicated to the salvation of mankind. By doing so, He has saved us from all the sins of the world, where Satan rules, intervenes, and accuses. By being baptized, in other words, Jesus took upon all the sins of this world that Satan the Devil had planted in us mankind. It was because Jesus had taken all the sins of mankind upon His own body through His baptism that He was nailed to the Cross, when, in fact, only sinners should have been crucified.

By doing so, Jesus has become the everlasting Savior who gives the remission of sin to all the generations to come who believe in and rely on His baptism and His blood on the Cross. It was because Jesus had carried the sins of the world through His baptism that He could be crucified. As our sins were passed onto the body of Jesus and He died on the Cross, He was lifted up high from this earth so that those who understand this with faith would be saved from all of their sins.

Why are we thankful to God? Human beings are so insufficient that they cannot help but commit so many sins while living in this world. It is not just in our past that we were insufficient, but we are still insufficient in the present, and we will continue to be insufficient in the future until the day we die. Yet despite this, Jesus the Savior was born of Mary as a human, and by being baptized by John in the Jordan River, He accepted and washed away all the sins that we commit throughout our entire lifetime from our very birth to our death—just how fortunate and thankful is this?

To be born again from sin, both the water with which Jesus was baptized and the blood that He shed on the Cross are absolutely indispensable. Put differently, it is by believing in this Jesus who was baptized and crucified to bear the punishment of sin that one can be born again by faith. This faith is the faith that enables us to be born through the gospel of the water, the blood, and the Spirit (1 John 5:6-8). All of us must return to the gospel of the water and the Spirit.

The Gospel of the Water and the Spirit Is The Truth of Real Salvation

Nicodemus asked Jesus in return, "How can a man be born again? Must he enter into his mother's womb twice?" Jesus Himself then answered him, saying, "To be born again, one must be born again of water and the Spirit." We must believe that the baptism by water Jesus received was the way for Him to wash away all our sins; we must also believe that it was because Jesus was baptized that He was crucified to death; and we must believe it is only by having faith in His resurrection that we can enter the Kingdom of God and see Him.

To explain how we can receive the remission of our sins

and be born again, Jesus first spoke about the "water." He mentioned the water first because before His crucifixion through which He bore the condemnation of sin, there was the water of His baptism, the procedure through which He took onto Himself all the sins of the world.

When Jesus was about to be baptized by John the Baptist, Jesus said to John, *"Permit it to be so now, for thus it is fitting for us to fulfill all righteousness" (Matthew 3:15).* Here the phrase "thus" means: 1) proper; 2) appropriate; and 3) no other way but this. The baptism Jesus received from John was in the form of "laying on of hands." As you may know, the laying of hands on the head of the scapegoat by the High Priest was to pass over the sins of the Israelites all at once to the sacrifice. Therefore, when the hands of John, the representative of all mankind, were laid on the head of Jesus, the sins of the world were transferred onto the body of Jesus once and for all. So, the next day of Jesus' baptism, John the Baptist cried out seeing Jesus coming toward him, *"Behold! The Lamb of God who takes away the sin of the world!" (John 1:29)*

For human beings, who are all sinners, to enter the Kingdom of God by believing in Jesus, they must first receive the remission of their sins and be born again. Sinners can never enter His Kingdom. They must be saved by believing that just as Moses lifted up the serpent in the wilderness, Jesus was lifted up high on the Cross and was condemned for their sins, for He had taken upon all the sins of mankind at the Jordan River through His baptism. They must overcome the Devil that is accusing and mocking them for their sinfulness by placing their faith in the Truth, that Jesus was baptized by John, that He washed away all their sins in their place, and shed His blood and died for their sake. Now, it is through our faith in the gospel of the water and the Spirit that we can possess the true faith, which makes it possible for us to be born again from all our sins. For a person to be born again, he must believe in the baptism of Jesus and His blood on the Cross.

As I mentioned previously at the beginning, one cannot be born again whether he sees some kind of vision, give prayers of repentance, or volunteer to serve the community. It is not through one's own effort that he is born again. It is by believing in the baptism of Jesus and His blood on the Cross that we are born again from our sins.

To enable us to be born again, God temporarily bound us under His Law, as we were ruled by Satan, and made us sinners. And when we were still sinners, God Himself came as the Savior of sinners incarnated in the image of man to make us His own people, the people of God. Then, He took upon all the sins of mankind by being baptized by John the Baptist in the Jordan River, and then He carried all of these sins of the world to the Cross where He shed His blood vicariously on behalf of the sinners of this world. He was condemned to pay off the wages of sin in their place, and has thereby saved them once for all. The baptism through which Jesus took upon our sins was an act of the remission of sin that He carried out to cleanse His believers' hearts of their sins. With these righteous acts, He has now made it possible for all those who believe that He is God Himself, and that He bore the condemnation of the Cross, to be born again

Jesus was not crucified for no reason. To enable us to be born again and to make it possible for our old selves to die and to become renewed once again by believing in God, the Lord was baptized by John, was crucified to death, and rose from the dead again. To be born of water and the Spirit means precisely this Word. It is to believe in this Word which tells us that our Lord was baptized by John and died on the Cross to blot out all our sins. It is this Truth that has made us new by washing away all the sins of our hearts and souls, and allowed us to lack nothing in becoming God's own people.

The Word of the water and the blood of Jesus is the real Truth of being born again. Jesus said so clearly to Nicodemus: "What makes it possible for sinners to be born again is faith in the gospel Word of the water and the Spirit." It was because Jesus was baptized that He could die on the Cross, and it is because we believe in the gospel of the water and the Spirit that we have been born again from all our sins and received everlasting life.

All These Things Were Fulfilled According to God's Plan

One should never think that his being born again from sin depends on his endeavors. It is something that God has completed to grant us according to His plan, and is not something that we have to strive for. To allow us to be born again from our sins, and to make us His own children in the likeness of His image, God planned to come Himself as a man, receive John's baptism on His body, be condemned and crucified to death, and through all these things, make it possible for us to be born again once more.

My fellow believers, the blessing of being born again from sin is the gift from God to the believers in the gospel of the water and the Spirit, which proclaims that the Savior Himself took upon all the sins committed by everyone in this world, and that He was crucified. The baptism that Jesus received from John was the baptism that washed away mankind's sins, and His blood on the Cross was the wages of our sins.

We are grateful for the baptism of Jesus Christ, for His crucifixion, for His resurrection also, and for His second coming as well. God had chosen us and predestined us in Christ before the foundation of the world, and it was to make us His own children that He created man on the sixth day after making the whole universe and everything in it.

When God made us to be born into this world, He had planned to make it possible for us to receive everlasting life as His eternal children. This is why God made man on the sixth day of His creation of the heavens and the earth. His plan was to enable those of us who believe in all of the spoken Word of God to be born again of water and the Spirit, and thereby make us into His own people. This is the very reason why God gave us the gospel of the water and the Spirit through His son, so that we humans would be born again from our sins once more.

Even the smallest insects in this world do not just disappear once born, but they transform themselves into imagoes that have wonderful wings. We, too, must be born again as the righteous by believing in the gospel of the water and the Spirit. Jesus came to give us the gospel of the water and the Spirit and deliver all those who believe in this Truth from the sins of the world. And in our place He was baptized, carried all our sins on His shoulders, died on the Cross on our behalf, and rose again from the dead. By doing all these things, Jesus paid off all the wages of our sins with His own baptism and crucifixion, and He has made it possible for the believers to be born again with new life.

Why Was Jesus Crucified?

Jesus was to be crucified because He had taken upon Himself all of our sins once and for all by being baptized by John the Baptist in the Jordan River. Yet the Christian religionists of the world do not know that Jesus was baptized by John and was crucified to blot out the sins of this world through the gospel Truth of the water and the Spirit. However, they must grasp the gospel Word of the water and the Spirit clearly, finding out "who, when, where, what, how, and why" this gospel was fulfilled. God's Word is not a lie. Nor is it superstition. What God has done for our salvation has no defect whatsoever, no matter how hard the heretics try to find it. His Word meets every inquiry and resolves every doubt from human reasoning.

Why were you born into this world? Why are human beings born as humans? What is the reason and purpose for God's creation of man? What is the reason for Jesus Christ's coming to this earth? It was for God to enable us to be born again from our sins, to make us be born anew, to turn us into God's children, and to make us sinless, that Jesus Christ came to this earth, was baptized, died on the Cross, and has thereby saved sinners from all of their sins and transgressions. We must believe in this Truth.

My fellow believers, we need to recognize that we cannot be born again by giving some prayers of repentance, or through any such effort of our own. We need to realize that our own effort has nothing to do with the Truth that enables us to be remitted from all of our sins. For us to be born again, we must realize that this Jesus Christ who was lifted up high on the Cross had first took on and carried our sins in the Jordan River through His baptism. With all our hearts we must believe in this Truth, that to suffer our own death in our place, to pay the wages of sin, death itself, and to fulfill God the Father's commanded Word in obedience, Jesus was baptized, shed His blood in the place of sinners, and thereby paid off their wages of sin.

Is there anything else that we need to do to be born again? There is nothing else for us to do but to only believe in this Jesus who came by the gospel of the water and the Spirit. Do we need to give prayers of repentance, climb a mountain to pray, fast, provide aid to the poor, go out into the mission fields, or embrace our martyrdom to be born again? No, none of these is necessary for us. "Should I offer money to God, or should I offer Him a great chapel building? Doesn't God like money?" To this God said, *"The silver is Mine, and the gold is Mine" (Haggai 2:8).* Our God is the Lord of creation who made the universe and all things in it. Would He then have any want for gold?

Would He want good deeds from us? Would He want us to utter absolutely strange sounds such as "allelluiah-lululala," trying to speak in tongues? Would God be pleased if we remember even more of our sins, list them all, and ask Him in tears to forgive us? No! What God wants from us is our faith in His Son who came by His water baptism and His blood on the Cross! For us to believe in Jesus Christ as our Savior is the will of God the Father, and He has given us the gift of being born again through the gospel of the water and the Spirit that Jesus has completed.

God has never demanded anything else from us apart from our faith in the gospel of the water and the Spirit. Even in this world, the rich do not ask for something from others. Why would then God ask for something small from us humans? What would God demand from you and me? Would He ask us to attend morning prayer meetings faithfully, to be devout, to offer our material belongings, to give Him our prayers of repentance, and to remind ourselves of our sins over and over again in our repeated prayers of repentance while shedding our tears? Even without all these things, we already have enough wrinkles on our foreheads as it is. So why on earth would the Lord be pleased to see us frown, calling on His name in our everyday suffering and sadness due to our sins? Is this who God is? Of course not! Jesus, God Himself, is the Savior of mankind in our hearts who was baptized and shed His blood on the Cross for us, and He is the God that has made it possible for us believers to be born again.

Jesus is our Savior. He is the One who has enabled us to be born again into this world. Our Lord has renewed the hearts of all believers with the gospel of the water and the Spirit, as it is written in 2 Corinthians 5:17, *"If anyone is in Christ, he is a new creation; old things have passed away; behold, all things have become new."* Eventually, God will also renew the bodies of us believers of the gospel of the water and the Spirit. God Himself came as our Savior, and through the baptism He received and the blood He shed on the Cross, He has allowed us to be born again. We must believe in the baptism and blood of Jesus. He was baptized to take upon himself our iniquities. He was pierced for our blemishes. He was injured as a result of taking upon our sins through the baptism He received from John.

Jesus Christ was crucified because He had taken upon Himself the sins of this world by being baptized by John, for you and me. It was to make it possible for all those who believe in Jesus to be born again, to turn them into God's children, to make us without sin, to enable us to be born again as the sinless—it was for all these things that Jesus was baptized by

John and shed His blood for us. It was not to just boast His compassion upon us that Jesus Christ was crucified. All of us must realize and believe that Jesus was crucified solely because He had been baptized. Because Jesus has perfectly saved us from all our sins through His baptism and bloodshed on the Cross, the believers in the gospel of the water and the Spirit have been born again from their sins.

Just as the Apostle Paul said, *"I have been crucified with Christ" (Galatians 2:20),* the reason why Jesus Christ was crucified was to make us be born again, to be condemned for our sins, to put our old selves to death and to make us be born again as new selves—all because He had received His water baptism in the Jordan River. We must all believe that Jesus shed His blood for us only after being baptized first.

Do you now understand the real Truth of being born again through the gospel of the water and the Spirit? Or do you still believe that you can somehow be born again if you would just give prayers of repentance everyday? This simply is not true. Anyone who claims that our sins can be blotted out just by giving prayers of repentance is someone who has not been born again yet.

It is written in John 10:10, *"The thief does not come except to steal, and to kill, and to destroy. I have come that they may have life, and that they may have it more abundantly."* Whoever only mentions prayers of repentance and does not speak about the gospel of the water and the Spirit is a robber and a thief. But he who preaches the gospel of the water and the Spirit is God's real servant.

My fellow believers, God has given us the gospel of the water and the Spirit to make us be born again, so that He would make us His children, allow us to be sinless and righteous, and transform us into His own people who can forever enjoy everything that God has and live eternally with Him. Those of us who believe in the baptism of Jesus and His blood have now been saved from our sins according to His providence. Do you accept it into your hearts that God has made you born again through the gospel of the water and the Spirit so that He would turn you into His own children to live forever? Do you really believe that the Word of the baptism of Jesus and of His blood is the Word of salvation that makes you born again?

What is to be born again? By believing that Jesus took upon all our sins with His baptism, we become sinless in our hearts and become the born-again people of God. To believe in this Truth, that Jesus took upon Himself all the iniquities of sinners with His baptism and was crucified to death in our place, all to solve the problem of our sins, and to believe that He rose from the dead in three days, and has thereby brought His believers to life—this is the very faith that enables us to be born again.

That, my fellow believers, is precisely the Truth of being born again of water and the Spirit. To believe in the Word of Truth that enables us to be born again of water and the Spirit believing that Jesus is God Himself, and it is believing that Jesus was baptized to wash away the sins of mankind. Jesus' blood on the Cross signifies the punishment of sin, and His baptism signifies the washing of our sins. The resurrection of Jesus has brought us new life.

What Is the Mark of Evidence Proving That Jesus Has Washed Away All Our Sins?

Jesus was baptized by John the Baptist to take upon the sins of this world (Matthew 3:15). It is written in 1 Peter 3:21,

"There is also an antitype which now saves us—baptism (not the removal of the filth of the flesh, but the answer of a good conscience toward God), through the resurrection of Jesus Christ." Previous to this passage, Peter the Apostle had discussed the water of Noah's flood. Therefore, he meant that the baptism of Jesus removed all the sins of the world as if the water of Noah's flood had swept away all the filth of the first world. That's why the Bible clearly states here that there is an antitype that now saves us—baptism through the resurrection of Jesus Christ.

What is this antitype that proves that the Savior came to this world as a man, washed away our sins, and made us sinless? It is the baptism that Jesus received from John! What is the evidence of salvation that made us be born again? It is written in the Word that Jesus has washed away our sins through His baptism and His blood on the Cross.

This is why it is written in 1 John 5:6-8, *"This is He who came by water and blood—Jesus Christ; not only by water, but by water and blood. And it is the Spirit who bears witness, because the Spirit is truth. For there are three that bear witness in heaven: the Father, the Word, and the Holy Spirit; and these three are one. And there are three that bear witness on earth: the Spirit, the water, and the blood; and these three agree as one."*

God Himself came to this earth, washed away all the sins of His believers with the water of His baptism, and then died on the Cross for us to pay the wages of our sins. God has given new life to us, to all of us who believe in the gospel Truth of the water and the Spirit. God has given us the gospel of the water and the Spirit as the gift of salvation.

"There is also an antitype which now saves us—baptism (not the removal of the filth of the flesh, but the answer of a

good conscience toward God), through the resurrection of Jesus Christ" (1 Peter 3:21). The baptism of Jesus is the Word that has made it possible for us to be born again from our sins, and it is the evidence of salvation through which He took upon Himself our sins in the Jordan River. His death on the Cross was to take the place of our own death and punishment of sin. The resurrection of Jesus Christ was to bring new life to His believers. The Lord is our Savior who has saved us forever from our sins through the Word of baptism and blood that enables sinners to be born again.

By believing in this, that Jesus was baptized, shed His blood and died on the Cross, and rose from the dead again, our souls can be brought to new life once again to live forever. The gospel of the water and the Spirit has therefore turned our consciences into good consciences before God. It has emboldened us so that we would not hesitate to go toward God. Had Jesus not been baptized and not been crucified high on the Cross, how could we have received the remission of our sins and go boldly to stand before the presence of God the Father? In other words, without the baptism of Jesus Christ and His bloodshed, we could never have boldly stood before God. Because Jesus Christ took upon Himself all our sins and cleansed them all away from our hearts by being baptized by John, because He died on the Cross and rose from the dead again in three days, and because we believe in this Word of God, of the Truth of the atoning water and blood, we have been saved all at once, so that our consciences may lack nothing to call God as our Father. In this way, Jesus has enabled us to boldly come before the presence of God the Father by this very faith. Even now, because Jesus was crucified to death, we were also crucified to death with Christ, and because He was resurrected, our souls and our spirits could also be resurrected.

This is the Truth of being born again. You must all accept this Truth into your hearts.

You and I are seemed to be born into this world once and to die once all too soon. But, is this all that there is to life? No! There is, after all, a new way of everlasting life to us. There are many life forms in this world that are born again. When even the maggots are born again as cicadas, and the larvae are born again as butterflies, wouldn't God allow us, who are the lords of all creation, be born again through the gospel of the water and the Spirit? By making us accept the baptism of Jesus and His blood, God has made us be born again from our sins.

My fellow believers, to believe in Jesus' baptism and His blood is none other than to be born again. Let's turn to Galatians here. Galatians 3:27 says, *"For as many of you as were baptized into Christ have put on Christ."* The phrase "as many of you" here means "whoever." In other words, our Lord said that whoever was baptized into Christ has put on Christ. To be baptized into Christ means to unite with Jesus by believing that Jesus took away all of our old selves with all of our sins through His baptism. What about you then? Were you baptized into Christ? If so, then you have put on the garment of salvation, along with Christ. The believers in this Truth have now become God's children. This Word is the Word of Truth and the Word of being born again.

Let us together turn to Romans 8 also. It is written in Romans 8:1-2, *"There is therefore now no condemnation to those who are in Christ Jesus, who do not walk according to the flesh, but according to the Spirit. For the law of the Spirit of life in Christ Jesus has made me free from the law of sin and death."* Precisely as stated in this passage, you have to believe that Jesus has indeed given new life to His believers, and that He has indeed enabled you to be born again of water and the

Spirit. My fellow believers, do you believe in the gospel of the water and the Spirit? If you do, then you have been baptized into Jesus and entered into Him by faith.

Have you put on Jesus Christ by being baptized into Him? It is written, *"There is no condemnation to those who are in Christ Jesus" (Romans 8:1).* My fellow believers, those who believe in the gospel of the water and the Spirit can never have sin. They have become absolutely righteous by faith. They have been born again definitively, for the gospel of the water and the Spirit has swept away all their sins perfectly.

"For the law of the Spirit of life in Christ Jesus has made me free from the law of sin and death" (Romans 8:2). Through what means has Jesus saved us? The Lord has saved us through His baptism and His blood on the Cross. He has saved us from the sins of the world with this new law called the law of the Spirit of God. It is through the law of the Spirit that give us life, this law of God, that the Lord has saved us from the law of sin and death, from the curses of the Law, from all the sins that derive from our human weaknesses, ignorance, powerlessness, and wickedness. It is not through our own goodness that God has saved us, but it is through the gospel of the water and the Spirit, the life-giving law of God's salvation. God Himself came as our Savior and gave us His baptism and blood, and He saved all of us who accepted this God-given remission of sin into our hearts.

My fellow believers, I am sure you now believe in the gospel of the water and the Spirit. Then, do you still have sin? No! Is there still condemnation waiting for you because of your sins? No! Is there no condemnation whatsoever? None whatsoever! But if you sin again by any chance, would you come to have sin again? No! You have already died and were brought to new life within the gospel of the water and the Spirit.

Have you received the spiritual baptism of salvation by faith in Jesus Christ? Have you really been baptized into Christ by faith? If you have done so, then you have come into Jesus Christ by believing in His water and blood. In contrast, however, he who does not believe in the water of the baptism of Jesus Christ and in His blood is one who is standing outside Jesus Christ.

Let us read Roman 8:3-4 together: *"For what the law could not do in that it was weak through the flesh, God did by sending His own Son in the likeness of sinful flesh, on account of sin: He condemned sin in the flesh, that the righteous requirement of the law might be fulfilled in us who do not walk according to the flesh but according to the Spirit."*

Could we ever keep the Law of God in our flesh? Of course not! Clearly, we human beings could never keep the Law of God because of the weaknesses of our flesh. This is precisely the reason why God sent His Son Jesus Christ to satisfy the righteous requirement of the Law for us. We can never satisfy that requirement because of the weaknesses of our flesh. The Law declares that the wages of sin is death. One who has sin in his heart must be put to death. In other words, every sinner must be sent to hell, sentenced to eternal death. But, the Son of God, our Lord, resolved the problem of sin and death that the Law speaks of. So our Lord Himself came to us and took care of not only our sins, but also all the consequences of sin, even death itself. And to blot out our sins, He was baptized by John.

God said, *"For what the law could not do in that it was weak through the flesh, God did by sending His own Son in the likeness of sinful flesh, on account of sin: He condemned sin in the flesh"* (Romans 8:3). What does it mean when it says here that "He condemned sin in the flesh?" This means that God passed our sins onto Jesus Christ who had come in the flesh of man. God the Father had His Son, Jesus, be baptized according to the established law to pass our sins to Him. Jesus' baptism was administered in the form of the laying on of hands in the Old Testament.

Through His baptism, Jesus took upon all the sins of this world, as it is written, *"God did by sending His Son in the likeness of sinful flesh, on account of sin: He condemned sin in the flesh" (Romans 8:3).* Jesus accepted all the sins of the world onto His own body through His baptism. The reason for this was for Jesus Christ to bear the condemnation of our sins, for we could never, ever abide by all of the Law of God until the day we die. "He condemned sin in the flesh" means that God the Father transferred all the sins specified by His Law, all the sins that we commit from our failure to keep this Law, onto Jesus Christ through His baptism.

God the Father sent His Son as the Savior of mankind, and He had His Son accept our sins through John the Baptist. Jesus, in turn, did not seek after the comfort of His flesh, but in obedience to the will of God the Father, was baptized by John in the Jordan River and thus accepted the sins of the world, and following this will of the Father, He gave up His body on the Cross. Jesus willingly laid down His life so that we would be born again from our sins. And by doing so, He fulfilled all the requirements of the Law and the commandments spoken by God the Father.

God told us to recognize our sins through the Law and then receive the remission of our sins. Because the Law of God was given to mankind once, and God could not repeal this commandment, He gave us the law of salvation that could deliver mankind from sin.

God commanded to all of us, *"You shall have no other*

gods before Me" (Exodus 20:3). But humans were too weak that they turned to worship other gods. Each and every one of them has his own idol, that is, something more precious than God Himself. And God also commanded, *"You shall not take the name of the LORD your God in vain" (Exodus 20:7).* Yet people are still taking the name of God in vain. Again, God ordered, "Keep the Sabbath holy. Honor your parents. Do not kill. Do not commit adultery. Do not steal. Do not bear false witness. Do not covet. If you fail to keep even one of these, you will die. Anyone who breaks any of these commandments will die."

However, human beings are weak in their flesh and they are incapable of living according to God's Law, even though they know that His Law is right, and they themselves desire to live accordingly. Although human beings are incapable of keeping this Law because of their weak flesh, this does not mean that God would somehow excuse them. Therefore, once their sins are established, they must submit to death. Everyone who fails to keep the Law must be put to death before God. "You shall die, for you have broken the Law of God." Once God issues His commandment, it must be fulfilled infallibly. What is written in Romans 6:23, that *"the wages of sin is death,"* must be fulfilled by God without fail. And since each and every human being is insufficient, the entire human race has fallen into being sinners that must be put to death before God. So the Bible states, *"Therefore, just as through one man sin entered the world, and death through sin, and thus death spread to all men, because all sinned" (Romans 5:12).*

Jesus' Baptism and Blood Have Fulfilled All the Requirements of the Law

However, God could not just abandon mankind to their death, for He so loved us humans. So, out of His love for us, He sent His only begotten Son to this earth to deliver us from our sins. By sending us His Son, God fulfilled all the requirements of the Law and lifted up all its curses, and has thereby saved us all. It was to fulfill the requirements of the Law that God sent Jesus Christ to this earth. Through His Son, God made it possible to fulfill the purpose of His love for us, as well as the requirements of the Law that He had established. The way to achieve this mission began with the baptism of our Lord, when He accepted all the sins of mankind once and for all and took them all upon His own body by being baptized by John. Then by giving up His body unto the Cross, He then bore the condemnation of sin in our place, was crucified and shed His blood to death. By doing so, Jesus paid off the wages of sin demanded by the Law with the price of death, and He fulfilled the law of the Spirit of life that saves us from the sins of the world.

The will of God was to give us the remission of our sins and eternal life through the gospel of the water and the Spirit in Jesus Christ. This baptism and the blood of the Cross through which God has brought us to life again constitute the very gospel of the water and the Spirit. To fulfill the law of salvation for us, our Lord carried our sins on His shoulders in our place by being baptized by John, was crucified to death, rose from the dead again, and has thereby brought to life again all the souls of those who believe in Jesus Christ. This is the Truth of being born again. Jesus met all the requirements of the Law of God by shedding His blood on the Cross, all the while bearing all the sins of this world through the baptism He received from John.

We have confirmed that the gospel of the water and the Spirit is the only Truth of salvation that is written in the Bible. Therefore, with all our hearts, we must believe in the gospel of the water and the Spirit through which God has enabled us to be born again from our sins. No matter what our thoughts may be, we must believe that the gospel of the water and the Spirit is the real Truth of salvation. God has made it possible, in other words, for the spirits of all those who believe in Jesus' water and blood to be born again through the baptism of Jesus and the Spirit.

My fellow believers, we humans are born as sinners without exception. Therefore, we need to realize that if we are to die just as we are, without being born again, then all that awaits us is our destruction. Now is the time for all sinners to be born again. And if we want to be born again from our sins, we must believe in the gospel, that Jesus Christ has saved us through the water and the blood that He has given us. We must believe, in short, in the gospel of the water and the Spirit. We must believe that the Lord took upon our sins through His baptism, washed our hearts clean once for all, and took away the sins of the world. We must believe that Jesus Christ died on the Cross in our place to pay the wages of all of our sins.

We must believe in God's law of love. For God to save us from our sins is the very will of God. Sending us His Son, passing our sins to Him, putting His Son to death in our place, resurrecting His Son, and thus making it possible for those who believe in His Son to be born again, all for the purpose of saving us from our sins—none other than this is the love of God. We must understand this will of our God and believe in this love of His.

It is through our faith in the gospel of the water and the Spirit that we are born again from our sins. If we believe in the gospel of the water and the Spirit, then we will be born again and enter the Kingdom of God, but if we do not believe in it, then we will be condemned for our sins and cast into the everlasting fire of hell. Unless we believe that God loves us, there can only be curses and never-ending agonies. Therefore, it is only when you and I believe in the gospel of the water and the Spirit that we can receive new life.

When we become God's children by faith and pray to Him, our prayers will surely be answered. Hence, if we want to be helped and blessed by God, we must believe in the gospel of the water and the Spirit. Only then can we receive eternal life and enter the Kingdom of Heaven. This is to be born again, and this brings to us tremendous blessings bestowed by God. Herein lies the reason why all of us must be born again.

God has allowed us to be born again out of His love. Through what has He done this? He has made us be born again through the gospel of the water and the Spirit. The Lord God Himself came in the likeness of the flesh of man, took our sins of mankind upon His body by being baptized, was condemned for us by shedding the blood of His flesh, and in body He rose from the dead again. Through all this, He has opened the way for us to be saved by faith. In other words, God Himself came to this earth and made it possible to be born again for all those who believe in the gospel of the water and the Spirit that He fulfilled. Our Lord has given us, to all the believers in the gospel of the water and the Spirit, the gift of being born again and the right to become God's children. This is the only way to be born again.

Christian legalists still lay undue emphasis on human deeds for one to be born again. Yet, we all have to realize here that being born again has absolutely nothing to do with our deeds at all. We need to grasp clearly that it is entirely through our faith in the gospel of the water and the Spirit that we can be born again, and that being born again is entirely a matter of faith. We should never be deceived by the legalists again. It is neither through our obedience to the Law, nor through our pious religious lives that we can be born again. In fact, our own rightfulness is like a filthy, used-up mop (Isaiah 64:6). It is God Himself who loved us so much that He became a man; it is God Himself who, to blot out all our sins, accepted these sins by being baptized by the representative of mankind in the Jordan River; it is God Himself who was crucified to fulfill the Law that declares the wages of sin to be death; and it is God Himself who has thus delivered us from sin and death. Our Lord has delivered us from our old selves, died in our place, and has made us be born again, receive new life, and live for Him.

Jesus Christ is now sitting at the right hand of the throne of God the Father. When His time comes, our Lord will come to take away His people, who are now eagerly waiting for Him apart from sin (Hebrews 9:27). These people are the ones who have become the brides of Jesus Christ. They are the ones who have become sinless by believing in the gospel of the water and the Spirit. Therefore, they are the righteous. They are the ones who will receive God in joy, never in fear. We thank God for this Truth. Since all that we have done is to just believe in the God-given gospel of baptism and blood, and we now lack nothing to be able to call God our own Father, we cannot thank Him enough.

Now then, what is our understanding of God? What kind of God is He to us? We understand Him to be the God of mercy who loves us. We know Him as the God of love. We know Him as the God who has enabled us to be born again of water and blood and brought us to new life. Before, we might have known Him as the fearsome God, the frightful God, and as the God of judgment, but now that we have been born again of water and the Spirit, this is no longer our understanding of Him. When Jesus came to this earth as a Man, He bore the condemnation of our sins and made it possible for us to be born again. Why would we then fear the Lord when He has made us God's own children while we are living on this earth?

The Evidence of the Fact That We Have Been Born Again by Believing in the Gospel of the Water and the Spirit

Once a larva turns into a dragonfly, it flies freely in the sky. You all know what a dragonfly is, right? Sometimes, when we stand and extend one of our fingers toward the sky, a dragonfly would come and sit on our fingertip. Imagine a certain dragonfly is striking a conversation with larvae. "Hey, guys. Do you believe that you are to be born twice? Do you believe that one day you will turn into dragonflies like me?" Some larvae say that they believe, but there are also others who say that they don't know. But the dragonfly says to the larvae, "You have to believe. You will also be changed like this. Someday, you, too, will become like me. Let's meet again when you turn into dragonflies later. Bye~"

Have you seen a midsummer cicada? In the summer cicadas would sing from the trees. Decorating midsummer with their beautiful songs from the trees, they praise God. How do you suppose these cicadas became what they are? Maggots, burrowed deep in the ground, transformed themselves into cicadas. A cicada might say to the maggots, "Look at me. I was born again like this. Get out of earth and climb up the tree. Become great cicadas like myself. I am so happy with my new state."

A dragonfly or a cicada no longer has anything to do with its larval stage. It has now become an imago that flies the sky freely. Like this, we were sinners before we were born again. But now, we have become completely sinless by believing in the gospel of the water and the Spirit. The very fact that we now have no sin in our hearts is the clear evidence that proves that we have indeed been born again.

We are the born-again believers in the gospel of the water and the Spirit, which is constituted by the baptism and blood of Jesus. Those who believe in God, who has allowed us to be born again, live the life of preaching the gospel of the water and the Spirit as they live on this earth. As we carry on with our lives on this earth, we testify, "I have been born again! I am now sinless! My salvation did not come through my own acts. It came through my faith. It was reached through my faith in the gospel of the water and the Spirit. Jesus Christ has allowed me to be born again of water and blood. The Truth of the water, the blood, and the Spirit is the Truth of being born again." We live our lives, in other words, testifying the gospel of the water and the Spirit.

To make it possible for you and me to be born again from our sins, our Lord came to this earth, and He lived and labored for 33 years. In His 33 years on this earth, through the gospel of the water and the Spirit, our Lord redeemed all those who had been under the curse of the Law from all their sins. Coming to this earth, the Lord was baptized at 30, died on the Cross at 33, rose from the dead in three days, bore witness to His resurrection for 40 days, and ascended to Heaven. He now sits at the right hand of the throne of God the Father. Our Lord has enabled us to see, even as such lowly life forms as cicadas and dragonflies, what it is to be truly born again. Our Lord is saying to every sinner all over the world, "Meet My children who have been born again of water and the Spirit. Believe in My servants' words, and you, too, shall be born again. I have made it possible for you to be born again of water and the Spirit."

Jesus Christ our Savior is now sitting at the right hand of the throne of God the Father. Now, Jesus Christ is no longer baptized, nor crucified, nor shedding His blood, nor bearing suffering for us. This is because He already did all these things and has completely fulfilled the gospel of the water and the Spirit. Now there is no longer any need for Him to come again to wipe out our sins, nor to be baptized again, nor to die on the Cross again, nor to be resurrected once more. Why? Because Jesus was already baptized by John, was already crucified, rose from the dead again, ascended to Heaven, and has thereby completed all our salvation to perfection, so that all that He now has to do is just return to this earth to take away His believers in due time. Until the day when the Lord judges unbelievers with fire, He has no more work to do for our salvation. All that He does now is just be with those who believe in the gospel of the water and the Spirit, the gospel of Truth that He has already fulfilled. And He gives them the gift of eternal life. He has sent the Holy Spirit to their hearts and sealed them.

Our Lord has blotted out all our sins with the gospel of the water and the Spirit. Our Lord therefore recognizes with approval the faith of all those who believe in the gospel of the water and the Spirit. God approves their faith to be right, saying, "You are righteous. You are without sin." God in fact seals the sinless people with the Holy Spirit.

In the work of God, there is no sense of the flesh. However, when one is remitted from his sins by believing in the gospel of the water and the Spirit, and thus the Holy Spirit comes into his heart, then the true peace of mind comes to him, not just fleeting, empty emotional experiences. The righteous have no sin. So when you first believed in the gospel of the water and the Spirit, you likely did not go through much emotional change.

Jesus has allowed those of us, who believe in His baptism and blood, to be born twice. He has brought us up spiritually and made us preach the gospel of the water and the Spirit. And He has given us eternal life, so that when the time comes, we would live forever in the Kingdom of God the Father.

For those who believe in the gospel of the water and the Spirit God has allowed us to be born again from our sins. Do you now accept this gospel of the water and the Spirit into your hearts? He who believes in the gospel of the water and the Spirit gives all his thanks to God. He who accepts the gospel Word of the water and the Spirit is blessed to be born again from all his sins before God.

The gospel of the water and the Spirit is the Word of blessings that makes us born again by faith once and for all. ✉

Do You Really Know God's Love?

< John 3:16 >

"For God so loved the world that He gave His only begotten Son, that whoever believes in Him should not perish but have everlasting life."

Because we believe in God, who loves us all, we live happily. Even today, we are working for God while serving Him and preaching the gospel of the water and the Spirit. Had we not known God's love, we would have had no choice but to live dark and empty lives. We would not be able to spread the gospel of the water and the Spirit in joy. Without knowing God's love, it would be too difficult for us to work for Him.

As we read God's Word, what do we realize? We realize that God loves us, and because we know this, we can lead our lives energetically everyday by trusting in this love. Our hearts are overflowing with joy because the love of God is in our hearts. Because God's love for the righteous is so great, we ourselves, who have been clothed in this love, also have loving hearts for all sinners.

God has a loving heart for us. The Apostle John proclaimed, *"We love Him because He first loved us" (1 John 4:19)*. We have come to love God because we have received His love through the gospel Word of the water and the Spirit. Because we now love God, we can also spread this love to others. If we really do not know God's love, not only would we be unable to be saved from this sinful world, but we would also be unable to earn eternal life. When we believe in the gospel of the water and the blood, the very fruit of God's love, we can receive the remission of our sins and spread His love of salvation to others as well.

Leo Tolstoy, a literary giant from Russia, left us a famous story titled, "What Men Live By?" By what do we live? It is by God's love that all of us live. God has a loving heart for us, and in fact, He fulfilled this love through the gospel of the water and the Spirit and has forever bestowed it on us.

I ask you again. By what do our souls live? It is by the love of God that our souls live. By what kind of strength do we preach the gospel of the water and the Spirit and serve the Lord? It is by the strength of God's love for us that we are serving and preaching the gospel of the water and the Spirit. Such a life is made possible only because of God's love. It is not because of the existence of the Truth per se that we love, but it is because we have been clothed in this love of Truth that we are able to love.

God So Loved the World

Let us turn to John 3:14-16, a passage that is very familiar to us. *"And as Moses lifted up the serpent in the wilderness, even so must the Son of Man be lifted up, that whoever believes in Him should not perish but have eternal life. For God so loved the world that He gave His only begotten Son, that whoever believes in Him should not perish but have everlasting life."*

Had there not been this passage from John 3:14-16, we might have not known His love and grace of salvation fully, and even those who have already been saved by the water and the Spirit might have concluded that it was insignificant to believe in Jesus.

When God made us, He did it with His purpose of love. He considered us to be the objects of His love. When God created us, He created us so He could truly love us. While it is true that angels are spiritual beings too, they were merely created to serve the holy God. They are not God's people.

We human beings are made differently from these angels. We were made as the objects of God's love. If the angels were made as the subjects that worship God and serve His children, you and I, that is, all human beings, were made as the objects on whom God would bestow His love. Simply put, the angels were created to be used by God, but mankind was clearly created to enjoy glory with God. When we have children, we take them as our own blood and flesh, and we want to love them and cherish them—God made us just like this.

It is by the grace of God that we live completely saved from our sins. To everyone and anyone, God has given His unconditional love that saves believers from all sins. Our Lord is telling us, "Do you believe that I love you? Because I love you, I was baptized and I shed My blood on the Cross to death. Then I rose from the dead again, and in this way I have saved you. By loving you with the gospel of the water and the Spirit, I have made you My own children." Because we have received God's love by believing in the gospel of the water and the Spirit, we lead a life of serving His gospel, no matter what difficulties we might encounter, we endure them all by faith and we continue to serve the gospel diligently.

Now, you and I, all of us, live by placing our faith in God's love. The strength for us to embrace martyrdom boldly before God also comes from our faith in the fact that the Lord loves us. The strength for us to serve the Lord, also comes wholly from His love. We are also determined to preach the gospel of the water and the Spirit until the end of this world because we know and believe that He loves us. It is because we believe in God's love that we can live in His Church until the end of the age. The Lord is testifying His love to us with the gospel of the water and the Spirit.

The true love of God is fully revealed in the gospel of Truth, the gospel of the water and the Spirit that saves us from the sins of the world. It is also because of God's love that our relationships are sustained and we trust each other and cherish one another. It is just like the role of the bands and the cords that combine each pillar into one strong structure for the fence of the Tabernacle (Exodus 27:17-19). Even though we are weak individually, we can do the work of God bravely in union with the other saints in His Church for we have kept the love of God in our hearts. Through our own strength, it is impossible for us to do anything spiritual or serve the Lord. It is only because of the Lord's love that we can do anything.

It is because we believe in God's love that we serve the Lord in joy. It is because the gospel of the water and the Spirit that I know is the gospel of Truth and too precious to be kept just for myself that I go out and preach this gospel throughout the world, so that it may be spread everywhere. If we do not know God's love, we will consider it as some kind of duty or chain imposed on us, and we will be far from thankful for it. Then we would not be able to do anything for God, no matter what precious and valuable work He might entrust to us. If we have no desire for it, how could God continue to urge us to accept His love? You can take a horse to the water, but you can't force to it drink. Likewise, if we do not believe in God's love and reject it, then God can never saved us. It is because of our love for God that we are doing His work; our sense of duty alone can never make this possible.

It is only because we have received God's overflowing love that we are now able to share this love with one another. Our task then is to support and admonish one another with God's love so that we will all understand it. Since God has brought us new life, our life now belongs to Him. It is God's love that has delivered us from our sins. It is God Himself who has saved us by giving us His water and blood. Thereby, He has made us His people and enabled us to enter the Kingdom of Heaven. And now that He has made us into His workers, we are so thankful to Him beyond all words. All these things have been permitted to us by God's love.

The Love of God Is Manifested by Jesus, Who Was Baptized by John and Who Shed His Blood for Us

In John 1:29, it is written, *"The next day John saw Jesus coming toward him, and said, 'Behold! The Lamb of God who takes away the sin of the world!'"* John the Baptist had baptized Jesus in the Jordan River. And the next day after His baptism, John bore witness to the people, saying "Behold! The Lamb of God who takes away the sin of the world!" This is clearly because John the Baptist himself had passed all the sins of the world to Jesus Christ through His baptism, and he could testify this Truth. Jesus indeed was the Lamb of God who took away the sins of the world. When the Son of God came to this earth, He shouldered all the sins of this world by being baptized by John the Baptist, and then carrying the world's sins to the Cross.

John the Baptist testifies once more, saying, *"Again, the*

next day, John stood with two of his disciples. And looking at Jesus as He walked, he said, 'Behold the Lamb of God!'" (John 1:35-36) "The Lamb of God" mentioned here means that Jesus would become the sacrifice for all sinners of this world by being baptized by John the Baptist on their behalf and then by shedding His blood on the Cross. Jesus could be represented as the Lamb of God because He had accepted all sins of the world through His baptism from John, and would carry them to the Cross.

About 2000 Years Ago, Jesus Blotted out the Sins of the World through the Baptism He Received from John and His Blood Shed on the Cross

As I write this book, it is 2005. I say this to underscore the fact that it has now been 2005 years since the coming of Jesus Christ. The Gregorian calendar is based on this date when Jesus Christ came to this earth, marking the period after His birth as A.D., and before His birth as B.C. History is therefore divided into these two periods, before and after the birth of Jesus Christ, based on the year He came to this world, and so now over 2000 years have passed since His coming.

In 30 A.D., Jesus Christ accepted all the worldly sins of mankind through His baptism by John the Baptist. The next day, John saw Jesus coming toward him. Then, he testified, *"Behold! The Lamb of God who takes away the sin of the world!" (John 1:29)* This meant, "Jesus carried all your sins. No matter what kind of sin you might have committed, the Son of God took them all away. Now whoever believes in Him is a righteous man." To all those who believe in the gospel of the water and the Spirit, God has given the gift of being born again, the gift of the remission of sin.

Sent by God the Father, Jesus took upon all the sins of the world, yours and mine alike. After passing all the sins of this world to Jesus through the baptism that John the Baptist gave to Him, John then testified regarding Jesus so that all would believe in Jesus as their Savior. John 1:7 states, *"This man came for a witness, to bear witness of the Light, that all through him might believe."* Had there been no testimony of John the Baptist, no Christian in this world would have known how Jesus received the sins of the world. The Bible makes it clear that Jesus died on the Cross because of the baptism that He received from John. John the Baptist was testifying that Jesus took upon the sins of the world when Jesus was baptized by him, and that Jesus Himself would carry them to the Cross.

It has been more than 2000 years since Jesus Christ came, and we do not know how many days remain for this world. As the Lord said, *"I am the Alpha and the Omega,"* *(Revelation 1:8),* surely there is an end to this world. Coming to this earth more than 2000 years ago, Jesus Christ took upon all the sins of mankind, that is, "the sins of the world," and carried them to the Cross. From the time He was baptized, it took Him three years to go to the Cross. During these three years after His baptism, Jesus preached the gospel, and after the three years, He was crucified and shed His blood to death.

"The world" in the passage of "the sin of the world" does not just refer to this planet earth, but it refers to every human being whoever lives on it, to you and me. And because God is the eternal Being, He can look through the past world, the present world, and the future world at a glance, and He can blot out the sins of the world to infinite dimensions. Since Jesus said that He already washed away all the sins of the world through His baptism and His blood shed on the Cross, all human beings, whether from the past, the future, or the present, have been freed from all their sins.

Let's Apply "the Sins of the World" to Ourselves

John 1:29 states, *"Behold! The Lamb of God who takes away the sin of the world!"* As you and I were born into this world and are now carrying on with our lives, it has been around 2000 years since Jesus shouldered the sins of the world. We lead our lives limited by the dimension of time but God doesn't.

We are committing sins while leading our lives on this earth within the time dimension He created. Does the time since we were born from our mothers' wombs until now, then, belong to the world or not? It surely belongs to the world. Once born, as babies grow up in their childhood to reach one, two, and three years old, do they continue to commit sin or not? They do. Instead of separating original sin from personal sins, let's consider them altogether. Did we or did we not commit sin in our childhood, when we were from ages 1-10? Of course we did.

But Jesus has already blotted out all these sins with the gospel of the water and the Spirit. All the sins that we had committed in this period were passed onto Jesus when He was baptized. What about when you were teenagers? Did you or did you not commit sin in your adolescence, when you were 11-20 years old? Of course you did. Were these sins then already passed onto Jesus about 2000 year ago also, or were they not passed? They were indeed all passed on. All the sins of this world were put onto Jesus during His baptism. Jesus took away all the sins that we have committed and will ever commit from the day we were born to the day we die. Then do we still have sin or not? There is no sin in our hearts. Jesus already has made an advanced payment for all the sins of world and took them all away beforehand.

How long do we live? Let's just say here that most of us will live until we are 70 years old. If assume that we are now 20 years old, and we weigh all the sins that we would commit for the 50 years of our remaining lives, just how heavy would all these sins be? If you could somehow weigh your sins, they would be so heavy that you would need hundreds of dump trucks to load them. If anything, your sins would be even heavier than this, but never lighter. Regardless of whether it is with your deeds or your hearts that you commit these sins, they are still unbelievably heavy.

Through His baptism, Jesus took upon all the sins of this world once and for all. Jesus definitely carried and took away all the sins of the world. If we were to say that Jesus took away only our original sin, and not our personal sins, then we would end up in hell despite our belief in Jesus. Just how many sins do we commit as we live in this world? Are all they included in the sins of the world or not? Of course, they all belong to the sins of the world. You commit sin when you are 21-30 years old also. These sins, too, are the sins that are committed in the world. And Jesus took them all away also.

Let's say we are 50 years old now. Did or did Jesus not atone for all the sins that we have committed in this world so far? Of course He did! How about the sins that will be committed by our children while they are growing older in the future? All those sins also have already been passed onto Jesus when He was baptized by John the Baptist. He is the very Jesus who blotted out all the sins of mankind.

Through this one man, the representative of mankind, the

Savior was baptized, and through this baptism He put onto Himself all the sins of mankind, all the sins of this world and by dying on the Cross, He freed everyone from the bondage of sin. The Lord, in other words, has atoned for all our sins. To fulfill such a great mission, God needed to send the proper servant who would prepare His way and actually play the great role of passing all the sins of the world to Jesus. Put differently, the Lord needed a representative of all mankind who would lay his hands on His head. This is why God the Father sent John the Baptist prior to Jesus, and said in Matthew 3:15, "Permit it to be so now, for thus it is fitting for us to fulfill all righteousness," commanding John the Baptist to baptize Him. Then Jesus Himself came to this earth and was baptized by this servant of God, John the Baptist.

My fellow believers, it is because John the Baptist has passed the sins of the world to Jesus through His baptism that we are saved by believing in this Jesus Christ. Do you and I have sin or not? We have no sin. Were our sins passed onto Jesus through His baptism? They were indeed passed on.

Because Jesus atoned for all the sins of the world through His baptism, who could then claim that there still is sin in this world? All of us can therefore be saved when we believe in the center of our hearts what John the Baptist and Jesus did for us. By being baptized, Jesus accepted all the sins of the world that each and every one of us have and will commit until the day we die, and He carried these sins of the world to the Cross and shed His blood for us to pay for them. By doing all these things, He has blotted out all our sins.

I have lived for over a half of a century. In retrospect, I have led a very varied and interesting life. I am sure that there are many among you who have seen all kinds of ups and downs in your lives. There are plenty of people other than me who have led difficult lives. All these lives are like a dayfly's life before God.

My fellow believers, how can people understand the gospel of Heaven that Jesus has fulfilled through His baptism and blood? Let's take a dayfly for instance. How many hours are in a dayfly's life? It's about 24 hours. Dayflies are said to live for only a day, and so just one day spans their entire lifetime. Of course, some dayflies live longer than a day, but the name itself essentially captures their ephemeral existence.

By the time dayflies live for 12 hours out of the 24-hour life span, just how many stories would they have to tell, since this is half of their entire lifetime? By the time they live for three-firths of their lifetime, it would be around 6 in the evening, and nightfall would already be setting in. Let's say that these dayflies got together at that time. They were already facing their twilight. Those that lived 24 hours actually have lasted a rather long time; some may have already died in 20 hours, saying, "I'll go first," while others may have lasted for just another hour.

We can imagine that they would chat of old times with their friends with retrospection of their childhood even though it all just happened in the morning in human eyes. When they died, they probably thought that the tiny, insignificant things that they had experienced in a day took place during their long and entire lifetime. But how is it when we look at them? From our perspective, as human beings that live for 70 or 80 years on average, wouldn't the lives of these dayflies seem so trivial to us? If we could somehow listen in to their conversation, it would seem so laughable. However, before God, we ourselves are precisely like these dayflies.

God is the Eternal Being. He existed even before He creates time. Existing in this eternàl time God is looking at us.

Do You Really Know God's Love?   307

Out of His eternal time dimension, He Himself came to this earth into our temporal dimension, took upon all the sins of mankind, all the sins of the world, and upon His death on the Cross, He declared, "It is finished." He then rose from the dead again in three days, and ascended to Heaven, the eternal world. He now abides in eternal time and is looking at us humans.

Let's take the example of the life a man. This man thinks, "I am only 30 years old, and yet I've already committed far too many sins. It's so horrendous and terrible, so how could I ever be forgiven?" But our Lord, who is abiding in eternal time, says to him, "Are you kidding Me? Do you suppose that I only took away the sins that you committed when you were 25 years old, or the sins that you committed until you turned 30? Do you think that this is all that I took away? No! I took away all the sins of the world. Can you see this now? Through My baptism, I accepted onto My body all the sins of every human being whoever lived in this world and will ever live, from Adam the first man to the very last man alive until the end of the age, of your children and generations after them."

Abiding in His everlasting time, our Lord is thus telling us. He is saying to us, "I have already atoned for your sins and all the sins of the world as well."

Jesus Has Completely Fulfilled the Gospel of the Water and the Spirit That Saves the Sinners of the World from All Their Sins

Let's turn to John 19:17-20. *"And He, bearing His cross, went out to a place called the Place of a Skull, which is called in Hebrew, Golgotha, where they crucified Him, and two others with Him, one on either side, and Jesus in the center. Now*

Pilate wrote a title and put it on the cross. And the writing was: JESUS OF NAZARETH, THE KING OF THE JEWS. Then many of the Jews read this title, for the place where Jesus was crucified was near the city; and it was written in Hebrew, Greek, and Latin."

Jesus was crucified on a hill called *Golgotha.* According to the Scripture, He was crucified at 9 o'clock A.M., and agonized for 6 hours on the Cross. When He was about to die, He said, "I thirst!" Then, people filled a sponge with sour wine, put it on hyssop, and put it to His mouth. After receiving the sour wine, He said, "It is finished!" and passed away (John 19:28-30). And Jesus Christ rose from the dead in three days and ascended to Heaven. By doing all these things, He completed all the salvation of mankind.

"The Laying on of Hands" (to Pass Sin) in the Old Testament Was a Shadow of Jesus' Baptism in the New Testament

Hebrews 10:1-9 states, *"For the law, having a shadow of the good things to come, and not the very image of the things, can never with these same sacrifices, which they offer continually year by year, make those who approach perfect. For then would they not have ceased to be offered? For the worshipers, once purified, would have had no more consciousness of sins. But in those sacrifices there is a reminder of sins every year. For it is not possible that the blood of bulls and goats could take away sins. Therefore, when He came into the world, He said: 'Sacrifice and offering You did not desire, But a body You have prepared for Me. In burnt offerings and sacrifices for sin You had no pleasure. Then I* said, 'Behold, I have come—In the volume of the book it is written of Me—To do Your will, O God.' Previously saying, 'Sacrifice and offering, burnt offerings, and offerings for sin You did not desire, nor had pleasure in them' (which are offered according to the law), then He said, 'Behold, I have come to do Your will, O God.' He takes away the first that He may establish the second."

It is written that the Law is a representation of good things to come. The sacrificial animals of the Old Testament, sheep and goats, that had accepted sin with the laying on of hands and were put to death, was a foretelling that Jesus Christ would come to this earth and atone for our sins in the same way, and blot them out with His death. All the people of faith in the Old Testament, such as David and Isaiah, believed in the coming of the Christ Savior by having faith in God's salvation from the sacrificial system written in the Word. The Word of the Old Testament foretold that the Savior would come, take upon all our sins by being baptized by John in this way, and die on the Cross for us like this. The people of the Old Testament's time believed in this, and were saved by faith. This is why the sacrificial system in the Law is a predictor of the good things to come.

However, the Bible says that that these sacrifices offered according to the Law can never wholly purify us. To perform sacrifices everyday whenever we sin involves bringing an animal, passing our sins to it by laying our hands on it and slaughtering it, and to do this all over again tomorrow, cannot make us perfect. This is why the Son of God, the perfect, eternal, and sinless One, Himself came to this world.

Coming to this earth, He said, *"Sacrifice and offering You did not desire, But a body You have prepared for Me. In burnt offerings and sacrifices for sin You had no pleasure. Then I* said, 'Behold, I have come—In the volume of the book it is written of Me—To do Your will, O God.' Previously saying, 'Sacrifice and offering, burnt offerings, and offerings for sin You did not desire, nor had pleasure in them' (which are offered according to the law), then He said, 'Behold, I have come to do Your will, O God.' He takes away the first that He may establish the second" (Hebrews 10:7-9).

The gospel of the water and the Spirit that God fulfilled is the Truth that Jesus Christ the Lamb of God was baptized and crucified to death to make us perfectly sinless. Therefore, we cannot be saved through the Law, but only by believing in the baptism and blood of Jesus can we be saved. According to the system established by God from the Word of the Old Testament, it is only by believing that Jesus Christ took away all our sins like this, that we have truly received the remission of our sins.

Let's turn to Hebrews 10:10. *"By that will we have been sanctified through the offering of the body of Jesus Christ once for all."*

Have you been sanctified or not? You surely have. What is "that will" here? It was for God the Father to send us His Son, to pass all our sins of the world to His Son, to judge this Son once for all, and to thereby free us from all the sins of the world—this was the very will of God the Father. My fellow believers, because Jesus Christ offered His body once and for all to save us, we have now been sanctified. Because Jesus Christ took upon all our sins once and for all, and because He was sacrificed, we have now become sinless.

As the Bible says, once born, it is appointed for us to die once, and to face our judgment after this (Hebrew 9:27). But instead of our death, Jesus Christ, having put all our sins on His own body, vicariously died in our place one time. If someone came along and paid off all the debts that I've had all my life and that I will run up in the future, would I owe anything? No. Precisely in this way, our Lord has paid off all the wages of our sins when He came to this earth. Our Lord has therefore saved all of us who believe in Him from all the sins of the world, so that you and I would neither die nor be condemned. The Old Testament's laying on of hands was the symbol of His baptism.

We Have Been Saved by Believing in Jesus According to the Written Word of the Scriptures

When it comes to believing in Jesus Christ, some people argue that we need some kind of scientific evidence to have concrete faith. But this Word of God itself is far more accurate and logical than any secular science. In the Old Testament, it is written in detail about the offering of sacrifices that were given for the remission of sin. These sacrifices had required the people of Israel to bring innumerable animals and sacrifice them every time they sinned, but in contrast, Jesus offered one everlasting sacrifice for sin with His body, who was baptized once and offered His body once to die on the Cross (Hebrews 10:12).

Do you still believe, in spite of this, that you can somehow be washed from your sins everyday by offering prayers of repentance every time you commit sins? If we still had to give such prayers of repentance everyday, we would return back to the age of the Old Testament. Who could ever be justified by never committing any sin until the day he dies, or by confessing all his sins perfectly including sins he committed by chance? Who could ever receive the remission of sins like this? Who would be able to not commit any sin at all, and who could ever be washed from his sins just by offering prayers of repentance? When there are so many sins that we have committed, how could we possibly repent all of them? We are beings such that the sins that we had committed in the morning are all forgotten by the evening, the evening's sins are also trivially passed over, and all our usual sins are pretty much forgotten in no time; hence, to say that we can wash away our sins by prayers of repentance simply makes no sense.

As it is written, *"By that will we have been sanctified through the offering of the body of Jesus Christ once for all"* *(Hebrews 10:10),* Jesus Christ offered His body once for all. And because of this, we have now been sanctified once for all. Our sanctification has been reached in an instant, not over an extended period of time or a series of steps. The claim that we are somehow sanctified gradually and incrementally is nothing more than Satan's deception. Our Lord has blotted out all our sins once for all with the gospel of the water and the Spirit.

Hebrews 10:11-18 states, *"And every priest stands ministering daily and offering repeatedly the same sacrifices, which can never take away sins. But this Man, after He had offered one sacrifice for sins forever, sat down at the right hand of God, from that time waiting till His enemies are made His footstool. For by one offering He has perfected forever those who are being sanctified. But the Holy Spirit also witnesses to us; for after He had said before, 'This is the covenant that I will make with them after those days, says the LORD: I will put My laws into their hearts, and in their minds I will write them,' then He adds, 'Their sins and their lawless deeds I will remember no more.' Now where there is remission of these, there is no longer an offering for sin."*

Did God say here that we have to offer some sacrifices for our sins? No! What does it mean by the phrase, "remission of these"? It is the written Word of the Scriptures proclaiming that God has blotted out sin itself, any and all the sins of the world.

Had John the Baptist not baptized Jesus Christ, could we have received the remission of our sins? On the other hand, even if God had established the representative of mankind as John the Baptist, if Jesus had not received baptism from this man, and therefore did not take upon the sins of the world, could He then have blotted out our sins? No. God's law is the law of justice. It is equitable and fair. If God says just by words, "You're the Savior. I have forgiven all your sins. I am your Messiah," this alone does not mean that our salvation is completed. He had to actually take upon all our sins. Why did Jesus come incarnated in the flesh of man? It was precisely to bear all our sins trough His baptism, to remove all the sins that we commit in both our flesh and our hearts (for He already knew them), and to blot them out with His bloodshed, that He came to this earth incarnated in the same flesh as ours.

My fellow believers, had Jesus Christ not been baptized by John the Baptist, our sins could not have been entirely atoned for. And had Jesus died on the Cross without first taking all our sins on Himself, His death would have been all in vain. This death would have been useless and completely irrelevant to us. This is why Jesus came to this earth incarnated in the flesh, quietly led an ordinary life until 30, and was then baptized. Then, He lived three years of His public life from His baptism until His death on the Cross.

His baptism was the beginning of His public life. Saying to John the Baptist, *"Permit it to be so now, for thus it is fitting for us to fulfill all righteousness" (Matthew 3:15)*, Jesus was then baptized. It was at this moment that the passage from John 1:29—*"Behold! The Lamb of God who takes away the sin of the world!"*—was fulfilled.

Because Jesus had accepted all our sins by being baptized, and because all these sins of ours, each and every sin of mankind, were wholly passed onto the body of Jesus, God the Father Himself turned away His eyes when His Son died on the Cross. Even God the Father could not bear to see His own Son dying, but because He did not choose to save His Son who was now shouldering all the sins of the world from His certain death, the Father could not help but let Him die. This is why darkness had descended upon the land for three hours before Jesus took His last breath, for God had turned His face. At the climax of His agony of death, Jesus Himself shouted out, *"Eli, Eli, lama sabachthani?"* that is, *"My God, My God, why have You forsaken Me?" (Matthew 27:45-46)* Jesus had shouldered the sins of the world in our place, and was punished and condemned on the Cross in our stead. This is how He has saved you and me. Can you now grasp this? Do you now believe?

Had Jesus Christ not been baptized by John the Baptist, and had He not accepted the sins of the world, He would not have been condemned. There was no reason for Jesus Christ to die on the Cross if He had not taken upon our sins from John the Baptist, who was the representative of all mankind prepared by God.

This is why, in speaking of John the Baptist, Jesus said, *"What did you go out into the wilderness to see? A reed shaken by the wind? But what did you go out to see? A man clothed in soft garments? Indeed, those who wear soft clothing are in kings' houses" (Matthew 11:7-8),* and added, *"But what did you go out to see? A prophet? Yes, I say to you, and more than a prophet" (Matthew 11:9).* Jesus also declared, *"Assuredly, I say to you, among those born of women there has not risen one greater than John the Baptist,"* and He went on to say, *"And from the days of John the Baptist until now the kingdom of heaven suffers violence" (Matthew 11:11-12).*

In all these things, Jesus is telling us that it was because John the Baptist had passed all the sins of the world to Himself that they could all be blotted out. You and I, having now seen the baptism given to Jesus and heard the testimony of John the Baptist, have come to believe in the Word of the remission of sin that Jesus fulfilled for us. This is how we became the righteous people without sin. Therefore, we can now call God as "God the Father."

It is written, *"Now where there is remission of these, there is no longer an offering for sin" (Hebrew 10:18).* There is no more sin in our hearts. If our bill is all paid off, do we still owe any debt? For example, let's say here that a certain father loved to drink, and so he ran huge tabs in every pub in town. But his son became rich and made advance payments for all the drinks that his father loved so much, and he even paid for all drinks his father would ever have in his entire lifetime. If so, would this father have any bill to pay, even if continued to drink for an entire lifetime? He would owe nothing! This is only an example, of course, but just like this illustration, our God put all our sins on Jesus, so that He may save us. Moreover, Jesus did not just take upon the sins of our lifetime alone, but He took upon all the sins of the world without exception. All our sins were passed onto Jesus Christ when He was baptized. They now all belong to Jesus. This is why whoever believes in this is saved from all his sins. It is because Jesus was baptized for you when He came to this earth that you receive the remission of your sins by believing in this.

The planet earth has been here long before we were born. It's not as if it came to exist after we came into existence. Jesus Christ, who has blotted out our sins, had already atoned for all of our sins long before you and I were born. Jesus atoned for each and every sin that all the disobedient sinners of this world have ever committed. My dear fellow saints, it is because the sins of the world were all passed onto Jesus that we have now become sinless, by believing in this Jesus who became the propitiation for all our sins.

My fellow believers, do you then still have sin? Of course not. What about tomorrow's sins then, you might ask? All the sins that you will commit tomorrow will also be atoned for by Jesus. God Himself, on His side, took away each and every sin of the world, and He bore all the condemnation of sin because of the sins that He put on Himself.

Introducing the baptism that Jesus received from John, the Gospel of Mark begins by saying, *"The beginning of the gospel of Jesus Christ, the Son of God" (Mark 1:1)*. This means that the Truth implied in Jesus' baptism is very good news to everybody. God says to us, "I have atoned for all your sins. I am Your Savior. I have atoned all your sins in this way." What is the gospel of truth? It's *'euaggelion'* or the good news. The Greek word for "gospel" is *"euaggelion."* And God is asking us whether we believe or not in this gospel (*euaggelion*), this joyful news that His Son Jesus has brought to us.

Yet among so many people in this world, only a very small number have actually answered, saying, "Yes, I believe as You say. Yes, Lord, I believe as You have done. Now that I heard the Truth, it is so simple, and yet all this time I had not known it." It is those who believe like this that God approves of, saying to them, "You are right. You are the righteous people like Abraham."

However, most people only say, "I don't think so, Lord. This gospel is something strange that I've never heard before." So when the Lord says to them, "Oh, yeah? Have I or haven't I blotted all your sins then?" they say, "Well, yes and no. You took away my original sin, but You didn't take away my personal sins." Being stunned by such misunderstanding, Jesus can only say to them, "Yes, you are so smart that you may have no need to learn from Me!" To such people, even Jesus would run out of words to say.

That these people would be cast into hell for refusing to believe that Jesus blotted out all their sins out of His love is a punishment that they will bear for the wages of their sins. As such, this is only their rightful punishment, not something that deserves compassion or sympathy. My fellow believers, it is not because one commits so many sins, nor the severity of such sins, that one is cast into hell. It is because one does not believe that Jesus has atoned for all sins that one is cast into hell. But whoever believes in the baptism of Jesus and the Cross can reach the Kingdom of Heaven by receiving his salvation.

Had Jesus not put all our sins on Himself by being baptized by John the Baptist, then our faith in Him would also be in vain. The baptism of Jesus is mentioned so many times in the Pauline Epistles. For instance, Galatians 3:27 says, *"For as many of you as were baptized into Christ have put on Christ."* Here, to be "baptized into Christ" means to come into Jesus Christ to be united with Him by believing in His baptism. It means that all our sins were put on Jesus through the hands of John the Baptist, and this, in short, means that all our sins were passed onto Him. Therefore, when He died, we also died. And when He rose from the dead again, we, too, were resurrected.

Romans 6:3 says, *"Or do you not know that as many of us as were baptized into Christ Jesus were baptized into His death?"* Again, Romans 6:10 says, *"For the death that He died, He died to sin once for all; but the life that He lives, He lives to God";* and John 1:12 says, *"But as many as received Him, to them He gave the right to become children of God, to those who believe in His name."* As these passages show that for all those who accept into their hearts what God has done for them, He has confirmed them as His own children.

In Colossians 1:13-14, it is written, *"He has delivered us from the power of darkness and conveyed us into the kingdom of the Son of His love, in whom we have redemption through His blood, the forgiveness of sins."* Hallelujah!

God has delivered us from the midst of all our sins through the water and the blood, the gospel of the water and the Spirit, and He has made us born again from all our sins. I praise God for saving us all. Hallelujah! ✉

Let Us Do Spiritual Work by Faith

< John 3:16-17 >

"For God so loved the world that He gave His only begotten Son, that whoever believes in Him should not perish but have everlasting life. For God did not send His Son into the world to condemn the world, but that the world through Him might be saved."

It is so difficult for human beings to live in this world. Struggling against the rapidly changing environment is hard enough, and many people have perished from recent heat waves. Every summer, we hear of news about how many people did not survive through the scorching heat waves and perished. Temperatures in my country during the summer have also gone up so high that it feels as though I live in a tropical climate, and simply taking in breaths is hard work. The world has yet to see far worse heat waves, and so my heart is determined to spread the gospel of the water and the Spirit to everyone throughout the world as soon as possible.

The world is falling ill now. In Botswana, a southern African country, almost 40% of the population is said to be HIV-positive. The crises of neighboring countries are almost the same. The situation is so bad that the very survival of these nations is now in doubts. UNAIDS, the joint United Nations program on HIV, reported that the average life span in Botswana is no more than 39. If the HIV infection rate of this country does not decrease, over two-thirds of its teens would pass away in the near future.

It is in such a tough world in which you and I are now living. For what reason should we live, and what purpose should we mark for our lives? We the born-again righteous who believe in the gospel of the water and the Spirit should know clearly what our purpose of life is.

There are so many things in this world for us to do, and yet there are so many difficulties that we are facing. Are you also struggling? For what purpose do you live? People in this world start to distance themselves from their lust of the flesh and begin to think about their souls only when they are nearing death, and it is only then that they desire to be washed from their sins, to become sinless before the presence of God. Because countless people try to take care of their souls only upon their imminent death, they are unable to receive the true salvation and remission of their sins, and therefore they ultimately end up going to hell.

You and I have the duty to live for the countless souls who still have not accepted the gospel of the water and the Spirit. We are doing all these works of service to spread the gospel of the water and the Spirit to them in any way possible. In doing so, our situation does not matter. Throughout this whole world, there are many people waiting for our helping hands. In underdeveloped countries, there are countless souls dying because of their ignorance of the good news. These people desperately need the Word of God, and we must do everything possible so that they may also believe in the gospel of the water and the Spirit that can save and renew their souls. Though they are struggling with hunger and diseases, I know that they would want their souls to be filled with God's abundant blessings just like us. They are calling us to be saved.

People in some developed countries, on the other hand, are proud of their past glory. They are proud of the achievements of their ancestors, boasting of their great castles, renowned artists, and cultural heritage left for the world. But the matter of fact is that their souls, too, are also dead spiritually. We must go to them also by sharing our gospel books. We need to share our books that hold the gospel of the water and the Spirit with everyone in the whole wide world. There is indeed much for us to do, for we must spread the gospel of the water and the Spirit to them, so that they may come to know and believe in Jesus, receive the remission of their sins, and enter the Kingdom of God.

What Is Our Purpose for Life in This Age and Time?

"For what purpose should we live?" This question is something that all of us must give some serious consideration to at least once. Human beings are fundamentally so weak that they cannot even survive through slightly more intense heat waves. The spread of the gospel of the water and the Spirit to such beings has now become our purpose in life. And this means that we have been permitted by God to receive strength from Him and to live fruitful and worthy lives. For the believers in the gospel of the water and the Spirit who have received the remission of sin, they are now living for this purpose of spiritual work and this is something to be greatly proud of.

It would be a shameful life if I were to lead my life simply to eat and drink, trying to make some pittance for my own survival. Money cannot be the goal of our lives. We only need it to survive in the flesh in order to serve the gospel of the water and the Spirit. As such, those who have now received the remission of their sins by believing in the gospel of the water and the Spirit must live for the salvation of other souls. It is crystal clear that unless one is remitted from his sins, he is bound to hell. Therefore, we should not fail to grasp God's desire, which has made us born again first through the gospel of the water and the Spirit, so that we may help others to prepare their next lives for Heaven rather than hell. If we instead live for our flesh, even after receiving the remission of our sins, and we do not make up our minds to spread this gospel for the rest of our lives, then we would be like the beasts that perish (Psalms 49:20). You need to realize here that when the born-again righteous do not live for God's righteousness, they have no reason for existence.

Our purpose in life is to spread the gospel of the water and the Spirit to others, so that they may receive the remission of their sins. The Lord said to us that life on this earth lasts only a moment, and all that remains thereafter is the judgment. This is why we must do the spiritual works that save souls. It is written, *"He who says he abides in Him ought himself also to walk just as He walked" (1 John 2:6).* If you have indeed become the righteous children of God by believing in the gospel of the water and the Spirit, then it is only proper for you to live for other souls just as Jesus Christ has done so.

Our thoughts, our minds, and our purpose must be clear and large. However, most people live lowly and hopeless lives because of their small aspirations and narrow minds. What would be sadder than having nothing worthy in their achievements on their headstones other than to note the years of their birth and death? The reality is that everyone on this earth who has not been born again is like this. The born-again who do not live for the gospel are also like this. You do not want to end up like these people, to leave a headstone that only says you were born in such a year, were born again by believing in the gospel of the water and the Spirit, but then lived to only feed yourselves, do you?

We do not serve because we want to be memorialized by someone down the road, but we serve because we do not want to lead the kind of life that we would not be proud of. Those of us who have been born again of the water and the Spirit should have our headstones read, "This man was born in such a year, was born again in such a year, and until he passed away and came to rest here, he preached the gospel to countless people and he saved countless souls." Only then have we led truly worthy lives.

Whether one's life would be something to be proud of or be ashamed of depends on how he decides to live his life. On one hand, there are those who are living for the immediate pleasures of the flesh, and on the other hand, there are those who are thinking about their future and wondering how they can live worthy and meaningful lives. How one ends his life depends on how he decides to live his life.

Human life, after all, lasts only 70-80 years, perhaps 90-100 years if we live long. Everyone is inevitably bound to die like this, for it is appointed for man to be born once and die once. But once we are born, we have to meet the Lord, receive remittance from all our sins, and live our lives to spread the gospel to everyone throughout the world. Just how eagerly are people waiting for our help?

Have you ever seen the Carnival in Rio de Janeiro, Brazil? The Brazilian dance Samba is world-famous. What a dizzy, sumptuous, and lively dance is it? But while seeing the magnificence of this Samba Carnival, suddenly I realized the emptiness of life, for in my eyes, these death-bound people shaking their bodies fervently in their dance were only desperately trying to forget their suffering temporarily. When I thought about how they had worked hard for a whole year just to enjoy the revelry during the Carnival, and how they had lived only to eat and drink like this, they seemed so pitiful to me. As I came to see the pity that lies behind the glittering splendor, my heart was convicted to spread the gospel to such people in Brazil first.

When we look at people, there are those who draw our compassion, and then there are those who do not. Those who seem fine in their outward appearance, and have adorned themselves, do not draw our compassion. But those who still retain their sadness and misery despite searching and trying hard to live their lives in true joy draw our compassion. It was our goal to spread the gospel to such poor people that we published our books in every language. These books are going into every nation to testify about the gospel of the water and the Spirit, and as a result, there have arisen many partners of the same faith as ours around the world. This is how we are able to meet those who were looking for the Truth.

God has entrusted us with the work that enables people to believe in the gospel of the water and the Spirit and receive remission for their sins. It is simply a joy to see people receiving the remission of sin and giving thanks to God. So we willingly and gladly do our best to carry out this work before God. This work is something that we do simply because God has commanded us to do so, and it is worthwhile because of the profound joy that is found in sharing the gospel with others; there is nothing we demand from them. We are only pleased with this work that makes it possible for dying souls to be saved. What is greater than this, to enable the dying to receive the remission of their sins and eternal life? People may not realize it, but to do this work that saves other souls is the greatest joy in the world.

When those who have received the remission of their sins before the gospel of the water and the Spirit are asked about the most memorable and worthwhile thing to happen in the whole life, they will likely say that the greatest joy for them is the fact that they have encountered the gospel. It is an utterly abundant and overflowing blessing to be saved. If you were interviewed at your deathbed, and were asked, "As your flesh is now deteriorating before God, what was the single most meaningful event to happen in your life on this earth, if any?" how would you answer this question? Wouldn't you say that the most worthwhile moment was when you received the remission of your sins? "That I met the Lord, came to believe in the gospel of the water and the Spirit, and have been remitted from all the sins in my heart, was my most meaningful event. This is the most worthwhile event in my life, that my heart has received the remission of all my sins and I have lived to spread the gospel." This is how you would answer.

Even though our circumstances and situations may get worse day by day, we still continue to spread the gospel of the water and the Spirit. It is not to blow our own horn to show others how hard we are working, but we work heartily to embrace everyone in the whole world. It is because we are spreading the gospel of the water and the Spirit that those who have subsequently heard and believed in it are now able to live their lives free from all their sins. Given this, we are indeed doing something that is profoundly worthwhile.

There is no one in this world who is greater than we, the born-again, who are serving and spreading this gospel. Those on this earth who boast of themselves are nobody. Those who are arrogant and boastful are akin to a pig with gold earrings in its ear and a diamond ring in its hoof. Is a pig transformed into a human just because it's wearing a diamond ring on its nose? No, it still remains nothing more than a pig. As it is written, *"As a ring of gold in a swine's snout, so is a lovely woman who lacks discretion" (Proverbs 11:22),* a life that is apart from God's will cannot be anything but worthless. Those who have been remitted from all their sins through the gospel of the water and the Spirit, who have embraced everyone in this whole world in their hearts, and who are living their lives for them as the witnesses of the gospel—these are the most admirable people on this earth.

You and I are now doing this very work. Through our literature, we are spreading the gospel throughout the whole world. It is because you and I, the believers in the gospel of the water and the Spirit, have united with God's Church, that we do various works for the sole purpose to spread the gospel throughout the entire world. All of us have done this together. You may not have designed the cover-arts of our books, edited our books, or translated them, but still, the gospel could be spread only because of you, who have prayed for this ministry, gave offerings, fulfilled your role as out of sight supporters, and served behind the scenes. We have all done this together.

My fellow believers, these books that we have made together are now making their way to every corner of the world. For the last few years, we have translated our books not only into major languages, but even into many tribal languages also. Soon, even people living in obscure countries that we've never seen or heard of will send us letters that confirm the same faith as our faith. In particular, many ministers and theologians will send us their letters that proclaim the same faith of ours.

There are many famous pastors throughout the world, but

few actually preach this gospel of the water and the Spirit. How do I know this? We can find this out using the Internet. Before we published our first book, some of our staff workers had surfed the Internet to find out if anyone else had the same faith as ours. But, unfortunately, we couldn't find any pastor who was preaching the gospel of the water and the Spirit. Another piece of evidence indicating that few people knew of the gospel of the water and the Spirit is that of the many reviews that we have received, none have ever said, "I've had the same gospel of the water and the Spirit before I came across this book. I am so happy to meet my family of faith!"

So, I wrote on inside cover of my first book, "This is the first book of our time to preach the gospel of the water and the Spirit in strict accordance with the Scriptures." By this, I meant that there has been no one who has preached the gospel of the water and the Spirit since the end of the Apostolic Age up to my first book. It's been proven that this is not an exaggerated advertisement. Many pastors were unable to hide their amazement, and have testified, "I have read many Christian books, but I never knew that Jesus' baptism held such significance. I didn't know that the gospel of the water and the Spirit is so blessed."

When we were about to print my first book, I said, "Soon our pastors and our brothers and sisters will be invited all over the world." What has actually happened so far? Truly, there have been too many people around the world who have invited us.

Countless pastors and theologians have published Christian books, marketing them on Internet bookstores such as Amazon.com. As I browsed through their books on the Internet, I came to deplore the fact that they all have written their books full of their own thoughts to make a show of their own limited knowledge. To spread the Christian faith in a book, it is only proper for the book to hold the Truth, which is the gospel of the water and the Spirit that enables one to receive the remission of sin through the Word of God. The gospel of the water and the Spirit is the Truth that was revealed first in the Apostolic Age.

My fellow believers, countless Christians say that they have no sin even when they believe only in Jesus' blood on the Cross. They still retain their sins everyday because they commit sin everyday, and they have no other recourse but to pray daily for repentance. These people, too, believe in the resurrection of Jesus, in His birth, and in the fact that Jesus is the Son of God, but they do not know how Jesus accepted their sins, and they consider it strange and incorrect that He accepted the sins of the world when He was baptized. This is how most Christians are.

My fellow believers, to believe in and preach only the blood of the Cross is only to spread religion. Yet despite this, few are actually preaching the gospel of the water and the Spirit besides us. That's why to preach the gospel of the water and the Spirit is so right, and those who do this work are so precious. We will preach this gospel to everyone in this entire world. As the Apostle Paul said, *"I am a debtor both to Greeks and to barbarians, both to wise and to unwise" (Romans 1:14),* we have to preach the gospel of the water and the Spirit to everyone throughout the whole world. We are the remarkable people who have the gospel of power to achieve this. We are now preaching this amazing gospel. This is why we truthfully think about spiritual works and do these works of God, regardless of the hot weather and difficult circumstances, and whether worldly thoughts arise in our minds or not.

The Scripture passage that we read today says, *"For God so loved the world that He gave His only begotten Son" (John*

3:16). My fellow believers, our God the Father told us that He sent His only begotten Son in order to save every one of us. The word "gave" here means that God sent His Son to this earth, and made Him save everyone by accepting all the sins of this world through His baptism, and that He let His Son be crucified for all those sins. God has saved everyone in this world by sending His only begotten Son. Because Jesus Christ has blotted out everyone's sins, all who believe in this Jesus who came to this earth, was baptized, died on the Cross, and rose from the dead again as their Savior, are the sinless who have been saved. They have become God's people, who have turned into the righteous, and they have received everlasting life.

God has already saved you and me from all our sins. Therefore, we are not bound by our sins that Jesus already took away from us, but we should be thinking about spiritual works for the future. We should think about what God has done for us to save us mankind, to save you and me from our sins, and we should preach this to many people as we possibly can.

The second half of John 3:16 reads, *"That whoever believes in Him should not perish but have everlasting life."* My fellow believers, when you believe that God the Father has saved you by sending His only begotten Son to this earth, then you will receive everlasting life. Do you want to receive this eternal life? Do you want to have everlasting life? With this everlasting life, do you want to live happily forever? Do you abhor death? If the answer to these questions is 'Yes,' then believe in our Lord. The Lord has not only blotted out our sins, but also all the sins of all the people in this world. Our Lord Himself has blotted out all the sins that we have committed out of our lustful flesh, and He has given us the remission of sin and eternal life.

Now we are able to do spiritual works because we have received everlasting life and the remission of our sins by believing in our Lord. And we can lead everyone to also receive this remission of sin, and we can continue to do the work that saves souls.

Our Lord said in John 3:17, *"For God did not send His Son into the world to condemn the world, but that the world through Him might be saved."* God did not send Jesus to condemn us. Why, then, did He send His Son? God clearly states here that He sent Jesus so that the world would be saved through Him.

My fellow believers, Jesus was sent to this earth by God the Father to save everyone in this world from sin. All the people in this world are waiting for their salvation. They wonder to themselves, "How can I be saved?" They are longing for God's salvation.

Our books, carrying the immutable Truth called the gospel of the water and the Spirit, are now reaching them and knocking on the doors of all those who yearn to be saved in every nook and corner of the world. Among those who have been touched by the Truth through our book, pastors in particular have responded very positively. Just as it takes a while to find out whether a certain medication is good or bad, if we continue to do God's work and wait a bit longer, even more numerous and better fruits will be borne.

A pastor in India once wrote us that too many groundless Christian books were coming into his country. It was in this climate that he came to receive and read my first book, and he testified that this book was truly like drinkable water. Saying that this book was a good book, he told us that he wanted to translate our books into his tribal language and share them with the Tamil-speaking people. So he translated our books into

Tamil language, and we willingly financed the cost of publication. This is a wonderful thing, since even if we ourselves do not go out to the mission field, if our coworkers work there on our behalf, people can continue to receive the remission sin.

Every place our books enter, the gospel of the water and the Spirit enters also, and everywhere this gospel of the water and the Spirit enters, people are receiving the remission of sin. If someone would only read one of our books, the book would bring about more positive result than a week's worth of my labor. This is why I love to preach the gospel of the water and the Spirit through the literature.

Some people wonder occasionally, "Can the gospel of the water and the Spirit be spread through books?" I believe that it surely can. No matter how insufficient we may be, the Truth of the water and the Spirit is indeed spread when we continue to publish our books throughout the whole world. If our books are spread throughout the world, they may very well become the bestsellers in this world. They not have been advertised enough though, but I am sure that when they are known more widely, they may actually follow the record of the Bible as the most consistent bestseller in the history of mankind. In fact, thanks to our books, people are being saved everyday through the gospel of the water and the Spirit.

Our Lord came to this earth, was baptized, and shed His blood for us. It is written in the Word that God the Father did not send His only begotten Son to condemn the world but to save it, and Jesus precisely fulfills the Word. This is why Jesus was baptized, and through this baptism He accepted all the sins of our entire lifetime. This essentially means that He has given salvation to entire mankind. It was to save mankind that the Lord came to this earth.

We must preach what our Lord did for us when He came to the world to all the ends of the earth. This is the primary goal of our spiritual work. However, you and I pursue many things of the flesh. Is it a sin to follow the flesh or not? It clearly is a sin. I don't mean to suggest here that we should determine to never commit any sin again, but that we should admit to God what is sin as sin. For us to follow the flesh is a sin, but our Lord has blotted out all these sins and entrusted us with the work of spreading the gospel of the water and the Spirit. Therefore, by placing our faith in this gospel, we can deny our flesh and do spiritual works.

The Lord has given us the truly amazing gospel of the water and the Spirit. And by believing in this gospel, we have received the remission of our sins. It gives me such joy that our lives are not the kinds of life that follows the flesh, but they are spiritual lives. I am happy that our lives are spent not to do carnal works, but to continue to do spiritual works. All of us must become the ones who do spiritual works by faith, and all of our hearts must desire to do these spiritual works by faith. You and I are all capable of doing spiritual works. With God's power we can lead everyone to be saved. This is because our Lord has already saved us from all our sins, and He has also blessed us to do spiritual works. To do these works, we must live by faith. And we must live for the purpose of spreading the gospel of the water and the Spirit throughout the whole world.

We are mortal beings, as it is written, *"As it is appointed for men to die once, but after this the judgment"* (Hebrews 9:27). But, there is another passage of hope that says, *"For God so loved the world that He gave His only begotten Son, that whoever believes in Him should not perish but have everlasting life."* This means that God has already given us His salvation and everlasting life. Let us, then, not try to take care of only our flesh, nor to pursue only our own selfish greed, but let us now live for the purpose of proclaiming the righteousness of God throughout the whole world.

Some people believe beyond any doubt that it is for their own families and their own flesh that they should live. Strictly speaking, however, their lives are not for anyone else, but for themselves. Nonetheless, God has taught us the way to live the kind of life that is worthy of His commendation, and it is right for us to follow it. It makes me so happy to think that our hearts have received the remission of sin by believing in the gospel of the water and the Spirit, and we are able to live our lives preaching the gospel of the water and the Spirit, so that our families may also receive the remission of sin by hearing and believing in this Truth, and, taking a step further, so that everyone throughout the whole world may be saved—I cannot think of anything else that would make us as happy as this.

Everyone must go out in search of his happiness, and he has the duty to live his life for a worthwhile cause. It is my sincerest hope and prayer for all of you that it would be in your spiritual lives that you find this calling. Though we are weak and insufficient, now that we have accepted our God-given salvation, we must live for our Lord. And instead of serving our flesh only for its own sake, we must live our lives to make it possible for other souls to be saved also. This is so we can lay up treasures in the Kingdom of Heaven as it is written in God's Word.

As human beings can only live up to 70-80 years, and 90-100 years at most, what would be left at their end? If we do not yearn for everlasting life, there is nothing else in our existence but eating, laboring, sleeping, going to the washroom, and then dying. Instead of narrowing our minds, we should let our hearts and minds grow bigger and bolder, and live to serve the gospel so that our lives may not be in vain. We must live for what is right, and then go to the presence of our Lord.

It is my hope and prayer that you and I will continue to be blessed in our lives, both in body and spirit. There is no other way to be blessed both in body and spirit, but to live for the Lord doing spiritual works and then coming face to face with the Lord. I thank God for the salvation that He has given us. ✉

HAVE YOU TRULY BEEN BORN AGAIN OF WATER AND THE SPIRIT?

PAUL C. JONG

Among many Christian books written about being born again, this is the first book of our time to preach the gospel of the water and the Spirit in strict accordance with the Scriptures. Man can't enter the Kingdom of Heaven without being born again of water and the Spirit. To be born again means that a sinner is saved from all his lifelong sins by believing in the baptism of Jesus and His blood of the Cross. Let's believe in the gospel of the water and the Spirit and enter the Kingdom of Heaven as the righteous who have no sin.

RETURN TO THE GOSPEL OF THE WATER AND THE SPIRIT

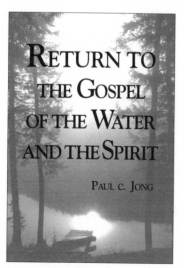

PAUL C. JONG

Let's return to the gospel of the water and the Spirit. Theology and doctrines themselves can't save us. However, many Christians still follow them, and consequently have not been born again yet. This book clearly tells us what mistakes theology and doctrines have made and how to believe in Jesus in the most proper way.

The Fail-safe Way for You to Receive the Holy Spirit

In Christianity, the most significantly discussed issue is salvation from sins and the indwelling of the Holy Spirit. However, few people have the exact knowledge of these two topics. Nevertheless, in reality people say that they believe in Jesus Christ while they are ignorant of true redemption and the Holy Spirit.

Do you know the true gospel that makes you receive the Holy Spirit? If you want to ask God for the indwelling of the Holy Spirit, then you must first know the gospel of the water and the Spirit and have faith in it. This book will certainly lead all Christians worldwide to receive the Holy Spirit through the remission of all their sins.

Our LORD Who Becomes the Righteousness of God (I) & (II)

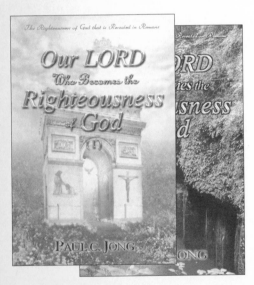

The teachings in these books will satisfy the thirst in your heart. Today's Christians continue to live while not knowing the true solution to the personal sins that they are committing daily. Do you know what God's righteousness is? The author hopes that you will ask yourself this question and believe in God's righteousness, which is dealt in detail in these books.

The Doctrines of Predestination, Justification, and Incremental Sanctification are the major Christian doctrines, which brought only confusion and emptiness into the souls of believers. But, dear Christians, now is the time when you must continue in the Truth which you have learned and been assured of.

These books will provide your soul with a great understanding and lead it to peace. The author wants you to possess the blessing of knowing God's righteousness.

IS THE AGE OF THE ANTICHRIST, MARTYRDOM, RAPTURE AND THE MILLENNIAL KINGDOM COMING? (I)

After the 9/11 terrorist attacks, traffic to "www.raptureready.com," an Internet site providing information on the end times, is reported to have increased to over 8 million hits, and according to a joint survey by CNN and TIME, over 59% of the Americans now believe in apocalyptic eschatology.

Responding to such demands of the time, the author provides a clear exposition of the key themes of the Book of Revelation, including the coming Antichrist, the martyrdom of the saints and their rapture, the Millennial Kingdom, and the New Heaven and Earth-all in the context of the whole Scripture and under the guidance of the Holy Spirit.

This book provides verse-by-verse commentaries on the Book of Revelation supplemented by the author's inspired sermons. Anyone who reads this book will come to grasp all the plans that God has in store for this world.

IS THE AGE OF THE ANTICHRIST, MARTYRDOM, RAPTURE AND THE MILLENNIAL KINGDOM COMING? (II)

Most Christians today believe in the theory of pre-tribulation rapture. Because they believe in this false doctrine teaching them that they would be lifted before the coming of the Great Tribulation of seven years, they are leading idle religious lives steeped in complacency.

But the rapture of the saints will occur only after the plagues of the seven trumpets run their course until the sixth plague is all poured-that is, the rapture will happen after the Antichrist emerges amidst global chaos and the born-again saints are martyred, and when the seventh trumpet is blown. It is at this time that Jesus would descend from Heaven, and the resurrection and rapture of the born-again saints would occur (1 Thessalonians 4:16-17).

The righteous who were born again by believing in "the gospel of the water and the Spirit" will be resurrected and take part in the Rapture, and thus become heirs to the Millennial Kingdom and the eternal Kingdom of Heaven, but the sinners who were unable to participate in this first resurrection will face the great punishment of the seven bowls poured by God and be cast into the eternal fire of hell.

The TABERNACLE: A Detailed Portrait of Jesus Christ (I)

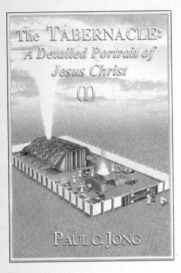

How can we find out the truth hidden in the Tabernacle? Only by knowing the gospel of the water and the Spirit, the real substance of the Tabernacle, can we correctly understand and know the answer to this question.

In fact, the blue, purple, and scarlet thread and the fine woven linen manifested in the gate of the Tabernacle's court show us the works of Jesus Christ in the New Testament's time that have saved the mankind. In this way, the Old Testament's Word of the Tabernacle and the Word of the New Testament are closely and definitely related to each other, like fine woven linen. But, unfortunately, this truth has been hidden for a long time to every truth seeker in Christianity.

Coming to this earth, Jesus Christ was baptized by John and shed His blood on the Cross. Without understanding and believing in the gospel of the water and the Spirit, none of us can ever find out the truth revealed in the Tabernacle. We must now learn this truth of the Tabernacle and believe in it. We all need to realize and believe in the truth manifested in the blue, purple, and scarlet thread and the fine woven linen of the gate of the Tabernacle's court.

The TABERNACLE: A Detailed Portrait of Jesus Christ (II)

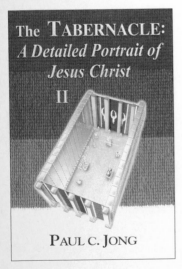

As God had commanded Moses to build the Tabernacle in the Old Testament, in the New Testament, God wants us to also build a Sanctuary in each of our hearts so that He may dwell in us. The material of faith with which we can build this Sanctuary in our hearts is the Word of the gospel of the water and the Spirit. With this gospel of the water and the Spirit, we must wash away all our sins and be cleansed. By telling us to build Him a Sanctuary, God is telling us to empty our hearts and believe in the gospel of the water and the Spirit. We must all cleanse our hearts by believing in the gospel of the water and the Spirit.

When we cleanse away all the sins of our hearts by believing in this gospel Truth, God then comes to dwell in them. It is by believing in this true gospel that you can build the holy Temples in your hearts. It is highly likely that until now, at least some of you have probably been offering your prayers of repentance to cleanse your hearts, trying to build the Temples by yourselves. But now is the time for you to abandon this false faith and be transformed by the renewing of your minds by believing in the gospel of the water and the Spirit.

The Elementary Principles of CHRIST

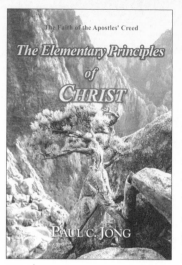

We must have the faith that the Apostles had and believe as they did, for their faith and beliefs came from the Holy Spirit. The Apostles believed in Jesus Christ, His Father, and the Holy Spirit as their God.

The Apostle Paul confessed that he died with Christ and was brought to new life with Him. He became an instrument of God by believing that he was baptized into Jesus Christ (Galatians 3:27). In God's gospel are found the baptism that Jesus received, the blood that He shed on the Cross, and the gift of the Holy Spirit that He has bestowed on everyone who believes in this true gospel of the water and the Spirit.

Do you know and believe in this original gospel? This is the very gospel that the Apostles had also believed. We, too, must therefore all believe in the gospel of the water and the Spirit.

The Gospel of Matthew (I) & (II)

There are countless new Christians throughout the world, who have just been born again by believing in the gospel of the water and the Spirit that we have been spreading. We are indeed yearning to feed on the bread of life to them. But it is difficult for them to have fellowship with us in the true gospel, for they are all far away from us.

Therefore, to meet the spiritual needs of these people of Jesus Christ, the King of kings, The author proclaims that those who have received the remission of their sins by believing in the Word of Jesus Christ, must feed on His pure Word in order to defend their faith and sustain their spiritual lives. The sermons in these books have been prepared as new bread of life that will nourish the born-again to edify their spiritual growth.

Through His Church and servants, God will continue to provide you with this bread of life. May God's blessings be on all those who have been born again of water and the Spirit, who desires to have true spiritual fellowship with us in Jesus Christ.

The First Epistle of John (I) & (II)

He who believes that Jesus, who is God and the Savior, came by the gospel of the water and the Spirit to deliver all sinners from their sins, is saved from all his sins, and becomes a child of God the Father.

The First Epistle of John states that Jesus, who is God, came to us by the gospel of the water and the Spirit, and that He is the Son of God the Father. The Book, in other words, mostly emphasizes that Jesus is God (1 John 5:20), and concretely testifies the gospel of the water and the Spirit in chapter 5.

We must not hesitate to believe that Jesus Christ is God and to follow Him.

Sermons on Galatians: From Physical Circumcision to the Doctrine of Repentance (I) & (II)

Today's Christianity has turned into merely a world religion. Most Christians nowadays live in a situation of being sinners because they haven't been born again by spiritual faith. It is because they have only relied on Christian doctrines without being aware of the gospel of the water and the Spirit until now.

Therefore, now is the time for you to know the spiritual fallacies of the circumcisionists and keep distance from such faith. You have to know the contradictoriness of the prayers of repentance. Now is the time for you to stand firmer than ever on the gospel of the water and the Spirit.

If you haven't believed in this true gospel so far, you have to believe in our Savior who came to us by the gospel of the water and the Spirit even now. Now, you have to be complete Christians with the faith of believing in the gospel Truth of the water and the Spirit.

The Fall of Man and the Perfect Salvation of God

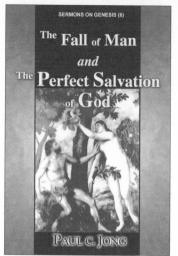

In the Book of Genesis, the purpose for which God created us is contained. When architects design a building or artists draw a painting, they first conceive the work that would be completed in their minds before they actually begin working on their project. Just like this, our God also had our salvation of mankind in His mind even before He created the heavens and the earth, and He made Adam and Eve with this purpose in mind. And God needed to explain to us the domain of Heaven, which is not seen by our eyes of the flesh, by drawing an analogy to the domain of the earth that we can all see and understand.

Even before the foundation of the world, God wanted to save mankind perfectly by giving the gospel of the water and the Spirit to everyone's heart. So although all human beings were made out of dust, they must learn and know the gospel Truth of the water and the Spirit to benefit their own souls. If people continue to live without knowing the dominion of Heaven, they will lose not only the things of the earth, but also everything that belongs to Heaven.

Paul C. Jong's Christian books have been translated into 51 major languages at this point: Albanian, Arabic, Bengali, Bulgarian, Burmese, Chichewa, Chinese, Croatian, Czech, Danish, Dutch, English, French, Georgian, German, Greek, Gujarati, Hebrew, Hindi, Hungarian, Indonesian, Iranian, Italian, Japanese, Javanese, Kannada, Khmer, Latvian, Malagasy, Marathi, Mongolian, Nepali, Polish, Portuguese, Romanian, Russian, Serbian, Slovak, Slovene, Spanish, Swahili, Swedish, Tagalog, Taiwanese, Tamil, Telugu, Thai, Turkish, Ukrainian, Urdu, and Vietnamese. They are also available now through our free e-book service.

E-book is digital book designed for you to feel a printed book on screen. You can read it easily on your PC monitor in your native language after downloading the viewer software and a text file. Feel free to visit our web site at http://www.nlmission.com http://www.bjnewlife.org to download our e-books, and you will get the most remarkable Christian e-books absolutely for free.

And, would you like to take part in having our free Christian books known to more people worldwide? We would be very thankful if you link your website to ours so that many people get an opportunity to meet Jesus Christ through our inspired Christian books. Please visit our site at http://www.bjnewlife.org/english/about/take_banners.php to take our banners to your website. In addition, we would be also very thankful if you introduce our website to the webmasters around you for adding our link.

The New Life Mission
Contact: John Shin, General Secretary
E-mail: newlife@bjnewlife.org